Metafiction

Metafiction

LONGMAN CRITICAL READERS

General Editor:

STAN SMITH, Professor of English, University of Dundee

METAFICTION

Edited and Introduced by

MARK CURRIE

LONGMAN
LONDON AND NEW YORK

Longman Group Limited,
Longman House, Burnt Mill,
Harlow, Essex CM20 2JE, England
and Associated Companies throughout the world.

*Published in the United States of America
by Longman Publishing, New York*

First published 1995

ISBN 0 582 212928 PPR

British Library Cataloguing-in-Publication Data

A catalogue record for this book is
available from the British Library

Library of Congress Cataloging-in-Publication Data

Applied for.

Set 19K in 9 on 11½ Palatino

Transferred to digital print on demand 2001

Printed and bound in Great Britain by Antony Rowe Ltd, Eastbourne

Contents

General Editors' Preface

The outlines of contemporary critical theory are now often taught as a standard feature of a degree in literary studies. The development of particular theories has seen a thorough transformation of literary criticism. For example, Marxist and Foucauldian theories have revolutionised Shakespeare studies, and 'deconstruction' has led to a complete reassessment of Romantic poetry. Feminist criticism has left scarcely any period of literature unaffected by its searching critiques. Teachers of literary studies can no longer fall back on a standardised, received, methodology.

Lecturers and teachers are now urgently looking for guidance in a rapidly changing critical environment. They need help in understanding the latest revisions in literary theory, and especially in grasping the practical effects of the new theories in the form of theoretically sensitised new readings. A number of volumes in the series anthologise important essays on particular theories. However, in order to grasp the full implications and possible uses of particular theories it is essential to see them put to work. This series provides substantial volumes of new readings, presented in an accessible form and with a significant amount of editorial guidance.

Each volume includes a substantial introduction which explores the theoretical issues and conflicts embodied in the essays selected and locates areas of disagreement between positions. The pluralism of theories has to be put on the agenda of literary studies. We can no longer pretend that we all tacitly accept the same practices in literary studies. Neither is a *laissez-faire* attitude any longer tenable. Literature departments need to go beyond the mere toleration of theoretical differences: it is not enough merely to agree to differ; they need actually to 'stage' the differences openly. The volumes in this series all attempt to dramatise the differences, not necessarily with a view to resolving them but in order to foreground the choices presented by different theories or to argue for a particular route through the impasses the differences present.

The theory 'revolution' has had real effects. It has loosened the grip of traditional empiricist and romantic assumptions about language and literature. It is not always clear what is being proposed as the new agenda for literary studies, and indeed the very notion of 'literature' is questioned by the post-structuralist strain in theory. However, the uncertainties and obscurities of contemporary theories appear much less worrying when we see what the best critics have been able to do with them in practice. This series aims to disseminate the best of recent criticism and to show that it is possible to re-read the canonical texts of literature in new and challenging ways.

RAMAN SELDEN AND STAN SMITH

The Publishers and fellow Series Editor regret to record that Raman Selden died after a short illness in May 1991 at the age of fifty-three. Ray Selden was a fine scholar and a lovely man. All those he has worked with will remember him with much affection and respect.

Acknowledgements

We are grateful to the following for permission to reproduce copyright material:

Helen Dwight Reid Educational Foundation for the article 'Metafiction, the Historical Novel and Coover's *The Public Burning*' by Raymond A. Mazurek from *Critique: Studies in Modern Fiction* 23, 2 (1982), 29–42, and the article 'The Art of Metafiction: William Gass's *Willie Masters' Lonesome Wife*' by Larry McCaffery from *Critique: Studies in Modern Fiction* XVIII, 1 (1976), 21–34, published by Heldref Publications, copyright © Helen Dwight Reid Educational Foundation; Eastern Michigan University for the article 'The Novel, Illusion and Reality: the Paradox of Omniscience in *The French Lieutenant's Woman*' by Frederick Holmes from *Journal of Narrative Technique*, 11, 3, Fall (1981), 184–98; Martin Secker and Warburg Ltd, part of Reed International Books, and Harcourt Brace and Company for the article 'Postmodernism, Irony, The Enjoyable' from *Reflections on the Name of the Rose* (US title *Postscript to the Name of the Rose*) by Umberto Eco, translated by William Weaver, pp. 61–81, copyright © 1983 by Umberto Eco, English translation copyright © 1984 by Harcourt Brace and Company; Mouton de Gruyter, a division of Walter de Gruyter and Company, for the article 'Metanarrative Signs' from *Narratology* by G. Prince (1982), pp. 115–28; the author, Susana Onega for her paper 'British Historiographic Metafiction in the 1980s', also to be published in a series on British postmodernist fiction edited by Theo D'haen and Hans Bertens; Routledge and the author, Elizabeth Dipple for the chapter 'A Novel, which is a machine for Generating Interpretations: Umberto Eco and *The Name of the Rose*' from *The Unresolvable Plot* (1988), pp. 117–39; Routledge and the author, Linda Hutcheon for the chapter 'Historiographic Metafiction: "the Pastime of Past Time"', from *The Poetics of Postmodernism: History, Theory, Fiction* (1988), pp. 105–23; Routledge and the author, David Lodge for the chapter 'The Novel Now: Theories and Practices' from *After Bakhtin: Essays on Fiction and Criticism* (1990), pp. 11–24; Routledge and the author, Patricia Waugh for the chapter 'What is Metafiction?' from *Metafiction: the Theory and Practice of Self-Conscious Fiction* (1984), pp. 1–19; the author, Robert Scholes for his article 'Metafiction' from *The Iowa Review* 1, Fall (1970), 100–15; Wesleyan

University for the article 'The Question of Narrative in Contemporary Historical Theory' by Hayden White from *History and Theory*, 23, 1 (1984), 1–33, copyright © 1984 Wesleyan University.

We have been unable to trace the copyright holder in the article 'The Literature of Exhaustion' by John Barth, originally published in the journal *Atlantic Monthly*, 220, 2, August (1967), 29–34, and would appreciate any information that would enable us to do so.

Introduction

Definitions and Marginal Cases

The first use of the term 'Metafiction' is attributed to William Gass in the late 1960s, who wanted to describe recent fictions that were somehow about fiction itself. As it was defined in the 1970s, metafiction was fiction with self-consciousness, self-awareness, self-knowledge, ironic self-distance. But this conception of metafiction has raised problems which compel a definition with a different emphasis. First, the idea of self-consciousness is strangely inconsistent with most postmodern literary theories which would attribute neither selfhood nor consciousness to an author, let alone a work of fiction. Second, there is a vertiginous illogicality about 'self-consciousness': that something which is defined by its self-consciousness must surely be conscious of its own definitive characteristic. It is not enough that metafiction knows that it is fiction; it must also know that it is metafiction if its self-knowledge is adequate, and so on in an infinite logical regress. Can it then be meaningful to say that metafiction is conscious of itself?

A third problem rises in the gap between a relatively new term and the well-established literary characteristics it describes. 'Metafiction' might have consolidated its place in the critical lexis as a descriptor of postmodern fictional preoccupations, but few commentators have proposed the absolute novelty of literary self-consciousness. The problem here is not merely that metafictional characteristics can be found throughout the prehistory of postmodernism. There is also something about postmodern fiction, the deep involvement with its own past, the constant dialogue with its own conventions, which projects any self-analysis backwards in time. Novels which reflect upon themselves in the postmodern age act in a sense as commentaries on their antecedents. 'Self-consciousness' is neither new nor meaningfully 'self' consciousness, since the metafiction refers to fictions other than itself, in its own history. The relationship between a critical term and its literary object becomes profoundly confused because the literary object itself performs a critical function. The definition of 'metafiction' as fictional self-consciousness does not acknowledge this complexity, and my continued use of the notion of self-consciousness here carries such problems within it.

This volume begins from the definition of metafiction as a borderline discourse, as a kind of writing which places itself on the border between fiction and criticism, and which takes that border as its subject. Far from being some marginal no-man's-land, this definition gives metafiction a central importance in the projects of literary modernity, postmodernity and theory which have taken this borderline as a primary source of energy. The borderline between fiction and criticism has been a point of convergence where fiction and criticism have assimilated each other's insights, producing a self-conscious energy on both sides. For criticism this has meant an affirmation of literariness in its own language, an increased awareness of the extent to which critical insights are formulated within fiction, and a tendency towards immanence of critical approach which questions the ability of critical language to refer objectively and authoritatively to the literary text. For fiction it has meant the assimilation of critical perspective within fictional narrative, a self-consciousness of the artificiality of its constructions and a fixation with the relationship between language and the world. The reciprocity of this relationship indicates that metafiction is only half, the fictional half, of a process of challenging the boundary between fiction and criticism, and therefore that its explanation requires that it be articulated across the boundary, connecting it to the self-consciousness of criticism. The rationale of this volume is therefore one of contextualising metafiction in its relation to metacriticism, or to open out the idea of self-consciousness to accommodate criticism as well as fiction.

The critical self-consciousness of metafiction once seemed to announce the death of the novel, appeared to be a decadent response to its exhausted possibilities, but now seems like an unlimited vitality: what was once thought introspective and self-referential is in fact outward-looking. John Updike recently described self-consciousness, in another context, as a 'mode of interestedness which ultimately turns outwards'. This was certainly the fate of self-consciousness in literary narrative the implications of which extended far beyond the boundaries of fiction. If narrative self-consciousness found its first extended expression in the so-called high culture of literary modernism, it soon flowed outwards into the more demotic realms of film, television, comic strips and advertising. If this self-consciousness ever seemed pertinent only to the logic of artifice, similar insights eventually took hold beyond the domain of art, on modes of historical and scientific explanation, and indeed on representation and language in general. Only in a few cases could this be considered an outward flow from metafiction, since self-consciousness must in a sense arise from within each specific discourse; but such ubiquity makes it impossible to see metafictional self-consciousness as an isolated and introspective obsession within literature.

To focus the issue of self-consciousness on the boundary between fiction and criticism is to acknowledge the strong reciprocal influence between discourses which seem increasingly inseparable. A simple explanation of this inseparability would be that the roles of writer and critic are often fulfilled by the same person. On the one hand, novelists often depend financially or intellectually on employment as critics, so that the writers of fiction are also, for example, the reviewers who assess fiction for newspaper readers. On the other hand, and perhaps more importantly for metafiction, academic literary critics have been increasingly successful as novelists, leading to a high level of critical awareness within their fictional productions. In many cases this awareness has been much more tangible than implicit expertise, especially in novels which take academic literary criticism as their subject matter. In this latest version of the novel of ideas, the practices and perspectives of modern literary theory have been disseminated, more widely than they would otherwise, in the novel form as a kind of in-built self-referentiality. In both cases the writer/critic is an inhabitant of Literatureland, the place where texts and acts of interpretation constitute the world of experience which the novelist, knowingly or unknowingly, represents. We have so many novels about Literatureland because novelists are so often not the integrated participants in the world that they would like to be and Literatureland – writing and reading – is both the realm of their expertise and the texture of their experience. The writer/critic is thus a dialectical figure, embodying both the production and reception of fiction in the roles of author and reader in a way that is paradigmatic for metafiction.

Writer/critics personify the boundary between fiction and criticism, and accordingly have a key role in this volume. But the personification of the boundary is of biographical explanatory value without in itself being metafictional. A metafiction is not definitively a novel whose author is both a writer and a critic, but a novel which dramatises the boundary between fiction and criticism, and to unify metafictions under this definition requires a rather loose interpretation of 'criticism'. A typology of metafiction has to acknowledge a difference between a novel like Lodge's *Small World*, which takes the world of professional literary criticism as its fictional object without explicitly highlighting the artificiality of the fictional process, and one like Fowles's *The French Lieutenant's Woman* which highlights the artificiality of its construction without reference to literary criticism. In the former, the academic 'criticism' within the novel evokes implicitly the critical judgements that will be made of the novel. In the latter, an intrusive authorial voice appropriates in self-commentary a less academic critical perspective attributed to a reader who exists within the novel only as an addressee. In one sense Lodge's novel dramatises the critic more explicitly than Fowles's, and in another it allows the critic no explicit self-conscious or illusion-breaking dramatic function. If Lodge's device seems pertinent to the boundary between fiction and criticism,

Fowles's does so only by articulating a critical perspective on the boundary between art and life.

This difference illustrates an important preliminary distinction in the way that metafictions dramatise the boundary between fiction and criticism, either as illusion-breaking authorial intervention or as integrated dramatisation of the external communication between author and reader. In both cases it is often through an internal boundary between art and life that the novel develops the self-commentary that gives it critical self-consciousness. This is where the definition of metafiction as the dramatisation of the fiction/criticism boundary allows for marginal cases. One such marginal case would be a novel like Conrad's *Heart of Darkness* where Marlowe is a dramatised narrator, a kind of surrogate author grappling with his ability as a storyteller and with the ability of words to communicate his experience. At the same time, Marlowe is a surrogate reader trying, as protagonist of the narrated journey to make sense of events and to interpret its significance in a manner analogous to that of the external reader. The external readership is given further surrogate representation in the form of Marlowe's audience, his fellow sailors who listen to the narration from within the boundaries of the fiction yet alongside the external readership. This internal dramatisation of the external relationship between Conrad and his readership allows complex articulations of self-consciousness and metafictional appropriations of readers' responses. But surrogate authors and readers are endemic in fiction. To see the dramatised narrator or novelist as metanarrative devices is to interpret a substantial proportion of fiction as metafiction. As Umberto Eco has pointed out the surrogate reader is as common in fiction as the figure of the detective or any similar dramatised interpreter whose role in the narrative is to make sense of unintelligible events or to grapple with a mystery.

Another marginal case would be the metafiction which depends upon intertextuality for its self-consciousness: narratives which signify their artificiality by obtrusive reference to traditional forms or borrow their thematic and structural principles from other narratives. In its reference to quest narratives, to Dante's 'Inferno' or to Coleridge's 'Rime of the Ancient Mariner', *Heart of Darkness* gives its literal journey symbolic and literary overtones. Joyce's *Ulysses* joins its portrait of Dublin inseparably to its reinterpretation of Homer. Coover's 'The Magic Poker' and Fowles's *The Magus* invoke the metaphors of Shakespeare's *The Tempest*. In each case an internal boundary between extratextual reference to real life and intertextual reference to other literature signifies the artificiality of the fictional world while simultaneously offering its realistic referential possibilities. The boundary of art and life within the fiction, by reproducing the boundary of art and life which surrounds the fiction, subverts its own referential illusion and in so doing places it on the boundary between fiction and criticism.

These cases are marginally metafictional in the sense that they are implicit about their relation to criticism or their own artificiality. This points to two contradictory problems which are returned to throughout the writings in this volume. First it implies that metafiction might be better understood not as a generic category but, in the words of Patricia Waugh, as 'a function inherent in all novels'. Second, it implies that metafiction in some cases is not inherent, in the sense that it is an objective property of the literary text, but that it depends upon a certain construal of fictional devices as self-referential, or metanarrative in function. Taken together, these problems indicate a double relevance to metafiction of the boundary between fiction and criticism. Not only is this boundary dramatised or signified within fiction as self-commentary, but also problematised by the idea that metafiction is less a property of the primary text than a function of reading. In this way the epistemological ambiguity of a metafiction which highlights the artificial invention of its object is duplicated in a critical ambiguity between the objective discovery and the subjective invention of the literary object. In short, the critical text is the literary text and vice versa, and in this tautology we find a succinct expression of the postmodern condition in fiction and criticism.

From modernism to new historicism

If metafiction characteristically internalises the relationship between authors and readers, fiction and criticism or art and life, we find its antecedents throughout literary history. Chaucer's elaborate framings of *The Canterbury Tales*, Shakespeare's plays within plays, the extensive use of epistolary forms in seventeenth- and eighteenth-century poetry and fiction, or the intrusive narrators of Fielding and Richardson, are all in a sense precursors of the metafictional paradox. Novelistic parodies like Laurence Sterne's *Tristram Shandy* or Jane Austen's *Northanger Abbey* are seen as early metafictions precisely because the basis of their comedy is in making the paradox visible. Many commentators have looked to such precursors for the origins of postmodern sensibility, and to parody in particular as an intertextual mode of writing with a clear critical function. But when postmodern retrospect discovers proto-postmodernism in this way it produces a spurious self-historicising teleology which confirms that critical texts construe their literary objects according to their own interests and purposes: postmodern discourses are seen as the endpoint of history and all prior discourses are construed as leading inexorably towards the postmodern. To acknowledge this co-implication of literature and criticism, the history that I want to sketch here for metafiction is not a unilinear literary history, but a conjunctural analysis which traces parallel events in fiction and criticism of the twentieth century.

Linguistic self-consciousness probably has two principal sources in the twentieth century – literary modernism and Saussurean linguistics. Both are places where the self-referentiality of language was emphasised alongside its ability to refer to an external world. In Saussure's *Course in General Linguistics* the emphasis comes from the thesis that referential meaning is a mere function of differences between signs, so that the explanation of meaning must refer to that system of differences rather than to a sub-linguistic reality. This does not mean, as many have claimed in recent decades, that reference is impossible or illusory, but rather that the referential function of language is implicitly also self-referential because it depends upon the hidden system of differences, systemic and contextual, which give each sign its value. According to this argument, language hides the conditions which permit meaning production, and the task of the structuralist analysis is therefore to make those conditions – differential relations, contextual factors and conventions – explicit. For reasons that remain unexplored, and perhaps unexplorable, an analogous attitude to language was taking hold, at the time Saussure formulated these ideas, in literary modernism, which sought to foreground the hidden conditions – structural principles, the process of production, the conventions and the artifice – which permitted the production of literary meaning.

The self-referential dimension of literary modernism consisted partly in rejecting conventions of realism, traditional narrative forms, principles of unity and transparent representational language in preference for techniques of alienation, obtrusive intertextual reference, multiple viewpoints, principles of unity borrowed from myth and music, and a more demanding, opaque, poeticised language. In modernist fiction these tendencies are of two kinds: those which foreground fictional conventions, and those which foreground language itself. In both cases, transparent and invisible verbal structures are transformed into defamiliarised and visible techniques, so that referential meaning is articulated alongside a self-reference to the conditions of its own possibility. A dramatised version of this conjunction would be the representation of an artist in fiction, as in Joyce's *Portrait of the Artist* in which the narrator becomes more alienated from the referential aspect of words, seeing them instead as a kind of material self-activity, at the same time as the novel experiments poetically with the representation of his thoughts. *Ulysses*, likewise, portrays Dublin in all its newly achieved extremes of naturalism, within a verbal and literary universe which paradoxically reminds us always of the artificiality of the portrait. The opacity of language in *Finnegans Wake* apparently abandons the attempt at representation for a radical self-referentiality which stages only language itself. In its tendency away from representation, the modernist fiction was placing new demands on the reader to make sense of the text which was no longer intelligible in conventional referential ways.

These tendencies in modernist fiction, which require no lengthy demonstration here, led critics in the first half of the century towards a formalist or language-based analysis. Under the influence of prolific writer-critics of the early modernist period like Eliot and Pound, the new critical attitude in the Anglo-American tradition was one in which the representational content of a literary work was categorically inseparable from or identical with its formal and verbal structure.

Saussurean linguistics and literary modernism may have had some untraceable historical connection in their approaches to reference, but they did not converge in literary formalism until much later. It was not until the 1960s that critics in Europe brought Saussurean structuralist perspectives to bear on the question of literary reference. In the work of Roman Jakobson, for example, the convergence of the two sources is found on the one hand as a concern with the question of realism in art and on the other as an attempt to internalise literary studies within the field of general linguistics. For Jakobson, Saussure's differential theory of the sign acts as a model for a differential theory of discourse which can account for the modernist insight that fictional realism is a mode of discourse which hides the formal and linguistic conditions of its own significance. Roland Barthes argued similarly from a Saussurean point of view that the signifier which did not declare its own systemic conditions was an 'unhealthy signifier' – language that pretends not to be language, to be uncomplicatedly transparent – a 'naturalisation' of language as a referential medium. Like Jakobson, Barthes used structuralist poetics as a way of responding to the new kind of literature, particularly the Nouveau Roman, which had developed the self-reflexivity that fictional realism lacked. On the basis of this contrast, Barthes distinguished between the 'readerly' and the 'writerly' text where the latter was a text for which the reading process was not a passive reception but a creative act of structuring. In the terms of this distinction, modernist fiction not only articulates its own reading by foregrounding the conditions of its meaning-production; the processes of reading and writing are further conflated by the idea that reading is itself a process of creating the text, of creating structure, and imbuing it with meaning.

In this respect, Barthes was a key figure for the history of self-consciousness in criticism. He was a figure in whom the influences of Saussure and literary modernism converged, he was a theoretician preoccupied with linguistic self-consciousness, and he was an important transition figure between structuralism and poststructuralism. If structuralist poetics operated initially with the belief that literary structure was a property of the object-text, Barthes' conflation of reading and writing processes pointed towards the idea that literary structure was a function of reading, or that critical metalanguage projected its own structure onto the object text in exactly the same way that language in general projected its structure onto the world. Thus, metalingual reference to language was no different in kind from reference in general, and criticism had to guard against naturalisation of its object by articulating a modernist self-consciousness. This insight that fiction and criticism shared a condition, that the role of the critical text was to articulate the self-consciousness that either the realist text lacked or that was immanent in the modernist text, and that at the same time the critical text must acknowledge reflexively its own structuration or literariness, was the gateway into poststructuralism through which criticism passed at the end of the 1960s.

The importance of Derrida's work in the late 1960s and in the 1970s is paramount for any analysis of the borderline of fiction and criticism. Like Jakobson and Barthes, Derrida's work developed attitudes to language that derived both from literary modernism and from Saussurean linguistics. In Derrida's work literature's boundary with philosophy, linguistics and criticism is transgressed in a way that imputes to literary language a new epistemological import. There is also a kind of closing of a circle in Derrida between literary modernism and postmodern criticism. Derrida always acknowledged, for example, the influence of Joyce's language on his various critiques of metalanguage, so that his writings on Joyce, which are closer to literary parodies than critical analyses, enact the reciprocal influence of fiction and criticism between modernism and postmodernism. Derrida's readings of Joyce question the ability of a critical text to refer transcendentally to a literary text and revert to the same intertextual modes of criticism that are developed by Joyce's own novels. Thus affirming the literariness of criticism, Derrida also affirms the metafictional critical functions of intertextuality, parody and anti-reference.

Derrida refuses to write criticism as if it were simply outside its literary object, and equally he refuses metalingual status to those discourses like Saussure's which, in order to be about language, seem to separate themselves from their object. A brief tour of Derrida's reading of Saussure is worthwhile here for the reciprocal relevance of poststructuralism and metafiction. It is the neutrality of Saussure's account, its apparent separateness from its object that Derrida focuses on. In the first place this focus takes the form of the now famous argument that when Saussure identifies his object as spoken, not written language, his neutrality is compromised. The exclusion of written language is, according to Derrida, a mere prejudice inherited by Saussure which assumes that spoken language is somehow closer to the signifying mind than writing. But

Saussure's own use of writing as an analogy to explain the nature of speech exposes this prejudice as an arbitrary imposition of boundaries which makes his study less than neutral from its inception.

As a counter-move to Saussure's exclusion Derrida uses the term 'writing' to refer to 'the entire field of linguistic signs', seeing the graphic signifier as no more exterior than the phonic, where both are representations of the signified. But the distinction of signifier and signified is like that of speech and writing in that each is an imposed structure based on the presupposition of internal and external elements of language. For Derrida, this presupposition specifically invokes both a signifying mind and a referent, since the binary idea of the sign retains a vestige of the theory of representation in which the 'thing itself' is understood as separate from the way in which it is represented. Saussure is therefore structuring language according to presuppositions rather than referring neutrally to it as an object. There are therefore already two levels at which the relationship between language and its referential object is a problem. First, there is the level I referred to earlier where Saussure's account suggests that language can only refer to the outside world because of its internal system of differences which both enable reference and impose structure on the referent. Second, there is the level at which Saussure's exclusions and methodological choices impose value-laden structure on language as an object despite masquerading as neutral or objective manoeuvres.

By pointing this out Derrida is reapplying the Saussurean insight to Saussure, reminding us that just as language structures its object so does metalanguage. But what of the third level of reference as structuration? What of Derrida's own text and its attempt to represent Saussure? Derrida's writing has two strategies which address this problem. The first is the idea of immanence: the idea that Derrida is trying not to refer to Saussure from the outside but to operate within his text, within his own terms. Derrida presents his argument as something which happens inside Saussure's, as a 'tension between gesture and statement', which is both a reading added on by Derrida afterwards, and a possibility which presided internally over the inception of his argument. Likewise Derrida's own terms – like 'writing' or 'différance' – are not really intelligible as autonomous concepts, but rather name problems and contradictions within Saussure's system of terms and oppositions. The second strategy is a kind of self-consciousness in Derrida's text which prevents his own terms from acquiring metalingual or objective status by foregrounding their paradoxical and difficult relation to the language they describe. Derrida's language is never that of academic, transparent objectivity, at times enacting the principles that it advances – as when he endorses the priority given to writing over speech in the graphic joke of 'différance' – and at times playing with the rhetorical and metaphorical dimension of his own writing to the point of irritation. Derrida's reading of Saussure is an intervention which articulates the reflexivity which Saussure lacks at the same time as it articulates a reflexivity of its own.

For this reason it has never been possible to define any autonomous theory of language that belongs to Derrida. In general, poststructuralist thought has abandoned the idea that theory is capable of abstracting the principles of language. Hence Barthes', definition of the theoretical:

> Theoretical does not of course mean abstract. From my point of view, it means 'reflexive', something which turns back on itself: a discourse which turns back on itself is by virtue of this very fact theoretical.

This is a characteristic poststructuralist attitude to theory which implies that a critical text is no more capable of theorising language than a fictional one, and that the metalingual text which, like Saussure's, aspires towards transparency in its own language is as untheoretical as a realist novel. Theory then is a writing practice with pangeneric and interdisciplinary potential which turns language back on itself to foreground the hidden determinants and assumptions in the structure of the objects of discourse.

But when exactly does a discourse turn back on itself and how does one draw the line between language which is and is not theoretical in this way? Here again we encounter the paradox that a literary text and its reading are inseparable and that reflexivity is as much a function of reading as an inherent property of a text. This characteristic deconstructionist conflation is compounded in the work of Paul de Man. Like Derrida, who saw the tension between gesture and statement in Saussure as something the text does to itself as well as something formulated by his own intervention, de Man understood texts, literary and non-literary, as caught in an undecidable tension between literal and tropological dimensions of language, and recommended a 'rhetorical reading' which sought to sustain and represent the contradiction between them. De Man designated the inseparability of a text and its analysis with the phrase 'allegory of reading', the ambiguous genitive of which confused the location of the metalingual allegory between the text and its reading, and attributed to texts the ability to formulate elaborate theories of the self-referentiality of language unknowingly. De Man's writing, like that of many of the American deconstructionists, passed between critical commentary and metalingual propositions in a way that not only gave literature a new metalingual and philosophical status, but which endorsed the idea that literature and criticism could be seen as part of a common endeavour to enact the opacity of language.

If 'reflexivity' is linguistic self-awareness which links the projects of metafiction with metacritical writings such as Derrida's, it has also played an important part in a range of other discourses from linguistics, philosophy, theology, archaeology, architecture, film and the visual arts – places where a certain opacity of signifying media has been affirmed in recent years. It would of course be impossible to sketch these larger contexts adequately, but one can refer for example to the influence of deconstruction in architecture or Biblical hermeneutics, or to the increasingly complex versions of reflexivity in film, to suggest that this is not a phenomenon isolated either in literary studies or universities. Some would claim that Derrida's work is merely a limited expression of insights developed by Nietzsche or Einstein, Wittgenstein, Montaigne or even Plato. But for the purposes of contextualising metafiction, the two most relevant domains of theoretical writing are those concerned with language and those concerned with the writing of history.

It is no surprise that in literary studies the influence of deconstruction receded in the late 1980s under widespread pressure to re-engage with history. Derrida and his American disciples were perceived as formalists who showed scant regard for the material historical processes which shaped language and literature. Twentieth-century literary studies in America had been dominated by a rather factitious and binary debate between historicism and formalism since the New Critics defined their project in opposition to literary historicism in the 1920s. Opposition to the New Criticism from without and within had always been articulated in the name of historicism, and it was in the context of this debate that Derrida's work made its impact in the early 1970s in America. In that period it was common to see Derrida represented as the long-awaited return to some kind of historical perspective after the dominance of New Criticism and the apparent continuity of its formalist preoccupations in the work of Northrop Frye and those few Saussurean structuralists whose work had reached the United States before Derrida's. Before long, however, perspective had altered. In the late 1970s, the mediation of Derrida's work in the United States stressed the formalist orientation of his analyses, and opposition to deconstruction had itself become an historicist encampment.

The confusion here emerged from the fact that, on the one hand, and particularly in those works first translated in the United States, Derrida seemed to reject the synchronic account of structure which structuralism had inherited from Saussure, while on the other hand, assembling a critique of historical explanation on metaphysical grounds. In *Positions* Derrida summarises this critique as an objection to both 'the general concept of history' and 'the concept of history in general', that is the idea on the one hand, of a single history which transcends all other discourses and to which those discourses are internal, and on the other hand, the idea that all historical narratives have some common denominator which unifies them and compels some definition of the essence of history. For

American literary studies, Derrida did not offer a procedure which would allow a re-engagement with history. Rather his work inclined towards an examination of the metaphysical presuppositions and structurality of historical explanation in the same way as it did for structural-linguistic explanation, for example taking a dialectical approach to the poles of language and history in *Of Grammatology*, which asserted and enacted the proposition that language was no more within history than history was within language. For the American debate between historicism and formalism this was insufficiently polemical.

In Europe the debate between historicism and formalism had a different and perhaps more political configuration. As many American commentators have now argued, the European context of Derrida's writing was dominated by a polemic between a range of Marxist positions all committed to the importance of historical analysis, and those perspectives which belonged either to the formalist-structuralist tradition or to the existentialist and phenomenological schools in philosophy, both of which effectively demoted history from its status as transcendent explanatory system. The basic opposition of formalism and historicism underlay many of the ongoing polemics of recent decades, particularly where Marxism and poststructuralism encountered each other, as for example in the differences between Frankfurt School critical theory and French deconstruction. Often the alignments in Europe were less clear cut than in American criticism, either through attempts to fuse the two perspectives, for example in the reception theory developed in Konstantz University by Hans Robert Jauss and others, or through internal squabbles which revealed positions within poststructuralism which allowed for historicist and Marxist commitment such as Foucault's in his debate with Derrida.

Historiographical interstices between Derrida and Foucault are quite minor in that both saw history as a value-laden, artificial and textual structure, but Foucault's work, more than Derrida's, offered a way of returning to historical writing as a strategic opposition to the values of traditional history. For Foucault in his 'archaeological' phase, the writing of history involved the reduction of the irreducibly complex discursive formation of a period or epoch to a simple, unified essence which could take its place in a continuous narrative. This process was a 'structure of exclusion', an imposition of boundaries around the object of analysis akin to Saussure's, which bespoke the values of the historian and gave the impression that one thing lead to another in a causal chain. In place of this, Foucault articulated the histories of the forgotten areas of human thought, of the people excluded by traditional histories, and emphasised discontinuity in the progress of the historical narrative. The 'structure of exclusion' of an historical explanation represented the structure of power and authority which sought to rearrange and efface the disparity of events to produce a stable, centred narrative. Foucault's revised historicism was a refusal to efface the 'multiplicity of force relations' that constitute an epoch, and a turn towards the notion of history's complex plurality that would subvert the traditional authoritarian commitment to trace a line, a causal sequence or a tradition through a disparate past. In conjunction with Foucault's later writing, which turned more explicitly to questions of power in discourse, these revised historiographical goals inspired American critics such as Jerome McGann and Steven Greenblatt in the 1980s to formulate a New Historicism which incorporated an awareness of the textuality of historical writing and the values that textual structures imposed upon the representation of their historical objects. It was with such directives that American literary criticism moved away from the language-based analyses of deconstruction in the 1980s towards a self-conscious, textualist historicism. The return to history in criticism in the 1980s was not governed in all cases by a poststructuralist paradigm oriented towards a critique of historical explanation. There was also a resurrection of materialist and Marxist approaches which reinstated historical perspective as an authority within which discourses could be understood symptomatically. But even if there was a tendency towards a transcendental historicism in some of the new historicisms, old conceptions of the relation between base and superstructure had given way to more sophisticated accounts of ideology as a kind of confusion of linguistic and phenomenal reality which placed issues of language and representation at the forefront of cultural analysis. These trends in Europe and the United States may have owed more to Foucault, Althusser and Adorno than to Derrida and de Man in their anti-formalist and increasingly political orientations, but the legacy of deconstruction was evident in a new emphasis on the role of language in the apprehension of political reality. Post-formalist historiography undoubtedly acknowledges the common ground between interpreting the world and interpreting a text, and the impossibility of separating or subordinating the relationship between language and history.

The development of a self-conscious historiography in criticism went hand in hand with the poststructuralist critique of narrative explanation in general. The unilinear causality of narrative and its teleological orientation towards relevation and closure were seen as operating principles which projected structure onto otherwise structureless experience. The ubiquity of the narrative explanation in general history, the history of ideas, the history of science, the history of literature, in politics, law, biography, in the construction of national consciousness or personal identity, gave to the project of uncovering its hidden philosophical and politics assumptions a universal import. Taken in combination with the developments that had dismantled the boundary between theoretical and fictional production and highlighted the formal and textual principles of historical narratives, the perception of an all-encompassing scope for narrative offered an extended remit to the self-conscious novel. Traditionally, the novel was the most artful and sophisticated expression of narrative control. In the very act of telling a story the novel was a kind of history: a retrospective account of events ordered sequentially and causally, often with an omniscient potential to examine the relations between individuals and social conditions. The self-conscious novel therefore had the power to explore not only the conditions of its own production, but the implications of narrative explanation and historical reconstruction in general. In this context, the self-conscious re-engagement with historical subjects in what have been called the historiographic metafictions of the 1980s seems to acknowledge the new theoretical relevance of the novel to questions of representation and the principles of organisation through which history becomes knowable.

The passage from modernism to new historicism in the novel has been tailing criticism from the front. Outside of literary studies, the transition from modernism to postmodernism is often understood as a radical disjunction from and rejection of the past in favour of futuristic experimentation followed by an ironic recovery and recontextualisation of historical forms. This is perhaps less marked in literary history, where modernism was always already engaged in the recontextualisation of past forms, as for example in the use of myth. There was also a face of literary modernism which concerned itself specifically with the problems of giving narrative form to individual memory, as in Proust's *A la Recherche du Temps Perdu* or Conrad's *Heart of Darkness*. But if the seeds of historiographical metafiction were planted in modernism, they flowered so spectacularly only because events in the related but non-fictional fields of philosophy, linguistics, and literary and cultural criticism created the right conditions to give historiographical metafiction new theoretical scope. Hence, the works of Robert Coover, Umberto Eco, A.S. Byatt, John Fowles, Kurt Vonnegut, Thomas Pynchon, Julian Barnes and others who have ruminated self-consciously on the fictional representation of history, are contributors to a new philosophy of historical representation in which the ideological function of story-telling is central.

Twentieth-century intellectual life has been dominated by the polemic between history and language, but as we approach the end of the century the poles have converged. It is no longer possible to discuss history without heeding its linguistic representational condition, just as it is no longer possible to discuss language without contextualising the discussion in social and historical frameworks. If modernism strove for a kind of disjunction from history (social and literary), that project has now itself become part of history, supplanted by a postmodernism which strives to return to history having assimilated the self-conscious textualism that modernism formulated. In this light the emergence of historiographical metafiction from metafiction, of postmodernism from modernism, or the transmutation of literary into cultural studies, represent expanded scope for tendencies in twentieth-century thought which once seemed to point unpromisingly towards self-analysis and self-absorption.

Metafiction and postmodernism

Metafiction is not the only kind of postmodern fiction, and nor is it an exclusively postmodern kind of fiction. It is neither a paradigm nor a subset of postmodernism. Though Hutcheon has claimed the former for historiographic metafiction and Zavarzadeh has claimed the latter for metafiction in general, both claims are obliged to prescribe definitions of metafiction and postmodernism to achieve coherence. Such definitions might provide some satisfaction for the typologically minded critic, but they also impose boundaries which have no essential justification. Metafiction cannot be defined essentially without proposing a categorical separation of literary types and critical constructions; and postmodernism is equally undefinable without some authority that could arbitrate between its meanings as a kind of art, an historical period, or some total ideological and political condition. Terms like 'metafiction' and 'postmodernism' are not sustained by any common essence among their referents.

How then is it different to define metafiction as a borderline discourse between fiction and criticism? There is a sense in which any definition of metafiction is a contradiction. Since metafiction concerns itself above all with a reflexive awareness of the conditions of meaning-construction, any typological definition of metafiction rooted in objective characteristics or essences will contradict the linguistic philosophy that it attempts to describe. Above all, metafiction is committed to the idea of constructed meanings rather than representable essences. What is needed is a non-essentialist definition, one which does not name a singular common essence between metafictions but which designates a kind of problem in the philosophy of language, an irreducible difference and a non-identity: not a precise typological configuration of the relation of metafiction to postmodernism, but a postmodern definition of metafiction. This is what can be achieved by a definition located on the border between a discourse and its representation, one which divides responsibility for the metafictional function between fiction and criticism.

Because metafiction is not strictly a kind of fiction, because previous definitions have not often confronted its complexity, the term 'metafiction' has never really established an assured place in the lexicon of critical terms. The most distant antonyms of 'metafiction' such as 'realism' are underwritten by ontological difference in no more demonstrable a way than its closest relations such as 'fabulation', 'surfiction' or 'magic realism'. But such vagaries need not deprive 'metafiction' of concepthood. They merely imply that metafiction is one function of literary language among others, potentially co-existing with others, and that this function is a dialectic composite of inherent characteristics and critical interpretations.

The dialectic of inherent characteristics and critical interpretations leads into categorical difficulties of two kinds. The first kind of categorical difficulty is a metafictional novel which cannot appropriate its own critical response by any amount of reflexivity. An example would be John Fowles's *The Magus* where metafictionality is generated in the relationship between Conchis, the surrogate author, and Nicholas, the surrogate reader. In a classic metafictional dynamic, this relationship stages a quest by Nicholas for an interpretation of the inexplicable and mysterious circumstances in which he finds himself, and of which Conchis is a kind of author-God. In the process of the quest, Nicholas formulates possible interpretations of the fiction constructed around him by Conchis, and in so doing, interpellates the external reader, who is in possession of no extra information, into analogous interpretative acts. Nicholas and the reader are yoked together by a fictional point of view in quest of an interpretation, so that critical perspectives are assimilated into the novel and represented as part of the fiction. The literary interpretative nature of Nicholas's quest is established throughout the novel by a level of intertextual reference which consolidates Conchis's surrogate-authorial role and blurs the boundary between reality and art within the fiction. Although this dynamic is one with built-in metafictional reflexivity, it is still necessary to distinguish between appropriated critical perspective represented in Nicholas's quest and the actual critical responses of external readers. That is to say, the real reader can always further distance him or herself from the critical responses built into the text and from the interpellative processes of narrative technique, remaining free to construct the text from some other critical perspective not appropriated by the text itself. In this sense there is no real difference between reading a metafictional novel and reading a realistic one, since metafictional reflexivity can never fully appropriate the response of the real reader. It is of course possible to read *The Magus* as straightforward realism in which the characters have perfectly plausible, but not illusion-breaking literary interests.

A second categorical difficulty militates against the idea that metafiction is a type of fiction. Take, for example, the case of Tom Wolfe, an outspoken critic of metafictional writing in recent years. Wolfe's case is that the novel's most significant energy is social realism, the ability of fiction to portray the real world. For Wolfe, metafictional self-reference to the godlike power of the author, appropriation of critical perspective and endless intertextual cross-referencing are merely decadent forms of self-absorption which deprive the novel of that significant energy. This case, first articulated in *The New Journalism*, is repeated in the preface of his novel *The Bonfire of the Vanities*, which attempts to portray New York without deviation into self-analysis. But realistic intent of this kind does not immunise Wolfe's text against metafictional interpretation. Like Fowles's *The Magus*, *Bonfire of the Vanities* also establishes an internal boundary between reality and its representation, this time in the difference between actual occurrences and their distortion by journalistic representation. *Bonfire* tells a story of 'real' events alongside an unfolding journalistic story. It contains authorial and readerly surrogacy in the figures of Peter Fallow, the scoop journalist, and Sherman McCoy, who reads Fallow's story as the unfolding of his own downfall. The blurring of the distinction between reality and representation in *Bonfire* enacts a central proposition that so-called real events are inseparable from their interpretations, creating an internal analogy for the text itself. Journalism within *Bonfire* corresponds to Wolfe's own attempt to write a journalistic novel in exactly the same way that Fowles's *Magus* corresponds to Fowles's own creative function. Add to this a list of implicit intertexts which shape Wolfe's narrative, to the genre of 'Yuppie Nightmare' films, or to Greek tragedy, and a case for the metafictionality of Wolfe's novel emerges. This point was made adequately by Brian de Palma's film of Wolfe's novel, which ironically transposes Fallow into an obtrusive narrator, and opens with a paradigmatic metafictional scenario in which Fallow receives an award for the novel of the story which is about to be narrated, and of which he is the surrogate author.

These examples show that metafiction can be located at the conscious and the unconscious level of the text. Whereas postmodern fiction can generally be regarded as conscious metafiction, postmodern readings can also identify metafiction as an aspect of the unconscious level of the text, against the grain of realist intention, and therefore beyond any temporal boundaries which might apply to the term 'postmodernism'. In other words, postmodernist fiction and criticism both aim to articulate the unconscious, and in particular the unconscious self-referentiality of non-metafictional fiction. If unconscious self-consciousness is the common critical object of metafiction and criticism, it does not stabilise the identity of either, since both metafiction and criticism are likewise produced by the discourses which represent them. (Rather than seek to impose some kind of stability in this predicament, we should treat the idea of 'unconscious self-consciousness' as a reminder of compound illogicalities in the definition of metafiction as self-consciousness.) Metafiction is not then simply a form of postmodernism. The postmodern context is not one divided neatly between fictional texts and their critical readings, but a monistic world of representations in which the boundaries between art and life, language and metalanguage, and fiction and criticism are under philosophical attack.

Part One

Defining Metafiction

1 Metafiction*

ROBERT SCHOLES

Robert Scholes is one of several writers who sought to give definition to William Gass's term 'metafiction' in the early 1970s. This article attempts to link that term to ideas which derive from John Barth's essay 'The Literature of Exhaustion' (see Part Three) to describe the attempts of experimental fictions of the 1960s to 'climb beyond Beckett and Borges' (the principal subjects of Barth's essay) towards 'things that no critic can discern'. These undiscernible things are best thought of as moments of critical vertigo in which the relations between real life and representation are no longer clear, either within or beyond the fiction.

In a volume dedicated to the idea that metafiction is a border-line territory between fiction and criticism, this essay has a special place. Its argument begins with the idea that there are four aspects of fiction (fiction of forms, ideas, existence and essence) which correspond to four critical perspectives on fiction (formal, structural, behavioural, and philosophical) in the sense that each critical perspective is the most appropriate response to the four aspects of fiction. The argument then moves on to claim that, because metafiction 'assimilates all the perspectives of criticism into the fictional process itself', this scheme offers a model for the typology of metafictions, so that four distinct directions in metafiction can be understood to pertain to these four aspects of both fiction and criticism. Like most typologies, Scholes's relies on relational rather than absolute categories, and difficulties of determining the dominant aspect of any given metafiction can present real problems to the critic. The interest of the essay lies mainly in the idea that when a novel assimilates critical perspective it acquires the power not only to act as commentary on other fictions, but also to incorporate insights normally formulated externally in critical discourse. Scholes seems to conclude that the critic, and even the 'metacritic', is redundant with regard to such insights, but only, I think, because he is writing in the immediate prehistory to the golden age of the American metacritic, an age in which criticism sought to incorporate the same kind of aporetic insight into subject and object relations.

*Reprinted from SCHOLES, ROBERT, 'Metafiction', *The Iowa Review*, 1, Fall (1970), 100–15.

This essay was originally published in *The Iowa Review* in conjunction with Robert Coover's short story 'The Reunion'.

Many of the so-called anti-novels are really metafictions.

(W.H. Gass)

And it is above all to the need for new modes of perception and fictional forms able to contain them that I, barber's basin on my head, address these stories.

(Robert Coover)

the sentence itself is a man-made object, not the one we wanted of course, but still a construction of man, a structure to be treasured for its weakness, as opposed to the strength of stones

(Donald Barthelme)

We tend to think of experiments as cold exercises in technique. My feeling about technique in art is that it has about the same value as technique in lovemaking. That is to say, heartfelt ineptitude has its appeal and so does heartless skill; but what you want is passionate virtuosity.

(John Barth)

I

To approach the nature of contemporary experimental fiction, to understand why it is experimental and how it is experimental, we must first adopt an appropriate view of the whole order of fiction and its relation to the conditions of being in which we find ourselves. Thus I must begin this consideration of specific works by the four writers quoted above with what may seem an over-elaborate discussion of fictional theory, and I ask the reader interested mainly in specifics to bear with me. In this discussion I will be trying not so much to present a new and startling view of fiction as to organize a group of assumptions which seem to inform much modern fiction and much of the fiction of the past as well. Once organized, these assumptions should make it possible to 'place' certain fictional and critical activities so as to understand better both their capabilities and limitations.

One assumption I must make is that both the conditions of being and the order of fiction partake of a duality which distinguishes existence from essence. My notion of fiction is incomplete without a concept of essential values, and so is my notion of life. Like many modern novelists, in fact like

most poets and artists in Western culture, ancient and modern, I am a
Platonist. One other assumption necessary to the view I am going to
present is that the order of fiction is in some way a reflection of the
conditions of being which make man what he is. And if this be
Aristotelianism, I intend to make the most of it. These conditions of being,
both existential and essential, are reflected in all human activity, especially
in the human use of language for esthetic ends, as in the making of
fictions. Imagine, then, the conditions of being, divided into existence and
essence, along with the order of fiction, similarly divided. This simple
scheme can be displayed in a simple diagram. [see Fig. 1.1].

fig. 1.1

FICTION	BEING
forms	existence
ideas	essence

The forms of fiction and the behavioral patterns of human existence
both exist in time, above the horizontal line in the diagram. All human
actions take place in time, in existence, yet these actions are tied to the
essential nature of man, which is unchanging or changing so slowly as to
make no difference to men caught up in time. Forms of behavior change,
man does not, without becoming more or less than man, angel or ape,
superman or beast. Forms of fiction change too, but the ideas of fiction are
an aspect of the essence of man, and will not change until the conditions of
being a man change. The ideas of fiction are those essential qualities which
define and characterize it. They are aspects of the essence of being human.
To the extent that fiction fills a human need in all cultures, at all times, it is
governed by these ideas. But the ideas themselves, like the causes of
events in nature, always retreat beyond the range of our analytical
instruments.

Both the forms of existence and the forms of fiction are most satisfying
when they are in harmony with their essential qualities. But because these
forms exist in time they cannot persist unchanged without losing their
harmonious relationship to the essence of being and the ideas of fiction. In
the world of existence we see how social and political modes of behavior
lose their vitality in time as they persist to a point where instead of
connecting man to the roots of his being they cut him off from this deep
reality. All revolutionary crises, including the present one, can be seen as
caused by the profound malaise that attacks men when the forms of
human behavior lose touch with the essence of human nature. It is similar
with fiction. Forms atrophy and lose touch with the vital ideas of fiction.
Originality in fiction, rightly understood, is the successful attempt to find

new forms that are capable of tapping once again the sources of fictional vitality. Because, as John Barth has observed, both time and history 'apparently' are real, it is only by being original that we can establish a harmonious relationship with the origins of our being.

Now every individual work of fiction takes its place in the whole body of fictional forms designated by the upper left-hand quadrant in Fig. 1.1. Among all these works we can trace the various diachronic relationships of literary genres as they evolve in time, and the synchronic relations of literary modes as they exist across time. As a way of reducing all these relationships to manageable order, I propose that we see the various emphases that fiction allows as reflections of the two aspects of fiction and the two aspects of being already described. Diagrammatically this could be represented by subdividing the whole body of fictional forms (the upper left-hand quadrant of Fig. 1.1) into four subquadrants, in [the manner shown in Fig. 1.2].

fig. 1.2	fiction of forms (romance)	fiction of existence (novel)
	fiction of ideas (myth)	fiction of essence (allegory)

Most significant works of fiction attend to all four of these dimensions of fictional form, though they may select an emphasis among them. But for convenience and clarity I will begin this discussion by speaking as if individual works existed to define each of these four fictional categories.

The fiction of ideas needs to be discussed first because the terminology is misleading on this point. By fiction of ideas in this system is meant not the 'novel of ideas' or some such thing, but that fiction which is most directly animated by the essential ideas of fiction. The fiction of ideas is mythic fiction as we find it in folk tales, where fiction springs most directly from human needs and desires. In mythic fiction the ideas of fiction are most obviously in control, are closest to the surface, where, among other things they can be studied by the analytical instruments of self-conscious ages that can no longer produce myths precisely because of the increase in consciousness that has come with time. Existing in time, the history of fiction shows a continual movement away from the pure expression of fictional ideas. Which brings us to the next dimension, the fiction of forms.

The fiction of forms is fiction that imitates other fiction. After the first myth, all fiction became imitative in this sense and remains so. The history of the form he works in lies between every writer and the pure ideas of fiction. It is his legacy, his opportunity and his problem. The fiction of forms at one level simply accepts the legacy and repeats the forms bequeathed it, satisfying an audience that wants this familiarity. But the movement of time carries such derivative forms farther and farther from the ideas of fiction until they atrophy and decay. At another level the fiction of forms is aware of the problem of imitating the forms of the past and seeks to deal with it by elaboration, by developing and extending the implications of the form. This process in time follows an inexorable curve to the point where elaboration reaches its most efficient extension, where it reaches the limits of tolerable complexity. Sometimes a form like Euphuistic fiction or the Romances of the Scudery family may carry a particular audience beyond what later eras will find to be a tolerable complexity. Some of our most cherished modern works may share this fate. The fiction of forms is usually labelled 'romance' in English criticism, quite properly, for the distinguishing characteristic of romance is that it concentrates on the elaboration of previous fictions. There is also a dimension of the fiction of forms which is aware of the problem of literary legacy and chooses the opposite response to elaboration. This is the surgical response of parody. But parody exists in a parasitic relationship to romance. It feeds off the organism it attacks and precipitates their mutual destruction. From this decay new growth may spring. But all of the forms of fiction, existing in time, are bound to decay, leaving behind the noble ruins of certain great individual works to excite the admiration and envy of the future – to the extent that the future can climb backwards down the ladder of history and understand the past.

The fiction of existence seeks to imitate not the forms of fiction but the forms of human behavior. It is mimetic in the sense that Erich Auerbach has given to the term 'mimesis'. It seeks to 'represent reality'. But 'reality' for the fiction of existence is a behavioristically observable reality. This behavioral fiction is a report on manners, customs, institutions, habits. It differs from history only, as Henry Fielding (and Aristotle) insisted, in that its truth is general and typical rather than factual and unique. The most typical form of behavioral fiction is the realistic novel (and henceforth in this discussion the term 'novel' will imply a behavioristic realism). The novel is doubly involved in time: as fiction in the evolution of fictional forms, and as a report on changing patterns of behavior. In a sense, the continual development of its material offers it a solution to the problem of formal change. If it succeeds in capturing changes in behavior it will have succeeded in changing its form: discovery will have created its appropriate technique. But as Mark Schorer has persuasively argued, it may be rather that new techniques in fiction enable new discoveries about human behavior to be made. So the great formal problem remains, even for behavioristic fiction. A further problem for the novel lies in the non-fictional adjuncts to its apprehension of behavior. How does the novelist perceive his reality? In general he perceives it with the aid of non-fictional systems of apprehension and evaluation. Notions like the control of personality by angels and devils, by humours in the body, by abstract 'ruling passions,' by phrenological or physiognomical characteristics, by hereditary gifts and failings, by environmental shapings and twistings, by psychological needs – all these have been indispensable to the novelist as ways of making human behavior manageable. Tracing the history of the novel, we trace the shift from religious perspectives on behavior through pseudo-scientific views toward a behavioral science which is perhaps close to achievement at last. If the study of human behavior should become truly scientific, it might limit the activities of novelists drastically. Currently, this danger seems to be driving writers of fiction away from behaviorism into other dimensions of narrative art, one of which is the fiction of essence.

The fiction of essence is concerned with the deep structure of being, just as the fiction of behavior is concerned with its surface structure. One route from behavior to essence is via depth psychology, and many novelists have taken that route, but there is some doubt whether it gets to the heart of the matter. The fiction of essence is characterized by an act of faith, by a leap beyond behavior toward ultimate values. This is a leap from behavioral realism to what Auerbach has called the 'figural realism' of Dante. In effect, it is the distinguishing characteristic of allegorical fiction. This is not to be confused with the petty allegory by which a character with a fictional name is used to point coyly at a historical personage with another. The fiction of essence is that allegory which probes and develops metaphysical questions and ideals. It is concerned most with ethical ideas and absolutes of value, where behavioral fiction emphasizes the relative values of action in practice. One of the great strengths of fiction has been its ability to be both allegorical and behavioral, to test ideals by giving them behavioristic embodiment, and to test conduct against the ideas of being. The problems of the allegorist lie partly in his management of the complex interrelations among the formal, behavioral, and essential dimensions of his art. They lie also, however, in his dependence on theological and philosophical systems of thought as approaches to the essence of being. These systems, of course, exist in time, and tend in time to lose whatever they may have captured of the essence of being.

The current retreat of philosophy into existential and behavioral postures presents special problems for the allegorist. Existentialism, for instance, in one of its aspects seeks to become purely active and situational. It is a theory which argues against theory. Thus the existential allegorist must often give us narratives of characters who make a discovery which cannot be communicated. They discover the truth, and in discovering it find that it is true-for-them-only. Thus the best of

contemporary allegorists (writers like Barth, Fowles, and Iris Murdoch) –
work closely with existentialist ideas and often find themselves moving
through the fiction of essence and back into the fiction of forms,
producing, instead of romances which turn into allegories, allegories
which turn into romances. The allegorist struggles with fictional form,
trying to make it express ultimate truth, just as the realist tries to make it
capture behavioral truth. John Barth has compared both of these struggles
to the myth of Proteus:

> The depressing thing about the myth is that he turns back into
> Proteus again. If the shifting of forms is thought of [in terms of]
> literary forms, what's particularly depressing is that he doesn't talk
> until he's turned back into old Proteus again, the thing that you
> seized in the first place, a dead end in a way.
>
> (From a symposium in *Novel*, Spring 1970)

It is the ideas of fiction which render Proteus mute except in his own
fictional form. The myth of Proteus symbolizes the unchanging laws that
govern that myth and all others, the ideas which exert their power
whenever man seeks to create in fictional forms.

The four-fold perspective on fiction presented here is intended to clarify
certain aspects of fictional creation. It should also serve to clarify the
relationship between certain kinds of criticism and certain kinds of fiction.
We can see the criticism of fiction as having four dimensions which
correspond to the four dimensions of fiction in a way described by Fig. 1.3.

fig. 1.3

formal criticism	behavioral criticism
structural criticism	philosophical criticism

Both formal criticism and structural criticism are concerned with the way
fiction works. But structural criticism is directed toward the essential ideas
of fiction. It treats the individual works as instances of the ideas or
principles that inform them. Both the French Structuralists of today and
the Russian Formalists of yesterday may be called structural critics in this
sense. (Which makes, alas, for an unfortunate terminological overlap.)
Because of their structural orientation some of the most successful and
influential work of the Russian Formalists has been based on myths and
folk-tales, where the ideas of fiction exist in their purest form. Propp's
Morphology of the Folk Tale is typical of the achievement of structural
criticism in general. Formal criticism is closely related to structural
criticism. But it is more concerned with individual works than with the
ideas that inform them. Formal criticism is also concerned with the formal

relationships among literary works as they exist in time. Where the structuralist looks for the ideas common to all fiction, as they relate to the human use of language and to other human activities, the formalist looks for the way fictional forms change in time to create generic patterns within which individual works take shape. The structuralist is mainly synchronic in his orientation; the formalist is diachronic. The ends of formal criticism are esthetic: what the artist has achieved in a particular work. The ends of structural criticism are scientific: the laws of fictional construction as they reveal themselves in many works. The self-conscious work which shows its awareness of fictional form by elaboration or parody is the particular delight of the formal critic: Fielding or Sterne, James or Joyce. This esthetically oriented criticism works best with esthetically oriented fiction – which is to say romance and anti-romance.

The formal and structural critics are concerned to explain how fiction works. The behavioral and philosophical critics are more interested in interpreting what fiction means. The behavioral critic in particular comes to fiction with strong convictions about the nature of existence. The rigid values of critics as different as Lukács and Leavis are characteristic of the social consciousness of behavioral criticism. The behavioral critic pronounced 'true' those works which agree with his ideological perspective and damns as 'false' those which see behavior differently or emphasize some dimension of fiction other than behavior. More than other literary critics, the behaviorists are in the world and aware of the world. The great behavioral critics have all been, in the broadest sense of the word, socialists. Marxist, Liberal, or Tory Radical, they have tended to see society as evolving in time towards a better life for all men, and have looked at literature in terms of its contribution to that evolution.

One would expect philosophical critics to be more detached and contemplative than the behaviorists, but it would be more correct to say that such philosophical criticism as we have had in recent years has been merely feeble and derivative. Too often our philosophical critics have been concerned with exegesis alone. W. H. Gass has made the case against this sort of criticism in an essay called 'Philosophy and the Form of Fiction':

> Still, the philosophical analysis of fiction has scarcely taken its first steps. Philosophers continue to interpret novels as if they were philosophies themselves, platforms to speak from, middens from which may be scratched important messages for mankind; they have predictably looked for content, not form; they have regarded fictions as ways of viewing reality and not as additions to it. There are many ways of refusing experience. This is one of them.

Yet the kind of truly philosophical criticism Gass calls for in this essay does in fact exist – in the work of the 'Geneva' critics, sometimes called phenomenological critics or 'critics of consciousness'. Their work parallels that of the structuralists, but is quite distinct from it. As the structuralist looks for the ideas that inform fictional structure and the laws that preside over the order of fiction, the critic of consciousness looks for the essential values that inhere in the experience of fiction. Clearly these two activities are connected, and language is the bridge that connects them. But the structuralists work out of the perspective of linguistic science, and the Geneva school out of the perspective of linguistic philosophy: crudely put, it is a matter of Saussure versus Merleau-Ponty. Perhaps Chomsky's *Cartesian Linguistics* is a bridge that may connect the two more closely. At any rate, it is fair to say that in recent years the most vigorous and important work in the criticism of fiction, which used to be done by formal and behavioral critics, has passed into the hands of structural and philosophical critics. The fact that most of this work has been done in the French language is perhaps to the shame of British and American criticism. But at the same time it must be said that criticism seems to have stifled fiction in France, while in the chaos and confusion of American critical thought a vigorous new fiction has developed. It is this new fiction, a metafiction, that I wish to consider in the second part of this discussion.

II

Metafiction assimilates all the perspectives of criticism into the fictional process itself. It may emphasize structural, formal, behavioral, or philosophical qualities, but most writers of metafiction are thoroughly aware of all these possibilities and are likely to have experimented with all of them. In the following pages I will be considering four works of metafiction by four young American writers: John Barth's *Lost in the Funhouse*, Donald Barthelme's *City Life*, Robert Coover's *Pricksongs and Descants*, and W. H. Gass's *In the Heart of the Heart of the Country*. All four of these books are collections of short pieces. This is not merely a matter of symmetry. When extended, metafiction must either lapse into a more fundamental mode of fiction or risk losing all fictional interest in order to maintain its intellectual perspectives. The ideas that govern fiction assert themselves more powerfully in direct proportion to the length of a fictional work. Metafiction, then, tends toward brevity because it attempts, among other things, to assault or transcend the laws of fiction – an undertaking which can only be achieved from within fictional form.

The four works chosen here are impressive in themselves: the products of active intelligence grappling with the problems of living and writing in the second half of the twentieth century. Any one of them might provide fruit for extended explication – and probably will. But that is not my

intention here. I will do justice to no author, no book, not even any single
story. Rather, I will use these four books to illustrate the range and vigor
of contemporary metafiction, and the depth of the problems confronted by
it. Each of the four books, taken as a whole, emphasizes one aspect of
metafiction which may be related to one of the aspects of fiction and
criticism as I presented them in the first part of this essay. This emphasis is
displayed diagrammatically in Fig. 1.4.

fig. 1.4

LOST IN THE FUNHOUSE (formal)	CITY LIFE (behavioral)
PRICKSONGS AND DESCANTS (structural)	IN THE HEART OF THE HEART OF THE COUNTRY (philosophical)

These four books, of course, do not fit into the four categories described
above like pigeons into pigeon-holes. Their metafictional resourcefulness
alone would ensure that. But each one does take a distinct direction, which
can be designated initially and tentatively by the above diagram. The
special emphasis of each work can be seen even in its title and the
selection and arrangement of the pieces included. *City Life*, for instance,
sounds behavioral – a book about life in the city. And in a sense that is
exactly what the book is, slices of life, but not cut in the old naturalistic
way of behavioral fiction. Oh no. Still, the book is dominated by a Dadaist
impulse to make funny art-objects out of found pieces of junk. The found
pieces in this case are mainly bits of intellectual and psychological debris,
worn and battered fragments of old insights and frustrations, 'tastefully'
arranged like a toilet rim halo perched jauntily on a bust of Freud.

In the Heart of the Heart of the Country sounds behavioral too, only
directed toward midwestern farms and villages rather than the urban east.
But there is one heart too many in that title, which gives us pause. Gass *is*
interested in behavior but he is always trying to see through it,
philosophically, to an essential order behind it: 'the quantity in the action,
the principle in the thing' – the heart of the heart. He rightly says that
Barthelme 'has managed to place himself in the center of modern
consciousness,' and Barthelme has done so by adopting a relentlessly
ironic vision which will tolerate no notion of essences, as he explains,
ironically, in 'Kierkegaard Unfair to Schlegel'. But there is a difference
between the center of consciousness and the heart of the heart. The woman
who narrates in 'Order of Insects' speaks with Gass's voice:

> I had always thought that love knew nothing of order and that life
> itself was turmoil and confusion. Let us leap, let us shout! I have

leaped, and to my shame I have wrestled. But this bug that I hold in my hand and know to be dead is beautiful, and there is a fierce joy in its composition that beggars every other, for its joy is the joy of stone, and it lives in its tomb like a lion.

I don't know which is more surprising: to find such order in a roach or such ideas in a woman.

('Order of Insects,' *Heart*, p. 170)

The difference between the approaches of Gass and Barthelme to the phenomena of behavior show clearly when we see them both looking at the same object, like a basketball:

Why do they always applaud the man who makes the shot?
Why don't they applaud the ball?
It is the ball that actually goes into the net.
The man doesn't go into the net.
Never have I seen a man going into the net.

('The Policemen's Ball,' *City*, p. 54).

Only the ball moves serenely through this dazzling din. Obedient to law it scarcely speaks but caroms quietly and lives at peace.

('In the heart ...,' *Heart*, p. 206)

Barthelme's ironic voice, with its remorseless Dick-and-Jane rhythms and its equally remorseless pseudo-logic, moves toward the absurdity of existence by generating a ridiculous vision of a man going through the net – man as object. Gass, using pronounced alliteration in a sentence which divided into an assonant iambic couplet: –

Obedient to law it scarcely speaks
But caroms quietly and lives at peace –

works in the opposite direction, raising the object to the level of sentient, harmonious life. Gass reaches for the poetic order behind prose. Barthelme exposes the banality of prosaic statement. The two writers share a view of modern behavior, but Gass's vision is enabled by this metaphysical idea of order, while Barthelme includes any idea of a metaphysical order within the irony of his behavioral perspectives.

In 'Brain Damage' Barthelme's voice mentions the 'brain damage caused by art. I could describe it better if I weren't afflicted with it'. And concludes with the parodic vision of brain damage falling like the snow that descends on the living and the dead in the last paragraph of another volume of stories of city life – Joyce's *Dubliners*:

And there is brain damage in Arizona, and brain damage in Maine, and little towns in Idaho are in the grip of it, and my blue heaven is black with it, brain damage covering everything like an unbreakable lease –

Skiing along on the soft surface of brain damage, never to sink, because we don't understand the danger –

('Brain Damage,' *City*, p. 146)

This is not simply a parody of Joyce and the quasi-religious perspective of the end of 'The Dead.' It is also a measure of how far we have come since *Dubliners*. This snow-like fallout of brain damage is not just a reminder of the pollution of our physical atmosphere, it is the crust of phenomenal existence which has covered our mental landscape, cutting us off from the essence of our being, afflicting even the artists. For Barthelme man has become a phenomenon among phenomena. 'WHAT RECOURSE?' ask the bold-type headlines of 'Brain Damage'. In 'Kierkegaard Unfair to Schlegel' Q and A discuss two possibilities, which are the two principal resources of metafiction: fantasy and irony:

Q: That's a very common fantasy.
A: All my fantasies are extremely ordinary.
Q: Does it give you pleasure?
A: A poor ... A rather unsatisfactory ...

(p. 84)

A: But I love my irony.
Q: Does it give you pleasure?
A: A poor ... A rather unsatisfactory ...

(p. 92)

What recourse, indeed, for those gripped by phenomenological brain damage? They are beyond good and evil, beyond being, barely existing, snowed under.

For Gass, this phenomenological despair is a tempting refuge which he cannot quite accept:

I would rather it were the weather that was to blame for what I am and what my friends and neighbours are – we who live here in the heart of the country. Better the weather, the wind, the pale dying snow ... the snow – why not the snow?

('In the Heart ...', *Heart*, p. 191)

But it is not the snow, the weather. Though the speaker tries to convince himself that 'body equals being, and if your weight goes down you are the less,' at the end of the title story (and of the volume) he is straining to hear 'through the boughs of falling snow' the 'twisted and metallic strains of a tune' that may or may not be 'Joy to the World'. Gass's world is full of snow, but there is always something active within it, like the mysterious killer in the black stocking cap who haunts the blizzard in 'The Pedersen Kid'. Gass's snow is not a crust that will support a man but a curtain that man must penetrate. It is not phenomenal but apocalyptic.

> He was in the thick snow now. More was coming. More was blowing down. He was in it now and he could go on and he could come through it because he had before. Maybe he belonged in the snow. Maybe he lived there, like a fish does in a lake. Spring didn't have anything like him.
>
> ('The Pedersen Kid', *Heart*, p. 72)

After the purgation of this snowborne violence, there may be a new life, peace, even joy:

> It was pleasant not to have to stamp the snow off my boots, and the fire was speaking pleasantly and the kettle was sounding softly. There was no need for me to grieve. I had been the brave one and now I was free. The snow would keep me. I would bury pa and the Pedersens and Hans and even ma if I wanted to bother. I hadn't wanted to come but now I didn't mind. The kid and me, we'd done brave things well worth remembering. The way that fellow had come so mysteriously through the snow and done us such a glorious turn – well it made me think how I was told to feel in church. The winter time had finally got them all, and I really did hope the kid was as warm as I was now, warm inside and out, burning up, inside and out, with joy.
>
> (pp. 78–9)

In *Pricksongs and Descants* and *Lost in the Funhouse* Coover and Barth are less directly concerned with the conditions of being than Gass and Barthelme, and more immediately interested in the order of fiction itself. This difference of emphasis is proclaimed in the titles of the works and developed in each collection. Both descants and pricksongs are contrapuntal music. They run counter to the 'cantus firmus' of behavior. But to run counter is not to run free. These songs must speak to us finally about reality, however roundabout their approach. There are also some puns in Coover's title which can be looked at later. The title of Barth's *Lost in the Funhouse* is taken from a story about a boy who 'actually' gets lost in a 'real' funhouse. But the story is also about the difficulty of writing a story about that 'real' experience, as the book is about the difficulty of the writer whose position in existence is distorted by his desire to find fictional equivalents for the conditions of being. For Barth, nature and Homer have a fearful symmetry – and they had it especially for Homer, he would add. 'For whom is the funhouse fun? Perhaps for lovers.' But not for artists and thinkers who alternate between making pricksongs and shouting, Stop the music. Trapped in life like a boy lost in a funhouse, this kind of man – intellectual man – seeks to maintain control over his being by *imagining* that he is lost in a funhouse, like Sartre's waiter in *Being and Nothingness* who seeks to control the problem of being a waiter by pretending to be a waiter. Barth's Ambrose is lost in a funhouse, so he 'pretends that it is not so bad after all in the funhouse'. The boy Ambrose, figure of thinking man, treats the problem of being lost in a 'real' funhouse by constructing an imaginary one:

> How long will it last? He envisions a truly astonishing funhouse, incredibly complex yet utterly controlled from a great central switchboard like the console of a pipe organ. Nobody had enough imagination. He could design such a place himself, wiring and all, and he's only thirteen years old. He would be its operator: panel lights would show what was up in every cranny of its cunning of its multifarious vastness; a switch-flick would ease this fellow's way, complicate that's, to balance things out; if anyone seemed lost or frightened, all the operator had to do was.
>
> ('Lost in the Funhouse,' *Funhouse*, p. 97)

Was what? Was what Ambrose can't think of without remembering that the funhouse he's in is not so well planned, so neatly equipped, is in fact 'real'. But he does remember.

> He wishes he had not entered the funhouse. But he has. Then he wishes he were dead. But he's not. Therefore he will construct funhouses for others and be their secret operator – though he would rather be among the lovers for whom funhouses are designed.
>
> (p. 97)

Because life is a rather badly made funhouse the artist tries to imagine a better one. 'God,' Barth has quipped, 'was not a bad novelist, only he was a realist'. The energizing power of Barth's universe is the tension between the imagination of man and the conditions of being which actually prevail. After the 'Frame-Tale' (A Moebius strip which reads, endlessly, 'ONCE UPON A TIME THERE WAS A STORY THAT BEGAN'), *Lost in the Funhouse* begins with 'Night-Sea Journey,' the tiny epic voyage of a spermatozoon caught in the inexorable motion of life, sex, and art. And it ends with the tale of an anonymous Greek writer (figure of Homer, father of fiction) who gets his inspiration by draining wine from nine amphorae (named after the Muses) which he then fills with sperm and fiction written on goatskin in a mixture of wine, blood, and squid ink. He casts these creations upon the waters to float like spermatozoa on some night-sea journey of impregnation. *Lost in the Funhouse* is concerned with philosophical questions, but its metaphysics is inside its esthetics (life is bad art); just as Barthelme's concern for essential values is lost in the 'Brain Damage' and 'Bone Bubbles' of *City Life*. For Barthelme, language is inside of behavior and cannot get outside it to establish a perspective beyond the disordered wanderings of damaged brains. For Barth, behavior is inside of language. Life is tantalizingly fictitious, a rough draft of what might be perfected as a supreme fiction. For Gass, there is a deep reality behind behavior, beyond the walls of the funhouse. 'Against the mechanical flutter of appearance' he places 'the glacial movement of reality'. To approach this inner truth is difficult, because the path through human behavior leads into ultimate falsehood as well as ultimate truth. The fear of this falsehood haunts the truth-seeking narrator of 'Mrs. Mean':

> Indeed I am not myself. This is not the world. I have gone too far. It is the way fairy tales begin – with a sudden slip over the rim of reality.
>
> ('Mrs. Mean,' *Heart*, p. 117)

For Robert Coover the way to truth leads precisely over the rim of reality and through the gingerbread house. He sees contemporary man as living in a contracting universe, forced to re-assume 'cosmic, eternal, supernatural (in its soberest sense) and pessimistic' perspectives. In such a world the writer must use

> the fabulous to probe beyond the phenomenological, beyond appearances, beyond randomly perceived events, beyond mere history. But these probes are above all – like [Don Quixote's] sallies – challenges to the assumptions of a dying age, exemplary adventures of the Poetic Imagination, high-minded journeys towards the New World and never mind that the nag's a pile of bones.
>
> ('Dedicatoria,' *Pricksongs*, p. 78).

Barth minds very much that the nag's a pile of bones. He feels that 'the narrator has narrated himself into a corner … and because his position is absurd he calls the world absurd' ('Title,' *Funhouse*, p. 112). He feels as imprisoned in the funhouse of fiction as Barthelme does in the brain damage of phenomena. But Coover, like Gass, senses an order beyond fiction and beyond phenomena, which may be discovered. But where Gass seeks to move through behavior to essence, Coover makes the parallel move through form to idea. This is why some of the most successful things in *Pricksongs* are reworkings of fairy tales which probe into the human needs behind them. Gass thinks of a 'real' Hansel and Gretel

> who went for a walk in a real forest but they walked too far in the forest and suddenly the forest was a forest of story with the loveliest little gingerbread house in it.
>
> ('Mrs. Mean,' *Heart*. p. 117)

But Coover thinks of a fictional Hansel and Gretel who find in a gingerbread house the door to reality:

> The children approach the gingerbread house through a garden of candied fruits and all-day suckers, hopping along on flagstones of variegated wafers. They sample the gingerbread weatherboarding with its caramel coating, lick at the meringue on the windowsills, kiss each other's sweetened lips. The boy climbs up on the chocolate roof to break off a peppermint-stick chimney, comes sliding down into a rainbarrel of vanilla pudding. The girl, reaching out to catch him in his fall, slips on a sugarplum and tumbles into a sticky garden of candied chestnuts. Laughing gaily they lick each other clean. And how grand is the red-and-white striped chimney the boy holds up for her! how bright! how sweet! But the door: here they pause and catch their breath. It is heart-shaped and blood-stone red, its burnished surface gleaming in the sunlight. Oh what a thing is that door! Shining like a ruby, like hard cherry candy, and pulsing softly, radiantly. Yes, marvelous! delicious! insuperable! but beyond: what is that sound of black rags flapping?
>
> ('The Gingerbread House,' *Pricksongs*, p. 75)

This gingerbread house is a garden of sexuality, with its phallic chimney and cherry-red door. Sex itself is the door that connects fictional form and mythic idea: which is why these tales are called pricksongs and descants, or 'death-cunt-and-prick songs,' as Granny calls them in the opening story, 'The Door'. Apertures and orifices are as dominant in *Pricksongs* as mirrors and containers are in the *Funhouse*. Coover's technique is to take the motifs of folk literature and explode them into motivations and relevations, as the energy might be released from a packed atomic structure. 'The Door' itself is a critical mass obtained by the fusion of 'Jack the Giant-Killer,' 'Beauty and the Beast,' 'Little Red Ridinghood,' and other mythic fictions. In the heavy water of this mixture there is more truth than in many surface phenomena. Granny is aware of this as she ruminates on the younger generation's preoccupation with epidermal existence:

> whose nose does she think she's twistin the little cow? bit of new fuzz on her pubes and juice in the little bubbies and off she prances into

that world of hers that ain't got forests nor prodigies a dippy smile on her face and her skirts up around her ears well I'll give her a mystery today I will if I'm not too late already and so what if I am? let her go tippytoin through the flux and tedium and trip on her dropped drawers a few times and see if she don't come running back to old Granny God preserve me whistlin a different tune! don't understand! hah! for ain't I the old Beauty who married the Beast?

('The Door,' *Pricksongs*, p. 16)

Granny is witch and wolf, wife and mother; she is the old Beauty who married the beast – 'only my Beast never became a prince' – she is temptress and artist, a Scheherazade who has 'veils to lift and tales to tell'; she is initiatrix into the mysteries of her own degradation and transfiguration:

for I have mated with the monster my love and listened to him lap clean his lolly after ... I have been split with the pain and terrible haste of his thick quick cock and then still itchin and bleedin have gazed on as he lept other bitches at random and I have watched my own beauty decline my love and still no Prince no Prince and yet you doubt that I understand? and loved him my child loved the damned Beast after all.

('The Door,' *Pricksongs*, p. 17)

The 'flux and tedium' of phenomenal existence is not reality but the thing which hides it. For Coover reality is mythic, and the myths are the doors of perception. Like a mind-blown Lévi-Strauss he is concerned to open those doors.

Coover's mythic vision can be defined partly by its distance from Barthelme's perspective on myth. Usually a fabricator of assemblages of 'flux and tedium,' in 'The Glass Mountain' Barthelme gives us a fairy tale of sorts. It seems there is this man climbing – 'grasping in each hand a sturdy plumber's friend' – a glass mountain 'at the corner of Thirteenth Street and Eighth Avenue'. In one hundred numbered sentences and fragments he reaches the top with its 'beautiful enchanted symbols'.

97. I approached the symbol, with its layers of meaning, but when I touched it, it changed into only a beautiful princess.
98. I threw the beautiful princess headfirst down the mountain ...

('The Glass Mountain,' *City*, p. 65)

This is myth enmeshed in phenomena. The 'symbol' in the story symbolizes symbolism, reducing it to absurdity. It becomes an object with

a sign on it that says 'beautiful enchanted symbol'. The magical
transformation of 'symbol' into 'princess' is simply a change of signs.
Barthelme is like a comic magician who removes a sign labeled 'rabbit'
from behind a sign labeled 'hat' in a parody of all magic. But when Coover
gives us a magician putting a lady in a hat in the last story of *Pricksongs*,
she is a real lady in a real hat:

> Pockets handkerchief. Is becoming rather frantic. Grasps hat and
> thumps it vigorously, shakes it. Places it once more on table, brim up.
> Closes eyes as though in incantations, hands extended over hat. Snaps
> fingers several times, reaches in tenuously. Fumbles. Loud slap.
> Withdraws hand hastily in angry astonishment. Grasps hat. Gritting
> teeth, infuriated, hurls hat to floor, leaps on it with both feet.
> Something crunches. Hideous piercing shriek.
>
> ('The Hat Act,' *Pricksongs*, p. 255)

Magic is real. The fairy tales are true. Beast and princess are not phony
symbols for Coover but fictional ideas of human essences. Barth and
Barthelme are the chroniclers of our despair: despair over the exhausted
forms of our thought and our existence. No wonder they laugh so much.
Coover and Gass are reaching through form and behavior for some
ultimate values, some true truth. No wonder they come on so strong. All
four are working in that rarefied air of metafiction, trying to climb beyond
Beckett and Borges, toward things that no critic – not even a metacritic, if
there were such a thing – can discern.

2 What is Metafiction and Why are They Saying Such Awful Things About it?*

PATRICIA WAUGH

Waugh's book *Metafiction: the Theory and Practice of Self-Conscious Fiction* is probably responsible more than any other for the prominence of the term in the Anglo-American critical lexis. Published in 1984 as part of Methuen's (now Routledge's) New Accents series, the study falls within the genre of student introductions to new directions in literary theory. But Waugh's book is not typical of that series in that its focus is, as the subtitle suggests, divided between literary theory and practice, identifying the common denominator among metafictional novelists as the exploration of 'a theory of fiction through the practice of writing fiction'. The problems of separating those fictions which do and do not explore fictional theory, and the definition of metafiction as fictional self-consciousness have been discussed in the introduction to this volume. Waugh's lucid analysis looks at metafiction's role in breaking down the distinction between a novel and the external world, and in merging the acts of creation and criticism into 'interpretation' and 'deconstruction'.

Waugh's double project here is to assemble an adequate definition of metafiction and to argue against its vilification by some commentators. With other contributors to this volume such as Barth, Hutcheon and Onega, the second of these projects aims to dissociate metafiction from connotations of the novel's death, and counter-argue that the critique of certain realist narrative assumptions gives the genre new power to describe our contemporary philosophical predicament.

What is metafiction?

The thing is this.
That of all the several ways of beginning a book which are now in practice throughout the known world, I am confident my own way of doing it is the best – I'm sure it is the most religious – for I begin with writing the first sentence – and trusting to Almighty God for the second.
(Laurence Sterne, *Tristram Shandy*, p. 438)

---

*WAUGH, P. *Metafiction: the Theory and Practice of Self-Conscious Fiction* (London: Methuen, 1984), pp. 1–19.

Fuck all this lying look what I'm really trying to write about is writing
not all this stuff...

(B.S. Johnson, *Albert Angelo*, p. 163)

Since I've started thinking about this story, I've gotten boils, piles, eye
strain, stomach spasms, anxiety attacks. Finally I am consumed by the
thought that at a certain point we all become nothing more than dying
animals.

(Ronald Sukenick, *The Death of the Novel and Other Stories*, p. 49)

I remember once we were out on the ranch shooting peccadillos
(result of a meeting, on the plains of the West, of the collared peccary
and the nine-banded armadillo).

(Donald Barthelme, *City Life*, p. 4)

Fiction is woven into all ... I find this new reality (or unreality) more
valid.

(John Fowles, *The French Lieutenant's Woman*, pp. 86–7)

If asked to point out the similarities amongst this disconcerting selection of
quotations, most readers would immediately list two or three of the
following: a celebration of the power of the creative imagination together
with an uncertainty about the validity of its representations; an extreme
self-consciousness about language, literary form and the act of writing
fictions; a pervasive insecurity about the relationship of fiction to reality; a
parodic, playful, excessive or deceptively naïve style of writing.

In compiling such a list, the reader would, in effect, be offering a brief
description of the basic concerns and characteristics of the fiction which
will be explored here. *Metafiction* is a term given to fictional writing which
self-consciously and systematically draws attention to its status as an
artefact in order to pose questions about the relationship between fiction
and reality. In providing a critique of their own methods of construction,
such writings not only examine the fundamental structures of narrative
fiction, they also explore the possible fictionality of the world outside the
literary fictional text.

Most of the quotations are fairly contemporary. This is deliberate. Over
the last twenty years, novelists have tended to become much more aware
of the theoretical issues involved in constructing fictions. In consequence,
their novels have tended to embody dimensions of self-reflexivity and
formal uncertainty. What connects not only these quotations but also all of
the very different writers whom one could refer to as broadly
'metafictional', is that they all explore a *theory* of fiction through the
practice of writing fiction.

The term 'metafiction' itself seems to have originated in an essay by the American critic and self-conscious novelist William H. Gass (in Gass 1970). However, terms like 'metapolitics', 'metarhetoric' and 'metatheatre' are a reminder of what has been, since the 1960s, a more general cultural interest in the problem of how human beings reflect, construct and mediate their experience of the world. Metafiction pursues such questions through its formal self-exploration, drawing on the traditional metaphor of the world as book, but often recasting it in the terms of contemporary philosophical, linguistic or literary theory. If, as individuals, we now occupy 'roles' rather than 'selves', then the study of characters in novels may provide a useful model for understanding the construction of subjectivity in the world outside novels. If our knowledge of this world is now seen to be mediated through language, then literary fiction (worlds constructed entirely of language) becomes a useful model for learning about the construction of 'reality' itself.

The present increased awareness of 'meta' levels of discourses and experience is partly a consequence of an increased social and cultural self-consciousness. Beyond this, however, it also reflects a greater awareness within contemporary culture of the function of language in constructing and maintaining our sense of everyday 'reality'. The simple notion that language passively reflects a coherent, meaningful and 'objective' world is no longer tenable. Language is an independent, self-contained system which generates its own 'meanings'. Its relationship to the phenomenal world is highly complex, problematic and regulated by convention. 'Meta' terms, therefore, are required in order to explore the relationship between this arbitrary linguistic system and the world to which it apparently refers. In fiction they are required in order to explore the relationship between the world *of* the fiction and the world *outside* the fiction.

In a sense, metafiction rests on a version of the Heisenbergian uncertainty principle: an awareness that 'for the smallest building blocks of matter, every process of observation causes a major disturbance' (Heisenberg 1972, p. 126), and that it is impossible to describe an objective world because the observer always changes the observed. However, the concerns of metafiction are even more complex than this. For while Heisenberg believed one could at least describe, if not a *picture* of nature, then a picture of one's *relation* to nature, metafiction shows the uncertainty even of this process. How is it possible to 'describe' anything? The metafictionist is highly conscious of a basic dilemma: if he or she sets out to 'represent' the world, he or she realizes fairly soon that the world, as such, cannot be 'represented'. In literary fiction it is, in fact, possible only to 'represent' the *discourses* of that world. Yet, if one attempts to analyse a set of linguistic relationships using those same relationships as the instruments of analysis, language soon becomes a 'prisonhouse' from which the possibility of escape is remote. Metafiction sets out to explore this dilemma.

The linguist L. Hjelmslev developed the term 'metalanguage' (Hjelmslev 1961). He defined it as a language which, instead of referring to non-linguistic events, situations or objects in the world, refers to *another* language: it is a language which takes another language as its object. Saussure's distinction between the signifier and the signified is relevant here. The signifier is the sound-image of the word or its shape on the page; the signified is the concept evoked by the word. A metalanguage is a language that functions as a signifier to *another language*, and this other language thus becomes its signified.[1]

In novelistic practice, this results in writing which consistently displays its conventionality, which explicity and overtly lays bare its condition of artifice, and which thereby explores the problematic relationship between life and fiction – both the fact that 'all the world is not of course a stage' and 'the crucial ways in which it isn't' (Goffman 1974, p. 53). The 'other' language may be either the registers of everyday discourse or, more usually, the 'language' of the literary system itself, including the conventions of the novel as a whole or particular forms of that genre.

Metafiction may concern itself, then, with particular conventions of the novel, to display the process of their construction (for example, John Fowles's use of the 'omniscient author' convention in *The French Lieutenant's Woman* (1969)). It may, often in the form of parody, comment on a specific work or fictional mode (for example, John Gardner's *Grendel* (1971), which retells, and thus comments on, the *Beowulf* story from the point of view of the monster; or John Hawkes's *The Lime Twig* (1961), which constitutes both an example and a critique of the popular thriller. Less centrally metafictional, but still displaying 'meta' features, are fictions like Richard Brautigan's *Trout Fishing in America* (1967). Such novels attempt to create alternative linguistic structures or fictions which merely *imply* the old forms by encouraging the reader to draw on his or her knowledge of traditional literary conventions when struggling to construct a meaning for the new text.

Metafiction and the novel tradition

I would argue that metafictional practice has become particularly prominent in the fiction of the last twenty years. However, to draw exclusively on contemporary fiction would be misleading for, although the *term* 'metafiction' might be new, the *practice* is as old (if not older) than the novel itself. *What I hope to establish* [...] is that metafiction is a tendency or function inherent in *all* novels. This form of fiction is worth studying not only because of its contemporary emergence but also because of the insights it offers into both the representational nature of all fiction and the literary history of the novel as genre. By studying metafiction, one is, in effect, studying that which gives the novel its identity.

Certainly more scholarly ink has been spilt over attempts to define the novel than perhaps for any other literary genre. The novel notoriously defies definition. Its instability in this respect is part of its 'definition': the language of fiction appears to spill over into, and merge with, the instabilities of the real world, in a way that a five-act tragedy or a fourteen-line sonnet clearly does not. Metafiction flaunts and exaggerates and thus exposes the foundations of this instability: the fact that novels are constructed through a continuous assimilation of everyday historical forms of communication. There is one privileged 'language of fiction'. There are the languages of memoirs, journals, diaries, histories, conversational registers, legal records, journalism, documentary. These languages compete for privilege. They question and relativize each other to such an extent that the 'language of fiction' is always, if often covertly, self-conscious.

Mikhail Bakhtin has referred to this process of relativization as the 'dialogic' potential of the novel. Metafiction simply makes this potential explicit and in so doing foregrounds the essential mode of all fictional language. Bakhtin defines as overtly 'dialogic' those novels that introduce a 'semantic direction into the word which is diametrically opposed to its original direction ... the word becomes the arena of conflict between two voices' (Bakhtin 1973, p. 106). In fact, given its close relation to everyday forms of discourse, the language of fiction is *always* to some extent dialogic. The novel assimilates a variety of discourses (representations of speech, forms of narrative) – discourses that *always* to some extent question and relativize each other's authority. Realism, often regarded as the classic fictional mode, paradoxically functions by suppressing this dialogue. The conflict of languages and voices is apparently resolved in realistic fiction through their subordination to the dominant 'voice' of the omniscient, godlike author. Novels which Bakhtin refers to as 'dialogic' resist such resolution. Metafiction *displays* and *rejoices in* the impossibility of such a resolution and thus clearly reveals the basic identity of the novel as genre.

Metafictional novels tend to be constructed on the principle of a fundamental and sustained opposition: the construction of a fictional illusion (as in traditional realism) and the laying bare of that illusion. In other words, the lowest common denominator of metafiction is simultaneously to create a fiction and to make a statement about the creation of that fiction. The two processes are held together in a formal tension which breaks down the distinctions between 'creation' and 'criticism' and merges them into the concepts of 'interpretation' and 'deconstruction'.

Although this oppositional process is to some extent present in all fiction, and particularly likely to emerge during 'crisis' periods in the literary history of the genre, its prominence in the contemporary novel is unique. The historical period we are living through has been singularly uncertain, insecure, self-questioning and culturally pluralistic. Contemporary fiction clearly reflects this dissatisfaction with, and breakdown of, traditional values. Previously, as in the case of nineteenth-century realism, the forms of fiction derived from a firm belief in a commonly experienced, objectively existing world of history. Modernist fiction, written in the earlier part of this century, responded to the initial loss of belief in such a world. Novels like Virginia Woolf's *To the Lighthouse* (1927) or James Joyce's *Ulysses* (1922) signalled the first widespread, overt emergence in the novel of a sense of fictitiousness: 'a sense that any attempt to represent reality could only produce selective perspectives, fictions, that is, in an epistemological, not merely in the conventional literary, sense' (Pfeifer 1978, p. 61).

Contemporary metafictional writing is both a response and a contribution to an even more thoroughgoing sense that reality or history are provisional: no longer a world of eternal verities but a series of constructions, artifices, impermanent structures. The materialist, positivist and empiricist world-view on which realistic fiction is premised no longer exists. It is hardly surprising, therefore, that more and more novelists have come to question and reject the forms that correspond to this ordered reality (the well-made plot, chronological sequence, the authoritative omniscient author, the rational connection between what characters 'do' and what they 'are', the causal connection between 'surface' details and the 'deep', 'scientific laws' of existence).

Why are they saying such awful things about it?

This rejection has inevitably entailed, however, a good deal of writerly and critical confusion. There has been paranoia, on the part of both novelists *and* critics for whom the exhaustion and rejection of realism is synonymous with the exhaustion and rejection of the novel itself. Thus B. S. Johnson bursts into (or out of?) *Albert Angelo* (1964) with the words which preface this chapter, 'Fuck all this lying'. His comment serves in the novel as much to voice a paranoid fear that his audience will misinterpret his fiction by reading it according to expectations based on the tradition of the realistic novel, as to demonstrate the artificiality of fictional form through a controlled metafictional discourse. At the end of the book he asserts:

a page is an area on which I place my signs I consider to communicate most clearly what I have to convey ... therefore I employ within the pocket of my publisher and the patience of my printer, typographical techniques beyond the arbitrary and constricting limits of the conventional novel. To dismiss such techniques as gimmicks or to refuse to take them seriously is crassly to miss the point.

(*Albert Angelo*, p. 176)

It reads rather like an anticipation of a hostile review. A similar defensiveness about the role of the novels it appears in Donald Barthelme's obsession with *dreck*, the detritus of modern civilization. It is expressed through John Barth's characters who – as much in the style of Sartre as in that of Sterne – 'die, telling themselves stories in the dark', desperately attempting to construct identities which can only dissolve into metalingual mutterings (*Lost in the Funhouse* (1968), p. 95). Extreme defensive strategies are common. Kurt Vonnegut's *Breakfast of Champions* (1973) is written to express the sense of absurdity produced by its author's paradoxical realization that 'I have no culture', and that 'I can't live without a culture anymore'; p. 15). Attempts at precise linguistic description continually break down. Crude diagrams replace language in order to express the poverty of the 'culture' which is available through representations of 'assholes', 'underpants' and 'beefburgers'.

The strategy of this novel is to invert the science-fiction convention whereby humans are depicted attempting to comprehend the processes of an alien world. Here, contemporary American society *is* the 'alien world'. Vonnegut defamiliarizes the world that his readers take for granted, through the technique of employing an ex-Earthling narrator who is now living on a different planet and has set out to 'explain' Earth to his fellow inhabitants. The defamiliarization has more than a satiric function, however. It reveals Vonnegut's own despairing recognition of the sheer impossibility of providing a critique of commonly accepted cultural forms of representation, from *with-in* those very modes of representation.

What is the novelist to do? Here the 'naïve' narrative voice, apparently oblivious of all our liberal value-systems and moral codes, reveals through its defamiliarizing effect their often *illiberal* and *amoral* assumptions and consequences. Beneath the fooling with representations of cows as beefburgers, however, lurks a desperate sense of the possible redundancy and irrelevance of the artist, so apparent in Vonnegut's *Slaughterhouse-Five* (1969). Indeed, Philip Roth, the American novelist, has written:

The American writer in the middle of the twentieth century has his hands full in trying to understand, describe, and then make credible much of American reality. It stupefies, it sickens, it infuriates, and

45

finally it is even a kind of embarrassment to one's own meagre
imagination. The actuality is continually outdoing our talents.
(Quoted in Bradbury 1977, p. 34).

In turning away from 'reality', however, and back to a re-examination of
fictional form, novelists have discovered a surprising way out of their
dilemmas and paranoia. Metafictional deconstruction has not only
provided novelists and their readers with a better understanding of the
fundamental structures of narrative; it has also offered extremely accurate
models for understanding the contemporary experience of the world as a
construction, an artifice, a web of interdependent semiotic systems. The
paranoia that permeates the metafictional writing of the sixties and
seventies is therefore slowly giving way to celebration, to the discovery of
new forms of the fantastic, fabulatory extravaganzas, magic realism
(Salman Rushdie, Gabriel García Márquez, Clive Sinclair, Graham Swift,
D. M. Thomas, John Irving). Novelists and critics alike have come to
realize that a moment of crisis can also be seen as a moment of
recognition: recognition that, although the assumptions about the novel
based on an extension of a nineteenth-century realist view of the world
may no longer be viable, the novel itself is positively flourishing.

Despite this renewed optimism, however, it is still the case that the
uncertain, self-reflexive nature of experimental metafiction will leave it
open to critical attacks. Yet metafiction is simply flaunting what is true of
all novels: their 'outstanding freedom to choose' (Fowles 1971, p. 46). It is
this instability, openness and flexibility which has allowed the novel
remarkably to survive and adapt to social change for the last 300 years. In
the face of the political, cultural and technological upheavals in society
since the Second World War, however, its lack of a fixed identity has now
left the novel vulnerable.

Hence critics have discussed the 'crisis of the novel' and the 'death of
the novel'. Instead of recognizing the *positive* aspects of fictional self-
consciousness, they have tended to see such literary behaviour as a form
of the self-indulgence and decadence characteristic of the exhaustion of
any artistic form or genre. Could it not be argued instead that
metafictional writers, highly conscious of the problems of artistic
legitimacy, simply sensed a need for the novel to theorize about itself?
Only in this way might the genre establish an identity and validity within
a culture apparently hostile to its printed, linear narrative and
conventional assumptions about 'plot', 'character', 'authority' and
'representation'. The traditional fictional quest has thus been transformed
into a quest for fictionality.

Metafiction and the contemporary avant-garde

This search has been further motivated by novelists' responses to another feature of contemporary culture life: the absence of a clearly defined avant-garde 'movement'. The existence of an unprecedented cultural pluralism has meant that post-modernist writers are not confronted with the same clear-cut oppositions as modernist writers were. An innovation in a literary form cannot establish itself as a new direction unless a sense of shared aims and objectives develops among experimental writers. This has been slow to take shape in recent years. An argument originally advanced by Lionel Trilling in *Beyond Culture* (Trilling 1966) and reiterated by Gerald Graff has suggested one reason for this: that the unmasking of the 'hypocritical bourgeois belief in the material and moral progress of civilization' (Graff 1975, p. 308) has been so thoroughly accomplished by modernism that the creative tension produced by opposing this 'bourgeois belief' is no longer clearly available to the novelist.

In eighteenth- and nineteenth-century fiction, the individual is always finally integrated into the social structure (usually through family relationships, marriage, birth or the ultimate dissolution of death). In modernist fiction the struggle for personal autonomy can be continued only through *opposition* to existing social institutions and conventions. This struggle necessarily involves individual alienation and often ends with mental dissolution. The power structures of *contemporary* society are, however, more diverse and more effectively concealed or mystified, creating greater problems for the post-modernist novelist in identifying and then representing the object of 'opposition'.

Metafictional writers have found a solution to this by turning inwards to their own medium of expression, in order to examine the relationship between fictional form and social reality. They have come to focus on the notion that 'everyday' language endorses and sustains such power structures through a continuous process of naturalization whereby forms of oppression are constructed in apparently 'innocent' representations. The literary-fictional equivalent of this 'everyday' language of 'common sense' is the language of the traditional novel: the conventions of realism. Metafiction sets up an opposition, not to ostensibly 'objective' facts in the 'real' world, but to the language of the realistic novel which has sustained and endorsed such a view of reality.

The metafictional novel thus situates its resistance *within* the form of the novel itself. Saussure distinguished between *langue* and *parole*: between the language system (a set of rules) and any act of individual utterance that takes place within this system. Each metafictional novel self-consciously sets its individual *parole* against the *langue* (the codes and conventions) of the novel tradition. Ostentatiously 'literary' language and conventions are paraded, are set against the fragments of various cultural codes, not because there is nothing left to talk about, but because the formal structures of these literary conventions provide a statement about the dissociation between, on the one hand, the genuinely felt sense of crisis, alienation and oppression in contemporary society and, on the other, the continuance of traditional literary forms like realism which are no longer adequate vehicles for the mediation of this experience. Metafiction thus converts what it sees as the negative values of outworn literary conventions into the basis of a potentially constructive social criticism. It suggests, in fact, that there may be as much to be learnt from setting the mirror of art up to its own linguistic or representational structures as from directly setting it up to a hypothetical 'human nature' that somehow exists as an essence outside historical systems of articulation.

The problem facing writers who attempt authentically to represent conditions of rapid social change is that they may themselves produce works of art which are ephemeral and even trivial. In the present situation 'even a single work will be sufficient grounds for declaring a style finished, exhausted' (Rochberg 1971, p. 73). The practitioners of so-called 'aleatory art' (which attempts to be totally random in order to suggest the chaotic, frenetic and colliding surfaces of contemporary technological society) are open to these charges. Literary texts tend to function by preserving a balance between the unfamiliar (the innovatory) and the familiar (the conventional or traditional). Both are necessary because some degree of redundancy is essential for any message to be committed to memory. Redundancy is provided for in literary texts through the presence of familiar conventions. Experimental fiction of the aleatory variety eschews such redundancy by simply ignoring the conventions of literary tradition. Such texts set out to resist the normal processes of reading, memory and understanding, but without redundancy, texts are read and forgotten. They cannot unite to form a literary 'movement' because they exist only at the moment of reading.

The metafictional response to the problem of how to represent impermanence and a sense of chaos, in the permanent and ordered terms of literature, has had a much more significant influence on the development of the novel as genre. Aleatory writing might imitate the experience of living in the contemporary world, but it fails to offer any of the comfort traditionally supplied by literary fiction through a 'sense of an ending' (Kermode 1966). Metafiction, however, offers both innovation *and* familiarity through the individual reworking and undermining of familiar conventions.

Aleatory writing simply responds with a reply in kind to the pluralistic, hyperactive multiplicity of styles that constitute the surfaces of present-day culture. What is mainly asserted in such novels is an anarchic individualism, a randomness designed to represent an avoidance of social control by stressing the impossibility of easily categorizing it or assimilating the reader to familiar structures of communication. An argument sometimes proposed to justify the strategies of such fictions is that they are 'radical' because they rupture the conventional linguistic contracts that certify and/or disguise orthodox social practices (as realism, for example, certifies concepts like 'eternal human nature' or the assumption that authority as manifested through the omniscient author is somehow free of both gender distinctions and of historically constructed and provisional moral values). Such novels supposedly expose the way in which these social practices are constructed through the language of oppressive ideologies, by refusing to allow the reader the role of passive consumer or any means of arriving at a 'total' interpretation of the text.

Although it is true that much of this should undoubtedly be the task of experimental fiction, it does seem questionable whether, for many readers, so-called 'aleatory writing' is going to accomplish all of this. Novels like John Fowles's *The French Lieutenant's Woman* or Robert Coover's *Pricksongs and Descants* (1969), though apparently less 'radical', are in the long run likely to be more successful. Both are metafictional novels in that they employ parody self-consciously. Both take as their 'object' languages the structures of nineteenth-century realism and of historical romance or of fairy-tales. The parody of these 'languages' functions to defamiliarize such structures by setting up various counter-techniques to undermine the authority of the omniscient author, of the closure of the 'final' ending, of the definitive interpretation. Although the reader is thereby distanced from the language, the literary conventions and, ultimately, from conventional ideologies, the defamiliarization proceeds from an extremely familiar base. Such novels can thus initially be comprehended through the old structures, and can therefore be enjoyed and remain in the consciousness of a wide readership which is given a far more active role in the construction of the 'meaning' of the text than is provided either in contemporary realist novels or in novels which convert their readers into frenetic human word-processors, and which 'last' only as long as it takes to read them.

The mirror up to art: metafiction and its varieties

It remains [...] briefly to examine some alternative definitions of self-conscious writing. These similar modes have been variously termed 'the introverted novel', 'the anti-novel', 'irrealism', 'surfiction', 'the self-begetting novel', 'fabulation'.[2] All, like 'metafiction', imply a fiction that self-consciously reflects upon its own structure as language; all offer different perspectives on the same process. But the terms shift the emphasis in different ways. The 'self-begetting novel', for example, is described as an 'account usually first person, of the development of a character to a point at which he is able to take up and compose the novel we have just finished reading' (Kellman 1976, p. 1245). The emphasis is on the development of the narrator, on the modernist concern of *consciousness* rather than the post-modernist one of *fictionality* (as in, for example, André Gide's *The Counterfeiters* (1925)).

The entry of the narrator into the text is also a defining feature of what has been called 'surfiction'. Raymond Federman's book of that name discusses the mode in terms of overt narratorial intrusion so that, as in the 'self-begetting novel', the focus appears to be on the ironist him/herself rather than on the overt and covert levels of the ironic text. Telling as individual invention, spontaneous fabrication at the expense of external reality or literary tradition, is emphasized rather than what has been stressed above: metafiction's continuous involvement in – and mediation of – reality through linguistic structures and pre-existent texts.

As defined here, of course, metafictional writing may include all or some of the strategies that critics have discussed in the terms that have been mentioned. Different categories, in fact, often compete for the same fictional texts: John Barth's *Lost in the Funhouse* (1968) is clearly 'self-begetting', 'surfictional' *and* 'metafictional'. As I have argued, metafiction is not so much a sub-genre of the novel as a tendency *within* the novel which operates through exaggeration of the tensions and oppositions inherent in all novels: of frame and frame-break, of technique and counter-technique, of construction and deconstruction of illusion. Metafiction thus expresses overtly what William H. Gass has argued is the dilemma of all art:

> In every art two contradictory impulses are in a state of Manichean war: the impulse to communicate and so to treat the medium of communication as a means and the impulse to make an artefact out of the materials and so to treat the medium as an end.
>
> (Gass 1970)

The expression of this tension is present in much contemporary writing but it is the *dominant* function in the texts defined here as metafictional.

The metafictions of Jorge Luis Borges and Vladimir Nabokov illustrate this point. In some of their work – Borges' *Labyrinths* (1964) and Nabokov's *Pale Fire* (1962), for example – fiction *explicitly* masquerades as formalized critical interpretation. In all their work, however, as in all other metafiction, there is a more complex *implicit* interdependence of levels than this. The reader is always presented with embedded strata which contradict the presuppositions of the strata immediately above or below. The fictional *content* of the story is continually reflected by its *formal* existence as text, and the existence of that text within a world viewed in terms of 'textuality'. Brian McHale has suggested that such contradictions are essentially *ontological* (posing questions about the nature and existence of reality) and are therefore characteristically post-modernist. He sees as modernist those *epistemological* contradictions which question how we can know a reality whose existence is finally not in doubt (McHale, forthcoming).

Borges' imaginary kingdom Tlön, discovered by the 'fortunate conjunction of a mirror and an encyclopaedia', is a post-modernist world. It is twice a fiction because it is suggested that, before its invention by Borges,it has already been invented by a secret society of idealists including Bishop Berkeley, and both, of course, are finally dependent upon the conventions of the short story (*Labyrinths*, p. 27). The fact that this 'imaginary' world can take over the 'real' one emphasizes more than the *epistemological* uncertainty of both of them (which would be the aim of the 'self-begetting novel'). 'Tlön Uqbar Orbis Tertius', the story, is about a story that invents an imaginary world, and it primarily and self-consciously *is* a story which, like all stories, invents an imaginary world. It implies that human beings can only ever achieve a metaphor for reality, another layer of 'interpretation'. (Borges' story 'Funes the Memorias' (1964) shows that this need not be cause for despair, for if indeed we could not create metaphorical images then we would all surely become insane.)

Metafictional novels (unlike 'surfiction' or 'the self-begetting novel') thus reject the traditional figure of the author as a transcendental imagination fabricating, through an ultimately monologic discourse, structures of order which will replace the forgotten material text of the world. They show not only that the 'author' is a concept produced through previous and existing literary and social texts but that what is generally taken to be 'reality' is also constructed and mediated in a similar fashion. 'Reality' is to this extent 'fictional' and can be understood through an appropriate 'reading' process.

Also rejected is the displacement of 'historical man' by 'structural man' advocated by Robert Scholes as the basis of what he calls 'fabulation' (Scholes 1975). David Lodge has pointed out that 'history may be in a philosophical sense, a fiction, but it does not feel like that when we miss a train or somebody starts a war'.[3] As novel readers, we look to fiction to offer us cognitive functions, to locate us within everyday as well as within philosophical paradigms, to explain the historical world as well as offer some formal comfort and certainty. Scholes argues that the empirical has lost all validity and that a collusion between the philosophic and the mythic in the form of 'ethically controlled fantasy' is the only authentic mode for fiction (Scholes 1967, p. 11). However, metafiction offers the recognition, not that the everyday has ceased to matter, but that its formulation through social and cultural codes brings it closer to the philosophical and mythic than was once assumed.

A brief comparison of two self-conscious novels, one obviously 'metafictional', the other more obviously 'fabulatory', shows how metafiction explores the concept of fictionality through an opposition between the construction and the breaking of illusion, while fabulation reveals instead what Christine Brooke-Rose (1980) has referred to as a reduced tension between technique and counter-technique: a 'stylization' which enables other voices to be *assimilated*, rather than presenting a conflict of voices.

Muriel Spark's *metafictional* novels lay bare the process of imposing form upon contingent matter through the discursive organization of 'plot'. She can, however, as David Lodge has said of Joyce, afford her metaphoric flights because of the stability of her metonymic base (Lodge 1977a, p. 111). She uses her 'flights', in fact, to comment on the very paradigms that they are in the process of constructing (this embedding of strata, of course, being fundamental to metafiction). In *Not to Disturb* (1971), for example, this highly obtrusive simile describes a storm:

> Meanwhile the lightning which strikes the clump of elms so that the two friends huddled there are killed instantly without pain, zigzags across the lawns, illuminating the lily-pond and the sunken rose garden like a self-stricken flash photographer, and like a zip-fastener ripped from its garment by a sexual maniac.
>
> (p. 86)

This appears to be a piece of highly stylized descriptive prose marked particularly by the appearance of extremely bizarre metaphors. To this extent it is very similar to Richard Brautigan's *fabulatory* novel, *Trout Fishing in America* (1967), which is full of similar metaphorical constructions where the extreme polarity of vehicle and tenor implicitly reminds the reader of the way in which metaphor constructs an image of reality by connecting apparently quite disparate objects. In this novel, for example, trout are described waiting in streams 'like airplane tickets' (p. 78), and the reader's imagination is stretched throughout by the incongruity of the comparisons. The novel is a celebration of the creative imagination: it is a 'fabulation'.

In the Spark example, however, there is a further, more subtle function that is part of a sustained metafictional display; for the vehicle of the metaphor is explicitly related to what is happening at the continuously unfolding level of the story. A group of entrepreneurial and enterprising servants have arranged the filming of the last moments of an eternal triangle of superannuated aristocrats. The servants know their masters are going to die and also know how to capitalize on their deaths. Aristocratic scandals provide excellent material for media sensationalism. The photographer and the zip fastener (which the mentally deficient aristocratic son is continually attempting to rip off in the excitement of his intermittent sexual energy) are important elements in the plot being constructed by the novelist (who also, as in the example, arranges appropriate climatic conditions) and, of course, by the characters. The reader is alerted to the way in which the explicitly artificial construction of these connections fits in with the larger designs of the novelist playing God. The elements at the metaphorical level of the construction break down not into 'natural' or randomly chosen components, but to another level of artifice: the level of the 'plot'. The reader is thus reminded that pure contingency in novels is always an illusion, although the lowest level of the artifice (what the Russian formalist Boris Tomashevsky has referred to as realistic motivation; see Lemon and Reis 1965, pp. 61–99) is assumed to be reality. Thus not only do the characters in this novel play roles, 'fictionalize' in terms of the *content* of the plot; they too are 'fictionalized', created, through the *formal construction* of the plot.

Metafiction explicitly lays bare the conventions of realism; it does not ignore or abandon them. Very often realistic conventions supply the 'control' in metafictional texts, the norm of background against which the experimental strategies can foreground themselves. More obviously, of course, this allows for a stable level of readerly familiarity, without which the ensuing dislocations might be either totally meaningless or so outside the normal modes of literary or non-literary communication that they cannot be committed to memory (the problem, already discussed, of much contemporary 'aleatory' writing). Metafiction, then, does not abandon 'the real world' for the narcissistic pleasures of the imagination. What it does is to re-examine the conventions of realism in order to discover – through its own self-reflection – a fictional form that is culturally relevant and comprehensible to contemporary readers. In showing us how literary fiction creates its imaginary worlds, metafiction helps us to understand how the reality we live day by day is similarly constructed, similarly 'written'.

'Metafiction' is thus an elastic term which covers a wide range of fictions. There are those novels at one end of the spectrum which take fictionality as a theme to be explored (and in this sense would include the 'self-begetting novel'), as in the work of Iris Murdoch or Jerzy Kosinski, whose formal self-consciousness is limited. At the centre of this spectrum are those texts that manifest the symptoms of formal and ontological insecurity but allow their deconstructions to be finally recontextualized or 'naturalized' and given a total interpretation (which constitute, therefore, a 'new realism'), as in the work of John Fowles or E.L. Doctorow. Finally, at the furthest extreme (which would include 'fabulation') can be placed those fictions that, in rejecting realism more thoroughly, posit the world as a fabrication of competing semiotic systems which never correspond to material conditions, as in the work of Gilbert Sorrentino, Raymond Federman or Christine Brooke-Rose.

Much British fiction fits into the first half of the spectrum, though problematically, and much American fiction into the other half, though with the same proviso. The novelist at either end, however – in confronting the problem that, 'whether or not he makes peace with realism, he must somehow cope with reality' (Dickinson 1975, p. 372) – has acknowledged the fact that this 'reality' is no longer the one mediated by nineteenth-century novelists and experienced by nineteenth-century readers. Indeed, it could be argued that, far from 'dying', the novel has reached a mature recognition of its existence as *writing*, which can only ensure its continued viability in and relevance to a contemporary world which is similarly beginning to gain awareness of precisely how its values and practices are constructed and legitimized.

Notes

1. See FREDERIC JAMESON's *The Prisonhouse of Language* (Princeton and London: 1972), p. 159. Also useful is Jameson's essay 'Metacommentary', *PMLA*, 86 (1971).

2. The 'introverted novel' is referred to by JOHN FLETCHER and MALCOLM BRADBURY, in *Modernism: 1890–1930* (Harmondsworth: Penguin, 1976). They distinguish between eighteenth-century introversion, which draws attention to the narrator (as in *Tristram Shandy*), and twentieth-century introversion, which draws 'attention to the autonomy of the fictive structure itself' (p. 394) – as in novels by Muriel Spark, Vladimir Nabokov and Günter Grass. 'Anti-novel' is a widely used but rather vague term covering any novel whose structure seems to form a protest against traditional fictional forms. For an introduction to 'surfiction', see RAYMOND FEDERMAN's *Surfiction: Fiction Now ... and Tomorrow* (Chicago, Ill.: University of Illinois Press, 1975). 'Metafiction' itself is first used as a term by WILLIAM H. GASS, in *Fiction and the Figures of Life* (New York: 1970), p. 25. It is discussed extensively in ROBERT SCHOLES's essay 'Metafiction', in *The Iowa Review*, I, Fall (1970), 100.

3. DAVID LODGE, 'The Novelist at the Crossroads', in MALCOLM BRADBURY (ed.), *The Novel Today* (London: Fontana, 1977), p. 109. See also Lodge's essay 'Towards a Poetics of Fiction: An Approach through Language', in MARK SPILKA (ed.), *Towards a Poetics of Fiction* (Bloomington, Ind., and London: 1977).

3 Metanarrative Signs*

GERALD PRINCE

This extract from Prince's *Narratology*, published in 1982, represents a highly systematic approach to the analysis of narrative signs. Based on the work of Roman Jakobson, this analysis also derives from narratological structuralist ideas in the work of Roland Barthes, Wayne Booth, Jean Genette and Tzvetan Todorov. The importance of this essay in the present volume is the emphasis it gives to the idea that metanarrative signs are inherent features of narrative in general, and not merely characteristics of metafictional novels. Like Jakobson, Prince takes the view that metalingual aspects of language happily co-exist with other linguistic functions such as the referential, the emotive and the poetic. Thus we can assume that for Prince, as for Jakobson, a metafiction would be a fictional narrative in which the metanarrative function of signs dominate other such functions of the narrative. Prince understands metanarrative signs as glosses on parts of a text and its underlying codes: as a metanarrative commentary which builds into the text instructions on how to read. Like Scholes's idea of 'assimilated critical perspective', Prince's idea of metanarrative self-commentary is a way of indicating within a text how a reading might proceed and in what it should consist. But for Prince, metanarrative signs do not only tell us how we read – they also specify the distance between a text's self-commentary (as an appropriation of reading) and the reading process of a given reader, reminding us that a text can never fully appropriate reading.

In the context of structuralist approaches to the issue of fictional self-consciousness, another excellent analysis appears in the chapter 'Fictionality Declared' in Michael Riffaterre's recent work *Fictional Truth* (1990).

When the subject of a discourse is language, we sometimes say that the discourse is metalinguistic. Similarly, when the subject of a discourse is

---

*Reprinted from PRINCE, G., *Narratology* (Berlin, New York and Amsterdam: Monton, 1982), pp. 115–28.

narrative, we may say that the discourse is meta-narrative. According to this very general definition of the term, there are many kinds of discourse which may be metanarrative: a philosophical essay on the ontology of narration, for instance, a history of the Russian novel, or the present study. Obviously, a verbal narrative itself may be metanarrative: a given tale may refer to other tales; it may comment on narrators and narratees; or it may discuss the act of narration. Just as obviously, a particular narrative may refer to itself and to those elements by which it is constituted and communicated. Consider the following, for example:

(47) There was in all this, as may have been observed, one personage concerned, of whom, notwithstanding his precarious position, we have appeared to take but very little notice; this personage in M. Bonacieux, the respectable martyr of the political and amorous intrigues which entangled themselves so nicely together at this gallant and chivalric period. Fortunately, the reader may remember, or may not remember, fortunately, that we promised not to lose sight of him.

(*Les Trois Mousquetaires*)

(48) Perhaps I shall eliminate the preceding chapter. Among other reasons, there is, in the last few lines, something that might be construed as an error on my part.

(*Epitaph of a Small Winner*)

(49) Thus, gentle reader, I have given thee a faithful history of my travels for sixteen years and above seven months: wherein I have not been so studious of ornament as of truth. I could, perhaps, like others, have astonished thee with strange improbable tales; but I rather chose to relate plain matter of fact, in the simplest manner and style; because my principal design was to inform and not amuse thee.

(*Gulliver's Travels*)

These self-referential aspects of narrative have attracted quite a lot of attention recently and some theorists have successfully argued that many a narrative ultimately discusses itself and actually constitutes a metanarrative.[1]

There is another possible definition of the term metanarrative, a stricter and perhaps more meaningful one. In a famous statement on linguistics and poetics, Roman Jakobson presented a rapid survey of the constitutive factors in any act of verbal communication:

The **addresser** sends **a message** to the **addressee**. To be operative the message requires a **context** referred to ('referent' in another somewhat ambiguous nomenclature), seizable by the addressee, and either verbal or capable of being verbalized; a **code** fully, or at least partially, common to the addresser and addressee (or in other words, to the encoder and decoder or the message); and, finally, a **contact**, a physical channel and psychological channel and psychological connection between the addresser and the addressee, enabling both of them to enter and stay in communication.[2]

To each of these factors corresponds a different function of language. Should a verbal act be oriented mainly towards the referent or context, as in

(50) John is handsome and intelligent

it would have a primarily **referential** function. Should it be focused on the addresser and express his attitude towards what he is saying, as in

(51) I am getting bored talking about it

it would have an **emotive** function. Should it be centered on the addressee, as in

(52) Hey, you! Listen carefully!

it would have a **conative** function. A verbal act may also be aimed primarily towards the contact; it may be used, for instance, to check whether the channel works or to establish and prolong communication, as in

(53) Hello! Can you hear me?

or

(54) Do you know what I mean?

In this case, it mainly has a **phatic** function. It may be focused on the message for its own sake and draw our attention to its sound patterns, diction, syntax, structure, etc., as in

(55) Peter Piper picked a peck of pickled peppers;

it would then fulfill a so-called **poetic** function. Finally, it may be oriented towards the code and convey information about it, as in

(56) 'Flicks' means 'movies';

this would fulfill a **metalinguistic** function.[3]

Like any verbal act and, indeed, any signifying process, any narrative can be described in terms of similar factors. Thus, should certain parts of the narrative pertain to the narrator and his attitude towards what he is narrating ('With pain we record it, this first ecstasy was soon disturbed', *Notre-Dame de Paris*), we could say that they have an emotive function; should they concentrate on the narratee ('The reader has no doubt turned over the admirable works of Rembrandt', *Notre-Dame de Paris*), we would say that they have a conative function; and should they be focused on the code of the narrative, we could say that they primarily fulfill a metanarrative function. In other terms, the metanarrative component of a given narrative does not consist of any and all passages referring to that narrative or its constituent parts and should not be confused with the self-referential component. Rather, it is made up of those passages which explicitly refer to its code and which I call metanarrative signs.

Let us define a metanarrative sign more precisely by patterning our definition on that of a metalinguistic sign. Consider the following statements made up of linguistic signs:

(57) Destruction is terrible
(58) 'Destruction' is terrible
(59) Killing is bad
(60) 'Killing' is a present participle
(61) Freshmen are always nice
(62) 'Freshmen' means first-year students

(57), (59) and (61) tell us something about the world (a certain world); more particularly, **destruction, killing** and **freshmen** designate certain objects or actions in that world and they, as well as the terms predicated on them, refer us to that world. On the other hand, (58), (60) and (62) do not tell us very much about the world; rather, they tell us something about words, about signs in a language. Specifically, **'destruction'**, **'killing'** and **'freshmen'** do not designate anything else but the word 'destruction', the word 'killing', the word 'freshmen', and the terms predicated on them merely refer us to these words as words, to these signs as signs. (58), (60), and (62) are metalinguistic statements and the predicates in them are metalinguistic signs. In other words, a sign is metalinguistic when it is predicated on a linguistic unit taken as an element in the linguistic code.[4]

In a given narrative, there are many elements – many series of signs – which tell us something about a certain world. But there may also be elements which explicitly comment on such and such another element x in the narrative and which provide an answer to such questions as 'What does x mean in the (sub-) code according to which the narrative is developed?' or 'What is x in the (sub-) code used?', or again 'How does x function in the (sub-) code according to which the narrative can be read?' Each one of the commenting elements constitutes a metanarrative sign: each one is a sign predicated on a narrative unit considered as an element in the narrative code.[5]

Note that, according to this definition, a narrative passage like

(63) Shirley, who had always been very cheerful, was crying all the time.

contains no metanarrative signs (though it may suggest that there is a mystery to be solved and lead to a question such as 'How is it that Shirley is crying all the time?') On the other hand,

(64) Shirley, who had always been very cheerful, was crying all the time. This was a mystery.

does: **this was a mystery** explicitly tells us that Shirley's behavior is a unit in the hermeneutic code framing the narrative and that it must be taken as constituting an enigma.

Furthermore, note that there may be passages in a narrative which explicitly teach us something about the conventions of the world of the narrated but which are not metanarrative. For instance,

(65) It is the idea of duration – of earthly immortality – that gives such a mysterious interest to our own portraits. Walter and Elinor were not insensible to that feeling, and hastened to the painter's room.

('The Prophetic Pictures')

(66) Polder behaves as though he has been placed under eternal obligation by Rickett ... It is the same everywhere. The men who would not take the trouble to conceal from you that you are an incompetent ass ... will work themselves to the bone in your behalf if you fall sick or into serious trouble.

(The Phantom 'Rickshaw')

(67) Apartment dwellers always hate their neighbors and so John hated Peter.

tell us something about certain laws governing certain worlds and explain certain feelings and attitudes in terms of these laws; but no part of (65)–(67)

is predicated on a narrative unit taken merely as an element in the code. Instead of answering such questions as

(68) What is the meaning of unit x in the (linguistic, proairetic, hermeneutic ...) code framing the narrative?

or

(69) What is the function of unit x in the (linguistic, proairetic, hermeneutic ...) code framing the narrative?

parts of (65)–(67) answer something like 'Why x?' (Why did Walter and Elinor hasten to the painter's room? Why does Polder act as though he has been placed under eternal obligation by Rickett? Why did John hate Peter?) Similarly, as I have indicated earlier, there may be various passages which underline the organization of the narrated or the act of narration but which do not constitute metanarrative signs. In

(70) Our readers must have already perceived that D'Artagnan was not a common man.

(Les Trois Mousquetaires)

and

(71) We have just said that, on the day when the Egyptian and the archdeacon died, Quasimodo was not to be found in Notre-Dame.

(Notre-Dame de Paris)

there is no element which explicitly answers questions like (68) or (69).[6]

Note also that passages which implicitly or indirectly refer to and comment on the nature, meaning or function of other passages need not be considered metanarrative. After all, any sign in a system may be said to carry within itself an implicit comment on the meaning (or nature, or function) of all other signs in that system since it makes sense only in relation to them and vice versa. Indeed, the meaning of a particular element may be arrived at not by reference to the code but by reference to the context, by an examination of its connections with the other elements making up the sequence within which it appears. Consider, for example, the following passage from *The Sun Also Rises*:

(72) 'She took a telegram out of the leather wallet ... "Por ustedes?" I looked at it. The address was: "Barnes, Burguete". Yes, it's for us.'

Yes, it's for us is obviously an answer to **Por ustedes?** and it can be concluded, therefore, that the latter expression means something like **Is it**

for you?. But **Yes, it's for us** cannot replace **Por ustedes**? in the linguistic code; it is not predicated on **Por ustedes**?; and it does not directly answer a question such as 'What does **Por ustedes**? mean in the linguistic code used?' The meaning of **Por ustedes**? is arrived at mainly through contextual operations.

Finally, note that it is not the shape of an element but its relation to another element which makes it metalinguistic or more generally, metanarrative. In

(73) Jogging is funny

and

(74) 'Jogging' is funny

we find the same predicate. But, in the former,

(75) is funny

is predicated of a certain event in a certain world and refers us to that world; whereas, in the latter, (75) is predicated of a linguistic sign and is, therefore, metalinguistic. In the same way, identical sets of elements may function differently in different narrative passages. Given

(76) John was handsome and he had reached adulthood

and

(77) John had his own house, which meant that he had reached adulthood.

(78) he had reached adulthood

functions metanarratively (metaculturally) in (77) only.

The most evident metanarrative signs – though not necessarily the most numerous or the most important – are probably those which comment on linguistic code units. A text may define an esoteric expression, a technical term, a regionalism, or even a perfectly ordinary phrase. In *Eugénie Grandet*, the narrator writes:

> In Anjou, the **frippe**, a colloquial word, designates what goes with bread, from butter spread on toast – the commonest kind – to peach preserve, the most distinguished of all the **frippes**:

and in *Le Père Goriot*, several terms belonging to the jargon of thieves are explained:

> **Sorbonne** and **tronche** are two energetic words of the thieves' vocabulary invented because these gentry were the first to feel the need of considering the human head from two standpoints. **Sorbonne** is the head of the living man, his intellect and wisdom. **Tronche** is a word of contempt, expressing the worthlessness of the head after it is cut off.

A narrator may also explain the meaning of an element in his lexicon because he is using it in a rather special way: fearing that his private diary – and, consequently, his aspirations to sainthood – may be discovered by his immediate family, the protagonist of *Journal de Salavin* decides to use 'tourist' and 'tourism' for 'saint' and 'sainthood' respectively and he informs us of his decision. Sometimes, it is a foreign word or idiom which is translated into the language of the text. In *The Sun Also Rises*, for instance, the narrator states 'A fición means passion. An aficionado is one who is passionate about the bull-fights', and in *La Chartreuse de Parme*, the narrator gives the French equivalents to many of the Italian phrases scattered in his narration. Sometimes, it is the meaning of an abbreviation which the text provides: because he finds 'tourist' and 'tourism' ridiculous and inadequate, the hero of *Journal de Salavin* chooses to use 'S.' and 'St.' instead and he announces it in his diary; moreover, referring to his work, he explains:

> Since last November, I am fulfilling the functions of secretary for advertising in the offices of Icpom. This grotesque word means: Industrial Company of Pasteurized and Oxygenated Milks.

Finally, a text may define the various proper names appearing in it. In fact, this kind of definition is common even when the narrator is not particularly inclined to give explanations. Within a few pages of Flaubert's 'Un Coeur simple,' for example, we find: 'Robelin, the farmer of Geffosses ... Liébard, the farmer of Toucques ... the Marquis de Gremanville, one of her uncles ... M. Bourais, a former lawyer ... Guyot, a poor devil employed at the town hall ...' Note that in a passage such as

(79) John got up and left

there is no metalinguistic definition since the predicates refer to the person named John; however, in

(80) John, the shoemaker, got up and left

the *shoemaker* may be said to have a metalinguistic function since it is predicated on the sign 'John' and indicates something like

(81) John is the name of the shoemaker

or

(82) 'John' means 'the shoemaker'

In many narratives, one may also find various passages referring to the non-linguistic codes subsumed under the narrative code. In such cases, the text does not comment on what a sentence, for instance, means in the linguistic system adopted; it informs us about the meanings which the signified of this sentence has in (some of) the other codes framing the narrative. If I read

(83) Fabrice was so shaken up that he answered in Italian: L'ho comprato poco fa (I just bought it now)

(*La Chartreuse de Parme*)

it is the meaning of the Italian sentence in terms of a linguistic code which is given to me. But if I read

(84) She had a rifle of her own, which meant that she had fought in the war

or

(85) She was carrying a red umbrella, which meant that she was a Communist

in neither case does the text answer any questions about the linguistic nature or significance of any of the words and sentences constituting it. Rather, in both cases, the text indicates explicitly the meaning of the state of things presented in terms of a sociocultural code; in other words, it specifically answers such questions as

(86) She had a rifle of her own. What did it mean according to the relevant sociocultural code?

and

(87) She was carrying a red umbrella. What did it mean according to the relevant sociocultural code?

Similarly, in 'Sarrasine,' when I read after the detailed description of a hideous old man accompanied by a ravishing young woman

(88) 'Ah! it was death and lifer indeed!'

it is not a linguistic meaning which is revealed to me but the meaning of the couple in a symbolic system. Given any narrative passage, metanarrative signs can thus indicate its functioning in a series of codes. They can explain its linguistic, sociocultural, or symbolic meaning. They can point out that a certain behavior or a certain state of things represents an enigma or a solution to that enigma: during the *petite madeleine* episode of *A la recherche du temps perdu*, Marcel underlines several times the mysterious nature of the extraordinary sensations he has; and in *Le Temps retrouvé* a great many passages are explicitly presented as the definitive solutions to this mystery. Metanarrative signs can also show that a series of events belong to the same proairetic sequence and they can name the sequence: think of chapter and section titles which indicate at least one of the meanings of a set of activities in a narrative; or else, consider the many demonstrative + noun groups which summarize a series of sentences or paragraphs, as in

(89) John punched Jim, then Jim kicked John, then they threw bottles at each other. This fight lasted a few seconds only

In short, metanarrative signs can illuminate any aspect of the constituent signs of a narrative.

Whether they mostly appear in the main body of a text (*Le Père Goriot, Eugénie Grandet*) or in the footnotes (*Les Bestiaires*) whether they are ostensibly introduced by a narrator or by a character (in the course of a dialogue, for instance, or in a letter sent by one character to another); whether they precede the signs they explain ('Fear, I said, that's what *miedo* means') or, as is usually the case, follow them

(I had taken six seats for all the fights. Three of them were barreras, the first row at the ring-side, and three were sobrepuertas, seats with wooden backs, half-way up the amphitheatre. *The Sun Also Rises*);

whether they are detailed and precise or, on the contrary, general and vague; whether they refer to linguistic units, hermeneutic units, or cultural ones; and whether they comment on the shape, the meaning, or the appropriateness of a given unit, metanarrative signs may fulfill several functions.

They may, for example, contribute to the rhythm of a narrative by regularly slowing the pace at which new events are presented: it is obvious that they do not so much bring new information on the narrated as they constitute an interpretation of old information. They may work as a characterization device: a character who states the symbolic meaning of an event or explains a foreign locution clearly differs from characters who never perform similar actions. They may also help define a narrator, his narratee and their relationship. In the first place, the number, the kind and the complexity of a narrator's metanarrative comments can contribute to masking him pompous or unassuming, modest or conceited, cunning or straightforward, and so on and so forth. Second, the mere presence of such comments may constitute precious information on the very identity of the narratee and ultimately underline an important dimension of the narrative. In *Journal de Salavin*, the numerous metanarrative signs peppering the protagonist's diary ('Mme Baratti, the concierge ... M. Mayer, the director of personnel, M. Amigorena, the deputy chief accountant ...,' etc.) indicate that, far from writing for himself only, as he asserts again and again, Salavin may be writing for other readers who, he hopes, will understand him and sympathize with his plight: why else would he explain terms which he knows perfectly well? Rather than a mere private diary, it is perhaps a kind of tale which Salavin composes, a tale in which he can play the part of the hero and thanks to which the most trivial incidents in his daily life acquire importance. *Journal de Salavin* may therefore represent not only the itinerary of an unhappy consciousness in the modern world but also a meditation on the magic of telling about oneself, of narrating one's life; and it is the metanarrative components of the novel which brings this forward. Finally, metanarrative signs tend to reveal how a given narrator views the knowledge and sophistication of the audience he is addressing: the metanarrative explanations which he feels obliged to provide and the degree of tact which he manifests in providing them show what he thinks of his narratee, whether he respects him, is well disposed towards him, or considers himself to be infinitely superior; and the distribution of these explanations may point to a change in the relationship between the two: if the narrator stops making metalinguistic statements, for instance, it may be because he has understood that his narratee can do without them.[7]

But their most obvious and most important function is probably an organizational and interpretative one. Above all, metanarrative signs are glosses on various parts of a text and on the codes underlying them. To some extent at least, they point out the set of norms and constraints according to which the text deploys itself and makes sense; they present a model for its decipherment; they put forward a program for its decoding. In other words, they partially show how a given text could be understood, how it should be understood, how it wants to be understood. As I have indicated earlier, reading a narrative, understanding it, implies organizing it and interpreting it in terms of several codes. Metanarrative signs do part of this work for us. In their absence, it is up to us to determine the various connotations of a given passage, the symbolic dimensions of a given event, the hermeneutic function of a given situation, and so on. Metanarrative signs provide us with some specific connotations; they make some symbolic dimensions explicit; they define the hermeneutic status of some situations. On the one hand, then, metanarrative signs help us understand a narrative in a certain way; on the other hand, they force us (try to force us) to understand it in this way and not another. They thus constitute the answer of a text to the question: 'How should we interpret you?'

Note that this is always a partial answer. We do not know of any narrative which makes the code framing it entirely and perfectly explicit, and for a very good reason: how would anyone compose a narrative in which every element or sequence of elements is accompanied by its definition and function in a variety of codes? Note too that the partial answer is not necessarily enlightening. Metanarrative signs may not come when we expect them most or they may come when we don't expect them anymore; they may never appear in passages which are quite complex, and on the contrary, they may abound in passages which seem to present no particular difficulties. Indeed, the explanations they supply may be trivial, redundant or tautological. In this case, their ultimate role is not so much to clarify the meaning of the specific elements they comment on but rather to underline their importance (or to minimize the significance of other elements which are not glossed). In Breton's *Nadja*, for example, there is a veritable profusion of metanarrative signs. However, they do not have a strongly explicative dimension. When the narrator writes that the word **haunt** 'says much more than it means,' when he states that the term **incantation** 'must be taken literally,' when he uses the expression **perverse objects** and adds that it must be understood 'the way I understand it and like it,' he does not really explain this word, this term, this expression. Rather, he provides a commentary which makes them more, not less, impenetrable. Similarly, when the narrator identifies an event as mysterious without even suggesting why, or when he reformulates one enigma – 'Who am I?' – into another one which is surely more bizarre – 'Whom do I haunt?' – he tends to obscure rather than illuminate the various hermeneutic terms along which his narrative is moving. Finally, when he names 'strange adventure' an explicitly strange sequence of events, he is being, at the very best, banal and redundant. Breton's metanarrative interventions do not increase our understanding of the signs to which they refer; but they certainly draw our attention to them and insist on their sign value, their sign nature. Instead of making a passage transparent, metanarrative signs in *Nadja* increase its opacity. They emphasize the sign rather than its meaning: Breton's novel, like life according to the surrealist, is full of signs and, like life, it takes on the appearance of a cryptogram.

Note also that metanarrative signs may lead us by indirection to a valid reading of a particular text. For it may happen that, instead of acting as aids to a proper decoding they constitute an obstacle to it. Put forward by an ill-informed (or ill-intentioned) narrator, or by an ignorant character, the explanations provided are sometimes incomplete – while being given as entirely satisfactory – and set the decoder on the wrong track. Sometimes also, they contradict other metanarrative comments and thus augment the difficulties of decipherment. Often, they provide totally wrong information which, if accepted, can only lead to faulty conclusions. In such cases, the reading ostensibly proposed by the text is a poor one and only by realizing it can we reach more satisfactory results.

Note finally that, if metanarrative signs guide our reading, they also help us understand better the stance taken by a narrative with regards to its own communicability and legibility as well as to the activity of reading in general. Their very presence in a text emphasizes the fact that portions of it, at least, are legible in certain ways. Their appearance is similar to that of a (fragmentary) text in the text, representing a language that is **other** in the language of the text and establishing some of the interpersonal coordinates of a communicative situation. Since they operate as decipherments of various passages and, as such, act as partial replacements for them, they help specify the assumptions of the text and the decoding contracts endorsed by it. In other words, they clarify the premises of textual communicability (if you read me according to the hermeneutic code, you will see how everything will fall into place; if you interpret me in terms of a symbolic code, you will understand that I am saying much more than I seem to; I will summarize for you this sequence of events and that one, but you will have to summarize the others). Furthermore, if reading a narrative means adding to it a metanarrative commentary, not only do they indicate what such a commentary may consist in and how it may intervene but they help specify the distance between a text's own metacommentary and the metacommentary of a given reader. After all, both the text and the individual reader can interpret certain passages in terms of the same (sub-)codes and reach the same conclusions; but it can also happen that the text summarizes a set of activities in one way and the reader in another; or that the text finds a certain event mysterious whereas the reader does not; or that the text indicates only one symbolic aspect of a situation while the reader thinks of several others. In short, metanarrative signs tell us how we read.

Notes

1. See, for instance, Roland Barthes, *S/Z*: 219; William Gass, *Fiction and the Figures of Life* (New York: 1970), pp. 24–5; Tzvetan Todorov, *Poétique de la prose* (Paris: 1971), pp. 66–91.

2. ROMAN JAKOBSON, 'Closing Statement: Linguistics and Poetics', in *Style and Language*, THOMAS SEBEOK (ed.), (Cambridge, Mass.: 1960), p. 353. Some scholars prefer to speak of seven factors: DELL HYMES, for example, divides *context* into *topic and setting*. See 'The Ethnography of Speaking', in *Readings in the Sociology of Language*, JOSHUA A. FISHMAN (ed.), (The Hague: 1970), pp. 110–13.

3. Cf. Roman Jakobson, 'Closing Statement: Linguistics and Poetics', pp. 353–7. Of course, a verbal act may have more than one major function.

4. For a good discussion of metalinguistic statements and signs, see JOSETTE REY-DEBOVE, *Etude linguistique et sémiotique des dictionnaires français contemporains* (The Hague and Paris: 1971), pp. 43–52.

5. For a similar definition, see GERALD PRINCE. 'Remarques sur les signes métanarratifs', *Degrés*, 11–12 (1977), e1–e10. See also PHILIPPE HAMON, 'Texte littéraire et métalangage', *Poétique*, 31 (1977), 261–284 and PIERRE VAN DEN HEUVEL, 'Le narrateur narrataire ou le narrateur lecteur de son propre discours', *Agorà*, 14–15 (1977), 53–77.

6. In other words, a narrator's intrusion or an explanation does not necessarily constitute a metanarrative sign.

7. Note that all of the explanations by the narrator (including non-metanarrative ones) similarly function as indications on his relationship with his narratee. More generally, all of the explanations in any text (including non-narrative texts) provide information on the relationship between the addresser and the addressee.

Part Two

Historiographic Metafiction

4 Historiographic metafiction*

LINDA HUTCHEON

Whereas 'radical metafiction' belongs to a late stage of modernism, for Hutcheon, the meeting of metafiction and historiography produces a new kind of experimental writing uniquely capable of fulfilling the 'poetics of postmodernism'. In this chapter of her *A Poetics of Postmodernism* Hutcheon discusses the ways in which historiographic metafictions have redefined the relationship between literature and history, specifically by challenging the separability of the two discourses. Against Paul de Man and the deconstructionist conflation of fact and fiction, Hutcheon argues that historiographic metafiction points to the continuing relevance of that opposition at the same time as it highlights discursive principles common to both. Readers of historiographic metafiction will respond to historical material in such novels with a double awareness of its fictionality and its basis in real events, thus entering into one of postmodernism's definitively unresolved contradictions.

The discussion here places such writers as Salman Rushdie, Robert Coover, Christa Wolf, Julian Barnes, John Fowles and Umberto Eco in the context of an ongoing debate between history and fiction, particularly as it has been transformed by the historiographical skepticism of Hayden White and Dominick LaCapra, the non-fictional novels of Hunter S. Thompson, Tom Wolfe and Norman Mailer, and a post-Vietnam distrust of official versions of contemporary history. In this context, the importance of historiographical metafiction is defined in terms of its ability to contest the assumptions of the 'realist' novel and narrative history, to question the absolute knowability of the past, and to specify the ideological implications of historical representations, past and present.

I

We theoreticians have to know the laws of the peripheral in art. The peripheral is, in fact, the non-esthetic set. It is connected with art, but

---

*Reprinted from Hutcheon, Linda, *The Poetics of Postmodernism: History, Theory, Fiction* (New York and London: Routledge, 1988), pp. 105–23.

the connection is not causal. But to stay alive, art must have new raw
materials. Infusions of the peripheral.

(Viktor Shklovsky)

In the nineteenth century, at least before the rise of Ranke's 'scientific
history,' literature and history were considered branches of the same tree
of learning, a tree which sought to 'interpret experience, for the purpose of
guiding and elevating man' (Nye 1966, 123). Then came the separation that
resulted in the distinct disciplines of literary and historical studies today,
despite the fact that the realistic novel and Rankean historicism shared
many similar beliefs about the possibility of writing factually about
observable reality (H. White 1976, 25). However, it is this very separation
of the literary and the historical that is now being challenged in
postmodern theory and art, and recent critical readings of both history and
fiction have focused more on what the two modes of writing share than on
how they differ. They have both been seen to derive their force more from
verisimilitude than from any objective truth; they are both identified as
linguistic constructs, highly conventionalized in their narrative forms, and
not at all transparent either in terms of language or structure; and they
appear to be equally intertextual, deploying the texts of the past within
their own complex textuality. But these are also the implied teachings of
historiographic metafiction. Like those recent theories of both history and
fiction, this kind of novel asks us to recall that history and fiction are
themselves historical terms and that their definitions and interrelations are
historically determined and vary with time (see Seamon 1983, 212–16).

In the last century, as Barbara Foley has shown, historical writing and
historical novel writing influenced each other mutually: Macauley's debt
to Scott was an overt one, as was Dicken's to Carlyle in *A Tale of Two Cities*
(Foley 1986a, 170–1). Today, the new skepticism or suspicion about the
writing of history found in the work of Hayden White and Dominick
LaCapra is mirrored in the internalized challenges to historiography in
novels like *Shame, The Public Burning,* or *A Maggot*: they share the same
questioning stance towards their common use of conventions of narrative,
of reference, of the inscribing of subjectivity, of their identity as textuality,
and even of their implication in ideology. In both fiction and history
writing today, our confidence in empiricist and positivist epistemologies
has been shaken – shaken, but perhaps not yet destroyed. And this is what
accounts for the skepticism rather than any real denunciation; it also
accounts for the defining paradoxes of postmodern discourses. I have been
arguing that postmodernism is a contradictory cultural enterprise, one that
is heavily implicated in that which it seeks to contest. It uses and abuses
the very structures and values it takes to task. Historiographic metafiction,
for example, keeps distinct its formal auto-representation and its historical
context, and in so doing problematizes the very possibility of historical

knowledge, because there is no reconciliation, no dialectic here – just unresolved contradiction.

The history of the discussion of the relation of art to historiography is therefore relevant to any poetics of postmodernism, for the separation is a traditional one. To Aristotle (1982, 1,451a–b), the historian could speak only of what has happened, of the particulars of the past; the poet, on the other hand, spoke of what could or might happen and so could deal more with universals. Freed of the linear succession of history writing, the poet's plot could have different unities. This was not to say that historical events and personages could not appear in tragedy: 'nothing prevents some of the things that have actually happened from being of the sort that might probably or possibly happen' (1,451b). History-writing was seen to have no such conventional restraints of probability or possibility. Nevertheless, many historians since have used the techniques of fictional representation to create imaginative versions of their historical, real worlds (see Holloway 1953; G. Levine 1968; Braudy 1970; Henderson 1974). The postmodern novel has done the same, and the reverse. It is part of the postmodernist stand to confront the paradoxes of fictive/historical representation, the particular/the general, and the present/the past. And this confrontation is itself contradictory, for it refuses to recuperate or dissolve either side of the dichotomy, yet it is more than willing to exploit both.

History and fiction have always been notoriously porous genres, of course. At various times both have included in their elastic boundaries such forms as the travel tale and various versions of what we now call sociology (Veyne 1971, 30). It is not surprising that there would be overlappings of concern and even mutual influences between the two genres. In the eighteenth century the focus of this commonality of concern tended to be the relation of ethics (not factuality) to truth in narrative. (Only with the passing of the Acts of Parliament that defined libel did the notion of historical 'fact' enter this debate – L.J. Davis 1983.) It is not accidental that, 'From the start the writers of novels seemed determined to pretend that their work is not *made*, but that it simply exists' (Josipovici 1971, 148); in fact, it was safer, in legal and ethical terms. Defoe's works made claims to veracity and actually convinced some readers that they were factual, but most readers today (and many then) had the pleasure of a double awareness of both fictiveness and a basis in the 'real' – as do readers of contemporary historiographic metafiction.

In fact Michael Coetzee's novel, *Foe*, addresses precisely this question of the relation of 'story'-and 'history'-writing to 'truth' and exclusion in the practice of Defoe. There is a direct link here to familiar assumptions of historiography: that every history is a history of some entity which existed for a reasonable period of time, that the historian wishes to state what is literally true of it in a sense which distinguishes the historian from a teller of fictitious or mendacious stories.

(M. White 1963, 4)

Foe reveals that storytellers can certainly silence, exclude, and absent certain past events – and people – but it also suggests that historians have done the same: where are the women in the traditional histories of the eighteenth century? As we have seen, Coetzee offers the teasing fiction that Defoe did not write *Robinson Crusoe* from information from the male historical castaway, Alexander Selkirk, or from other travel accounts, but from information given him by a subsequently 'silenced' woman, Susan Barton, who had also been a castaway on 'Cruso''s [sic] island. It was Cruso who suggested that she tell her story to a writer who would add 'a dash of colour' to her tale. She at first resisted because she wanted the 'truth' told, and Cruso admitted that a writer's 'trade is in books, not in truth' (1986, 40). But Susan saw a problem: 'If I cannot come foreward, as author, and swear to the truth of my tale, what will be the worth of it? I might as well have dreamed it in a snug bed in Chichester' (40).

Susan does tell Foe (he added the 'De' only later, and so lost Coetzee's irony) her tale and his response is that of a novelist. Susan's reaction is irritation:

You remarked it would have been better had Cruso rescued not only musket and powder and ball, but a carpenter's chest as well, and built himself a boat. I do not wish to be captious, but we lived on an island so buffeted by wind that there was not a tree did grow twisted and bent.

(1986, 55)

In frustration, she begins her own tale: 'The Female Castaway. Being a True Account of a Year Spent on a Desert Island. With Many Strange Circumstances Never Hitherto Related' (67), but discovers that the problems of writing history are not unlike those of writing fiction: 'Are these enough strange circumstances to make a story of? How long before I am driven to invent new and stranger circumstances: the salvage of tools and muskets from Cruso's ship; the building of a boat ... a landing by cannibals ...?'(67). Her final decision is, however, that 'what we accept in life we cannot accept in history'(67) – that is, lies and fabrications.

The linking of 'fictitious' to 'mendacious' stories (and histories) is one with which other historiographic metafictions also seem to be obsessed: *Famous Last Words, Legs, Waterland, Shame*. In the latter, Rushdie's narrator addresses openly the possible objections to his position as insider/outsider writing about the events of Pakistan from England – and in English:

Outsider! Trespasser! You have no right to this subject! ... I know: nobody ever arrested me [as they did the friend of whom he has just written]. Nor are they ever likely to. *Poacher! Pirate! We reject your authority. We know you, with your foreign language wrapped around you like a flag: speaking about us in your forked tongue, what can you tell but lies?* I reply with more questions: is history to be considered the property of the participants solely? In what courts are such claims staked, what boundary commissions map out the territories?

(1983, 28)

The eighteenth-century concern for lies and falsity becomes a postmodern concern for the multiplicity and dispersion of truth(s), truth(s) relative to the specificity of place and culture. Yet the paradox is still there: in *Shame* we learn that when Pakistan was formed, the *Indian* history had to be written out of the Pakistani past. But who did this work? History was rewritten by immigrants, in Urdu and English, the imported tongues. As the narrator puts it, he is forced – by history – to write in English 'and so for ever alter what is written'(38).

There has also been another, long tradition, dating (as we have just seen) from Aristotle, that makes fiction not only separate from, but also superior to history, which is a mode of writing limited to the representation of the contingent, and the particular. The romantic and modernist assertions of the autonomy and supremacy of art led, however, as Jane Tompkins (1980b) has shown, to a marginalization of literature, one that extremes of metafiction (like American surfiction or the French New New Novel) only exacerbate. Historiographic metafiction, in deliberate contrast to what I would call such late modernist radical metafiction, attempts to demarginalize the literary through confrontation with the historical, and it does so both thematically and formally.

For example, Christa Wolf's *No Place on Earth* is about the fictionalized meeting of two historical figures, dramatist Heinrich von Kleist and poet Karoline von Günderrode: 'The claim that they met: a legend that suits us. The town of Winkel, on the Rhine, we saw it ourselves.' The 'we' of the narrating voice, in the present, underlines the metafictive historical reconstruction on the level of form. But on the thematic level too, life and art meet, for this is the theme of the novel, as Wolf's Kleist tries to break down the walls between 'literary fantasies and the actualities of the world' (1982, 12), contesting his colleagues' separation of poets from praxis: 'Of all the people here, perhaps there is none more intimately bound to the real world than I am'(82). It is he, after all, who is trying to write a romantic historical work about Robert Guiscard, Duke of Normandy. The metafictive and the historiographic also meet in the intertexts of the novel, for it is through them that Wolf fleshes out the cultural and historical context of this fictive meeting. The intertexts range from Günderrode's own letters to canonic romantic works like Hölderlin's *Hyperion*, Goethe's

Torquato Tasso, and Brentano's *Gedichte* – but, in all, the theme is the conflict between art and life. This novel reminds us, as did Roland Barthes much earlier (1967) that the nineteenth century could be said to have given birth to both the realist novel and narrative history, two genres which share a desire to select, construct, and render self-sufficient and closed a narrative world that would be representational but still separate from changing experience and historical process. Today history and fiction share a need to contest these very assumptions.

II

> To the truth of art, external reality is irrelevant. Art creates its own reality, within which truth and the perfection of beauty is the infinite refinement of itself. History is very different. It is an empirical search for external truths, and for the best, most complete, and most profound external truths, in a maximal corresponding relationship with the absolute reality of the past events.
>
> *(David Hackett Fischer)*

These words are not without their ironic tone, of course, as Fischer is describing what he sees as a standard historian's preconception about the relation of art to history. But it is not far from a description of the basic assumptions of many kinds of formalist literary criticism. For I.A. Richards, literature consisted of 'pseudo-statements' (1924); for Northrop Frye (1957), art was hypothetical, not real – that is verbal formulations which imitate real propositions; not unlike Sir Philip Sidney, structuralists argued that

> literature is not a discourse that can or must be false ... it is a discourse that, precisely, cannot be subjected to the test of truth; it is neither true nor false, to raise this question has no meaning: this is what defines its very status as 'fiction'.
>
> (Todorov 1981a, 18)

Historiographic metafiction suggests that truth and falsity may indeed not be the right terms in which to discuss fiction, but not for the reasons offered above. Postmodern novels like *Flaubert's Parrot, Famous Last Words,* and *A Maggot* openly assert that there are only *truths* in the plural, and never one Truth; and there is rarely falseness *per se,* just others' truths. Fiction and history are narratives distinguished by their frames (see B.H. Smith 1978), frames which historiographic metafiction first establishes and then crosses, positing both the generic contracts of fiction and of history. The postmodern paradoxes here are complex. The interaction of the historiographic and the metafictional foregrounds the rejection of the claims of both 'authentic' representation and 'inauthentic' copy alike, and the very meaning of artistic originality is as forcefully challenged as is the transparency of historical referentiality.

Postmodern fiction suggests that to re-write or to re-present the past in fiction and in history is, in both cases, to open it up to the present, to prevent it from being conclusive and teleological. Such is the teaching of novels like Susan Daitch's *L.C.*, with its double layer of historical reconstruction, both of which are presented with metafictional self-consciousness. Parts of the journal of the fictive protagonist, Lucienne Crozier, a woman implicated in, yet marginalized as a witness of the historical 1848 revolution in Paris, are edited and translated twice: once by Willa Rehnfield and once by her younger assistant after her death. The recent interest in archival women's history is given an interesting new twist here, for the two translations of the end of Lucienne's diary are so vastly different that the entire activity of translation, as well as research, is called into question. In the more traditional Willa's version, Lucienne dies of consumption in Algiers, abandoned by her revolutionary lover. In the version of her more radical assistant (a veteran of Berkeley in 1968, being sought by the police for a terrorist bombing), Lucienne just stops writing, while awaiting arrest for revolutionary activities.

Other historiographic metafictions point to other implications of the rewriting of history. Ian Watson's *Chekhov's Journey* opens in the manner of a historical novel about Anton Chekhov's 1890 trip across Siberia to visit a convict colony. The next chapter, however, sets up a tension between this and a 1990 frame: at a Russian Artists' Retreat in the country, a film-maker, a scriptwriter, and a Chekhov look-alike actor meet to plan a film about that historical trip of 1890. The plan is to hypnotize the actor and tape his entry into Chekhov's personality and past. From these tapes, a script will emerge. However, they encounter a serious problem: the actor begins to *alter* the dates of verifiable historical events, moving the Tunguska explosion from 1888 to 1908. We are told that, from this point on, 'the film project foundered further into a chaos of unhistory' (1983, 56). Suddenly a third narrative intervenes: a spaceship in the future is about to launch backwards into time past. (Meanwhile, at the Retreat, fog isolates the writing team in a timeless world; telephone circuits turn back on themselves; all links to the outside are cut.) The spaceship commander realizes that he is experiencing the rewriting of history: the 1908 explosion has regressed and become that of 1888, and both prefigure (repeat?) atomic blasts of an even later date. He is caught in a time loop which renders any firm sense of history or reality impossible. (At the Retreat, new books are found in the library, rewritten versions, not of history, but of literature: *Apple Orchard, Uncle Ivan, Three Cousins, Snow Goose*. Not that history remains unscathed: Joan of Arc, Trotsky, and others get changed out of recognition, in an allegory of not only Russian revisionary history, but also all our rewritings of the past, deliberate and accidental.)

This world of provisionality and indeterminacy is made even more complex when a consultation with the *Soviet Encyclopedia* confirms the actor's altered version of the Tunguska expedition. The team decides that their film, to be entitled (like the novel) *Chekhov's Journey*, will not be the experimental one they had envisaged, but *cinéma vérité*, despite the reader's awareness that it was the hypnotic tampering with time that brought on the time warp that blasted the *Cherry Orchard* and mutated the *Sea Gull* into a *Snow Goose*. As one of the team says:

> Past events can be altered. History gets rewritten. Well, we've just found that this applies to the real world too ... Maybe the real history of the world is changing constantly? And why? Because history is a fiction. It's a dream in the mind of humanity, forever striving ... towards what? Towards perfection.
>
> (1983, 174)

The text provides the ironic context in which to read this last statement: the next thing mentioned is Auschwitz, and the echo of Joyce in the passage reminds us that, for him, history was not a dream, but a nightmare from which we are trying to awaken.

The problematizing of the nature of historical knowledge, in novels like this, points both to the need to separate and to the danger of separating fiction and history as narrative genres. This problematizing has also been in the foreground of much contemporary literary theory and philosophy of history, from Hayden White to Paul Veyne. When the latter calls history 'a true novel' (1971, 10), he is signalling the two genres' shared conventions: selection, organization, diegesis, anecdote, temporal pacing, and employment (14, 15, 22, 29, 46–8). But this is not to say that history and fiction are part of the 'same order of discourse' (Lindenberger 1984, 18). They are different, though they share social, cultural, and ideological contexts, as well as formal techniques. Novels (with the exception of some extreme surfictions) incorporate social and political history to some extent, though that extent will vary (Hough 1966, 113); historiography, in turn, is as structured, coherent, and teleological as any narrative fiction. It is not only the novel but history too that is 'palpably betwixt and between' (Kermode 1968a, 235). Both historians and novelists *constitute* their subjects as possible objects of narrative representation, as Hayden White (1978a, 56) has argued (for history alone, however). And they do so by the very structures and language they use to present those subjects. In Jacques Ehrmann's extreme formulation: 'history and literature have no existence in and of themselves. It is we who constitute them as the object of our understanding' (1981, 253). This is the teaching of texts like Doctorow's *Welcome to Hard Times*, a novel about the attempt to write history that shows historiography to be a most problematic act: do we, in writing our past, even create our future? Is the return of the Bad Man from Bodie the past re-lived, or the past re-written?

Postmodernism deliberately confuses the notion that history's problem is verification, while fiction's is veracity (Berthoff 1970, 272). Both forms of narrative are signifying systems in our culture; both are what Doctorow once called modes of 'mediating the world for the purpose of introducing meaning' (1983, 24). And it is the constructed, imposed nature of that meaning (and the seeming necessity for us to make meaning) that historiographic metafiction like Coover's *The Public Burning* reveals. This novel teaches that 'history itself depends on conventions of narrative, language, and ideology in order to present an account of "what really happened"' (Mazurek 1982, 29). Both history and fiction are cultural sign systems, ideological constructions whose ideology includes their appearance of being autonomous and self-contained. It is the metafictionality of these novels that underlines Doctorow's notion that

> history is kind of fiction in which we live and hope to survive, and fiction is a kind of speculative history ... by which the available data for the composition is seen to be greater and more various in its sources than the historian supposes.
>
> (1983, 25)

Fredric Jameson has argued that historical representation is as surely in crisis as is the linear novel, and for much the same reasons:

> The most intelligent 'solution' to such a crisis does not consist in abandoning historiography altogether, as an impossible aim and an ideological category all at once, but rather – as in the modernist aesthetic itself – in reorganizing its traditional procedures on a different level. Althusser's proposal seems the wisest in this situation: as old-fashioned narrative or 'realistic' historiography becomes problematic, the historian should reformulate her vocation – not any longer to produce some vivid representation of history 'as it really happened,' but rather to produce the *concept* of history.
>
> (1984c, 180)

There is only one word I would change in this: the word 'modernist' seems to me to be less apt than ' postmodernist,' though Jameson would never agree (see 1983; 1984a). Postmodern historiographic metafiction has done exactly what Jameson calls for here, though there is more a problematizing than just a production of a *'concept* of history' (and fiction). The two genres may be textual constructs, narratives which are both non-originary in their reliance on past intertexts and unavoidably ideologically laden, but they do not, in historiographic metafiction at least, 'adopt equivalent representational procedures or constitute equivalent modes of cognition' (Foley 1986a, 35). However, there are (or have been) combinations of history and fiction which do attempt such equivalence.

III

> The binary opposition between fiction and fact is no longer relevant: in any differential system, it is the assertion of the space *between* the entities that matters.
>
> Paul de Man

Perhaps. But historiographic metafiction suggests the continuing relevance of such an opposition, even if it be a problematic one. Such novels both install and then blur the line between fiction and history. This kind of generic blurring has been a feature of literature since the classical epic and the Bible (see Weinstein 1976, 263), but the simultaneous and overt assertion and crossing of boundaries is more postmodern. Umberto Eco has claimed that there are three ways to narrate the past: the romance, the swashbuckling tale, and the historical novel. He has added that it was the latter that he intended to write in *The Name of the Rose* (1983, 1984, 74–5). Historical novels, he feels, 'not only identify in the past the causes of what came later, but also trace the process through which those causes began slowly to produce their effects' (76). This is why his medieval characters, like John Banville's characters in his *Doctor Copernicus*, are made to talk like Wittgenstein, for instance. I would add, however, that this device points to a fourth way of narrating the past: historiographic metafiction – and not historical fiction – with its intense self-consciousness about the way in which all this is done.

What is the difference between postmodern fiction and what we usually think of as nineteenth-century historical fiction (though its forms persist today – see Fleishman 1971)? It is difficult to generalize about this latter complex genre because, as theorists have pointed out, history plays a great number of distinctly different roles, at different levels of generality, in its various manifestations. There seems little agreement as to whether the historical past is always presented as individualized, particularized, and past (that is, different from the present) (see Shaw 1983, 26; 48; 148) or whether that past is offered as typical and therefore present, or at least as sharing values through time with the present (Lukás 1962). While acknowledging the difficulties of definition (see also Turner 1979; Shaw 1983) that the historical novel shares with most genres, I would define historical fiction as that which is modelled on historiography to the extent that it is motivated and made operative by a notion of history as a shaping force (in the narrative and in human destiny) (see Fleishman 1971). However, it is Georg Lukács' influential and more particular definition that critics most frequently have to confront in their defining, and I am no exception.

Lukács felt that the historical novel could enact historical process by presenting a microcosm which generalizes and concentrates (1962, 39). The protagonist, therefore, should be a type, a synthesis of the general and particular, of 'all the humanly and socially essential determinants'. From this definition, it is clear that the protagonists of historiographic metafiction are anything but proper types: they are the ex-centrics, the marginalized, the peripheral figures of fictional history – the Coalhouse Walkers (in *Ragtime*), the Saleem Sinais (in *Midnight's Children*), the Fevvers (in *Nights at the Circus*). Even the historical personages take on different, particularized, and ultimately ex-centric status: Doctor Copernicus (in the novel of that name), Houdini (in *Ragtime*), Richard Nixon (in *The Public Burning*). Historiographic metafiction espouses a postmodern ideology of plurality and recognition of difference; 'type' has little function here, except as something to be ironically undercut. There is no sense of cultural universality. The protagonist of a postmodern novel like Doctorow's *Book of Daniel* is overtly specific, individual, culturally and familially conditioned in his response to history, both public and private. The narrative form enacts the fact that Daniel is not a type of anything, no matter how much he may try to see himself as representing the New Left or his parents' cause.

Related to this notion of type is Lukác's belief that the historical novel is defined by the relative unimportance of its use of detail, which he saw as 'only a means of achieving historical faithfulness, for making concretely clear the historical necessity of a concrete situation' (1962, 59). Therefore, accuracy or even truth of detail is irrelevant. Many readers of historical fiction would disagree, I suspect, as have writers of it (such as John Williams 1973, 8–11). Postmodern fiction contests this defining characteristic in two different ways. First, historiographic metafiction plays upon the truth and lies of the historical record. In novels like *Foe*, *Burning Water*, or *Famous Last Words*, certain known historical details are deliberately falsified in order to foreground the possible mnemonic failures of recorded history and the constant potential for both deliberate and inadvertent error. The second difference lies in the way in which postmodern fiction actually uses detail or historical data. Historical fiction (*pace* Lukács) usually incorporates and assimilates these data in order to lend a feeling of verifiability (or an air of dense specificity and particularity) to the fictional world. Historiographic metafiction incorporates, but rarely assimilates such data. More often, the process of *attempting* to assimilate is what is foregrounded: we watch the narrators of Ondaatje's *Running in the Family* or Findley's *The Wars* trying to make sense of the historical facts they have collected. As readers, we see both the collecting and the attempts to make narrative order. Historiographic metafiction acknowledges the paradox of the *reality* of the past but its *textualized accessibility* to us today.

Lukács's third major defining characteristic of the historical novel is its relegation of historical personages to secondary roles. Clearly in post-modern novels like *Doctor Copernicus, Kepler, Legs* (about Jack Diamond), and *Antichthon* (about Giordano Bruno), this is hardly the case. In many historical novels, the real figures of the past are deployed to validate or authenticate the fictional world by their presence, as if to hide the joints between fiction and history in a formal and ontological sleight of hand. The metafictional self-reflexivity of postmodern novels prevents any such subterfuge, and poses that ontological joint as a problem: how do we know the past? What do (what can) we know of it now? For example Coover does considerable violence to the known history of the Rosenbergs in *The Public Burning*, but he does so to satiric ends, in the name of social critique. I do not think that he intends to construct a wilful betrayal of politically tragic events; perhaps, however, he does want to make a connection to the real world of political action through the reader – by making us aware of the need to question received versions of history. Historiographic metafiction's overt (and political) concern for its reception, for its reader, would challenge the following distinction:

> The discursive criterion that distinguishes narrative history from historical novel is that history evokes testing behavior in reception; historical discipline requires an author-reader contract that stipulates investigative equity. Historical novels are not histories, not because of a penchant for untruth, but because the author-reader contract denies the reader participation in the communal project.
>
> (Streuver 1985, 264)

In fact [...] historiographic metafiction's emphasis on its enunciative situation – text, producer, receiver, historical, and social context – reinstalls a kind of (very problematic) communal project.

While the debates still rage about the definition of the historical novel, in the 1960s a new variant on the history/fiction confrontation came into being: the non-fictional novel. This differed from the treatment of recent factual events recounted as narrative history, as in William Manchester's *The Death of a President*. It was more a form of documentary narrative which deliberately used techniques of fiction in an overt manner and which usually made no pretence to objectivity of presentation. In the work of Hunter S. Thompson, Tom Wolfe, and Norman Mailer, the authorial structuring experience was often in the forefront as the new guarantee of 'truth', as narrators individually attempted to perceive and impose pattern on what they saw about them. This metafictionality and provisionality obviously link the non-fictional novel to historiographic metafiction. But there are also significant differences.

It is probably not accidental that this form of the New Journalism, as it was called, was an American phenomenon. The Vietnam War created a real distrust of official 'facts' as presented by the military and the media, and in addition, the ideology of the 1960s had licenced a revolt against homogenized forms of experience (Hellmann 1981, 8). The result was a kind of overtly personal and provisional journalism, autobiographical in impulse and performative in impact. The famous exception is Truman Capote's *In Cold Blood*, which is a modern rewriting of the realist novel – universalist in its assumptions and omniscient in its narrative technique. But in works like *The Electric Kool-Aid Acid Test, Fear and Loathing: On the Campaign Trail '72*, and *Of a Fire on the Moon*, there was a very 'sixties' kind of direct confrontation with social reality in the present (Hollowell 1977, 10). The impact of the new mixing of fiction and fact is clear on popular, if not academic, history in the years following: in *John Brown's Journey*, Albert Fried broke the rules and showed the tentative groping movement of his becoming interested in his historical topic. The book is 'marked by the feeling of an historian in the act of grappling with his subject' (Weber 1980, 144), as the subtitle underlines: *Notes and Reflections on His America and Mine*.

Perhaps, too, the non-fictional novel in its journalistic variety influenced writers like Thomas Keneally who write historical novels, often of the recent past. The self-consciousness of the author's note that prefaces *Schindler's Ark* makes clear the paradoxes of Keneally's practice:

> I have attempted to avoid all fiction, though, since fiction would debase the record, and to distinguish between reality and the myths which are likely to attach themselves to a man of Oskar's stature. Sometimes it has been necessary to attempt to reconstruct conversations of which Oskar and others have left only the briefest record.
>
> (1982, 9–10)

At the beginning of the novel, Keneally points to his reconstructions (which he refuses to see as fictionalizations) by self-reflexive references to the reader ('In observing this small winter scene, we are on safe ground.' – 13) or by conditional verb forms. Nevertheless, there is a progression from initial statements of possibility and probability ('it is possible that ...' and '[they] now probably paid attention') to a generalized use of the (historical) past tense and a single authoritative voice, as the story continues. This is not historiographic metafiction, however much it may seem so in its early pages. Nor is it quite (or not consistently) an example of the New Journalism, despite its commitment to the 'authority of fact' (Weber 1980, 36).

The non-fictional novel of the 1960s and 1970s did not just record the contemporary hysteria of history, as Robert Scholes has claimed (1968, 37). It did not just try to embrace 'the fictional element inevitable in any reporting' and then try to imagine its 'way toward the truth' (37). What it did was seriously question who determined and created that truth, and it was this particular aspect of it that perhaps enabled historiographic metafiction's more paradoxical questioning. A number of critics have seen parallels between the two forms, but seem to disagree completely on the form that parallel might take. For one, both stress the overt, totalizing power of the imagination of the writers to create unities (Hellmann 1981, 16); yet, for another, both refuse to neutralize contingency by reducing it to unified meaning (Zavarzadeh 1976, 41). I would agree with the former as a designation of the non-fictional novel, though not of all metafiction; and the latter certainly defines a lot of contemporary self-reflexive writing more accurately than it does the New Journalism. Historiographic metafiction, of course, paradoxically fits both definitions: it installs totalizing order, only to contest it, by its radical provisionality, intertextuality, and, often, fragmentation.

In many ways, the non-fiction novel is another late modernist creation (see Smart 1985, 3), in the sense that both its self-consciousness about its writing process and its stress on subjectivity (or psychological realism) recall Woolf and Joyce's experiments with limited, depth vision in narrative, though in the New Journalism, it is specifically the author whose historical presence as participant authorizes subjective response. Postmodern novels like Rudy Wiebe's *The Scorched-Wood People* parody this stance, however: Pierre Falcon, the narrating participant in the historical action, was real, but is still fictionalized in the novel: he is made to tell the tale of the historical Louis Riel from a point of time after his own death, with all the insights of retrospection and access to information he could not possibly have had as participant.

There are non-fictional novels, however, which come very close to historiographic metafiction in their form and content. Norman Mailer's *The Armies of the Night* is subtitled *History as a Novel, the Novel as History*. In each of the two parts of the book there is a moment in which the narrator addresses the reader on the conventions and devices used by novelists (1968, 152) and historians (245). His final decision seems to be that historiography ultimately fails experience and 'the instincts of the novelist' have to take over (284). This self-reflexivity does not weaken, but on the contrary, strengthens and points to the direct level of historical engagement and reference of the text (cf. Bradbury 1983, 159). Like many postmodern novels, this provisionality and uncertainty (and the wilful and overt constructing of meaning too) do not 'cast doubt upon their seriousness' (Butler 1980, 131), but rather define the new postmodern seriousness that acknowledges the limits and powers of 'reporting' or writing of the past, recent or remote.

IV

> History is three-dimensional. It partakes of the nature of science, art, and philosophy.
>
> > *Louis Gottschalk*

Postmodern novels raise a number of specific issues regarding the interaction of historiography and fiction that deserve more detailed study: issues surrounding the nature of identity and subjectivity; the question of reference and representation; the intertextual nature of the past; and the ideological implications of writing about history. A brief overview at this point will show where these issues fit into the poetics of postmodernism.

First of all, historiographic metafictions appear to privilege two modes of narration, both of which problematize the entire notion of subjectivity: multiple points of view (as in Thomas's *The White Hotel*) or an overtly controlling narrator (as in Swift's *Waterland*). In neither, however, do we find a subject confident of his/her ability to know the past with any certainty. This is not a transcending of history, but a problematized inscribing of subjectivity into history. In a novel like *Midnight's Children*, nothing, not even the self's physical body, survives the instability caused by the rethinking of the past in non-developmental, non-continuous terms. To use the (appropriate) language of Michel Foucault, Saleem Sinai's body is exposed as 'totally imprinted by history and the process of history's destruction of the body' (1977, 148). As we shall see in Chapter 10, postmodernism establishes, differentiates, and then disperses stable narrative voices (and bodies) that use memory to try to make sense of the past. It both installs and then subverts traditional concepts of subjectivity; it both asserts and is capable of shattering 'the unity of man's being through which it was thought that he could extend his sovereignty to the events of the past' (Foucault 1977, 153). The protagonist's psychic disintegration in *Waterland* reflects such a shattering, but his strong narrative voice asserts that same selfhood, in a typically postmodern and paradoxical way. So too do the voices of those unreliable narrators of

Burgess's *Earthly Powers* and Williams's *Star Turn*, the former 'uncommitted to verifiable fact' (1980, 490) and the latter a self-confessed liar.

As we shall see in the next chapter, one of the postmodern ways of literally incorporating the textualized past into the text of the present is that of parody. In John Fowles's *A Maggot*, the parodic intertexts are both literary and historical. Interspersed throughout the book are pages from the 1736 *Gentleman's Magazine*, but there are many references to eighteenth-century drama as well, allusions that are formally motivated by the presence of actors in the plot. But it is to the fiction of the period that Fowles refers most often: its pornography, its prurient puritanism (as in Richardson's novels), but most of all, its mixing of fact and fiction, as in the writing of Defoe, whose 'underlying approach and purpose' the narrator has consciously borrowed (1985, 449).

Postmodern intertextuality is a formal manifestation of both a desire to close the gap between past and present of the reader and a desire to rewrite the past in a new context. It is not a modernist desire to order the present through the past or to make the present look spare in contrast to the richness of the past (see Antin 1972, 106–14). It is not an attempt to void or avoid history. Instead it directly confronts the past of literature – and of historiography, for it too derives from other texts (documents). It uses and abuses those intertextual echoes, inscribing their powerful allusions and then subverting that power through irony. In all, there is little of the modernist sense of a unique, symbolic, visionary 'work of art'; there are only texts, already written ones. Walter Hill's film *Crossroads* uses the biography and music of Robert Johnson to foreground the fictional Willie Brown and Lightening Boy, who pick up the Faustian challenge from the devil of his song, 'Crossroads' Blues'.

To what, though, does the very language of historiographic metafiction refer? To a world of history or one of fiction? It is commonly accepted that there is a radical disjunction between the basic assumptions underlying these two notions of reference. History's referents are presumed to be real; fiction's are not. But [...] what postmodern novels teach is that, in both cases, they actually refer at the first level to other texts: we know the past (which really did exist) only through its textualized remains. Historiographic metafiction problematizes the activity of reference by refusing either to bracket the referent (as surfiction might) or to revel in it (as non-fictional novels might). This is not an emptying of the meaning of language, as Gerald Graff seems to think (1973, 397). The text still communicates – in fact, it does so very didactically. There is not so much 'a loss of belief in a significant external reality'(403) as there is a loss of faith in our ability to (unproblematically) *know* that reality, and therefore to be able to represent it in language. Fiction and historiography are not different in this regard.

Postmodern fiction also poses new questions about reference. The issue is no longer 'to what empirically real object in the past does the language of history refer?'; it is more 'to which discursive context could this language belong? To which prior textualizations must we refer?' This is true in the visual arts as well, where the issue of reference is perhaps clearer. Sherrie Levine has framed Andreas Feininger's photographs of real subjects and has called *her* work 'Photographs by Andreas Feininger'. In other words, she frames the existing discourse to create a double remove from the real. In dance, Merce Cunningham's influence has led to postmodern choreography that not only uses visual or musical discourses, but also looks to concepts that would make movement freer of direct reference, in either a sculptural or expressive sense (Kirby 1975, 3–4).

Postmodern art is more complex and more problematic than extreme late modernist auto-representation might suggest, with its view that there is no presence, no external truth which verifies or unifies, that there is only self-reference (B.H. Smith 1978, 8–9). Historiographic metafiction self-consciously suggests this, but then uses it to signal the discursive nature of all reference – both literary and historiographical. The referent is always already inscribed in the discourses of our culture. This is no cause for despair; it is the text's major link with the 'world,' one that acknowledges its identity as construct, rather than as simulacrum of some 'real' outside. Once again, this does not deny that the past 'real' existed; it only conditions our mode of knowledge of the past. We can know it only through its traces, its relics. The question of reference depends on what John Searle (1975, 330) calls a shared 'pretense' and what Stanley Fish calls being party to a set of 'discourse agreements which are in effect decisions as to what can be stipulated as a fact' (1980, 242). In other words, a 'fact' is discourse-defined; an 'event' is not.

Postmodern art is not so much ambiguous as it is doubled and contradictory. There is a rethinking of the modernist tendency to move away from representation (Harkness 1982, 9) by both installing it materially and subverting it. In the visual arts, as in literature, there has been a rethinking of the sign/referent relation in the face of the realization of the limits of self-reflexivity's separation from social practice (Menna 1984, 10). Historiographic metafiction shows fiction to be historically conditioned and history to be discursively structured, and in the process manages to broaden the debate about the ideological implications of the Foucaldian conjunction of power and knowledge – for readers and for history itself as a discipline. As the narrator of Rushdie's *Shame* puts it:

> History is natural selection. Mutant versions of the past struggle for dominance; new species of fact arise, and old, saurian truths go to the wall, blindfolded and smoking last cigarettes. Only the mutations of the strong survive. The weak, the anonymous, the defeated leave few

marks ... History loves only those who dominate her: it is a
relationship of mutual enslavement.

(1983, 124)

The question of *whose* history survives is one that obsesses postmodern
novels like Timothy Findley's *Famous Last Words*. In problematizing almost
everything the historical novel once took for granted, historiographic
metafiction destabilizes received notions of both history and fiction. To
illustrate this change, let me take Barbara Foley's concise description of the
paradigm of the nineteenth-century historical novel and insert in square
brackets the postmodern changes:

> Characters [never] constitute a microcosmic portrayal of
> representative social types; they experience complications and
> conflicts that embody important tendencies [not] in historical
> development [whatever that might mean, but in narrative plotting,
> often traceable to other intertexts]; one or more world-historical
> figures enters the fictive world, lending an aura of extratextual
> validation to the text's generalizations and judgments [which are
> promptly undercut and questioned by the revealing of the true
> intertextual, rather than extratextual, identity of the sources of that
> validation]; the conclusion [never] reaffirms [but contests] the
> legitimacy of a norm that transforms social and political conflict into
> moral debate.
>
> (1986a, 160)

The premise of postmodern fiction is the same as that articulated by
Hayden White regarding history: 'every representation of the past has
specifiable ideological implications' (1987b, 69). But the ideology of
postmodernism is paradoxical, for it depends upon and draws its power
from that which it contests. It is not truly radical; nor is it truly
oppositional. But this does not mean it has no critical clout. The Epiloguist
of *A Maggot* may claim that what we have read is indeed 'a maggot, not an
attempt, either in fact or in language, to reproduce known history' (Fowles
1985, 449), but that does not stop him from extended ideological analyses
of eighteenth-century social, sexual, and religious history. Thomas
Pynchon's obsession with plots – narrative and conspiratorial – is an
ideological one: his characters discover (or make) their own histories in an
attempt to prevent themselves from being the passive victims of the
commercial or political plots of others (Krafft 1984, 284). Similarly
contemporary philosophers of history like Michel de Certeau have
reminded historiographers that no research of the past is free of socio-
economic, political, and cultural conditions (1975, 65). Novels like *The
Public Burning* or *Ragtime* do not trivialize the historical and the factual

in their 'game-playing' (Robertson 1984), but rather politicize them through their metafictional rethinking of the epistemological and ontological relations between history and fiction. Both are acknowledged as part of larger social and cultural discourses which various kinds of formalist literary criticism have relegated to the extrinsic and irrelevant. This said, it is also true that it is part of the postmodern ideology not to ignore cultural bias and interpretative conventions and to question authority – even its own.

All of these issues – subjectivity, intertextuality, reference, ideology – underlie the problematized relations between history and fiction in postmodernism. But many theorists today have pointed to narrative as the one concern that envelops all of these, for the process of narrativization has come to be seen as a central form of human comprehension, of imposition of meaning and formal coherence on the chaos of events (H. White 1981, 795; Jameson 1981a, 13; Mink 1978, 132). Narrative is what translates knowing into telling (H. White 1980, 5), and it is precisely this translation that obsesses postmodern fiction. The conventions of narrative in both historiography and novels, then, are not constraints, but enabling conditions of possibility of sense-making (W. Martin 1986). Their disruption or challenging is bound to upset such basic structuring notions as causality and logic – as happens with Oskar's drumming in *The Tin Drum*: narrative conventions are both installed and subverted. The refusal to integrate fragments (in novels like *The White Hotel*) is a refusal of the closure and telos which narrative usually demands (see Kermode 1966, 1967). In postmodern poetry too, as Marjorie Perloff has argued, narrative is used in works like Ashbery's 'They Dream Only of America' or Dorn's *Slinger*, but used in order to question 'the very nature of the *order* that a systematic plot structure implies' (1985, 158).

The issue of narrativity encompasses many others that point to the postmodern view that we can only know 'reality' as it is produced and sustained by cultural representations of it (Owens 1982, 21). In historiographic metafictions, these are often not simple verbal representations, for *ekphrases* (or verbal representations of visual representations) often have central representational functions. For example in Carpentier's *Explosion in a Cathedral*, Goya's 'Desastres de la guerra' series provides the works of visual art that actually are the sources of the novel's descriptions of revolutionary war. The seventh of that series, plus the 'Dos de Mayo' and 'Tres de Mayo,' are particularly important, for their glorious associations are left aside by Carpentier, as an ironic signal of his own point of view. Of course, literary intertexts function in the narrative in a similar way. The details of Estaban and Soffa's house in Madrid come, in fact, from Torres Villaroel's *Vida*, a book which Estaban had read earlier in the novel (see Saad 1983, 120–2; McCallum 1985).

Historiographic metafiction, like both historical fiction and narrative history, cannot avoid dealing with the problem of the status of their 'facts' and of the nature of their evidence, their documents. And, obviously, the related issue is that of how those documentary sources are deployed: can they be objectively, neutrally related? Or does interpretation inevitably enter with narrativization? The epistemological question of how we know the past joins the ontological one of the status of the traces of that past. Needless to say, the postmodern raising of these questions offers few answers, but this provisionality does not result in some sort of historical relativism or presentism. It rejects projecting present beliefs and standards onto the past and asserts, in strong terms, the specificity and particularity of the individual past event. Nevertheless, it also realizes that we are epistemologically limited in our ability to know that past, since we are both spectators of and actors in the historical process. Historiographic metafiction suggests a distinction between 'events' and 'facts' that is one shared by many historians. Events, as I have been suggesting, are configured into facts by being related to 'conceptual matrices within which they have to be imbedded if they are to count as facts' (Munz 1977, 15). Historiography and fiction, as we saw earlier, *constitute* their objects of attention; in other words, they decide which events will become facts. The postmodern problematicization points to our unavoidable difficulties with the concreteness of events (in the archive, we can find only their textual traces to make into facts) and their accessibility. (Do we have a full trace or a partial one? What has been absented, discarded as non-fact material?) Dominick LaCapra has argued that all documents or artifacts used by historians are not neutral evidence for reconstructing phenomena which are assumed to have some independent existence outside them. All documents process information and the very way in which they do so is itself a historical fact that limits the documentary conception of historical knowledge (1985b, 45). This is the kind of insight that has led to a semiotics of history, for documents become signs of events which the historian transmutes into facts (B. Williams 1985, 40). They are also, of course, signs within already semiotically constructed contexts, themselves dependent upon institutions (if they are official records) or individuals (if they are eye-witness accounts). As in historiographic metafiction, the lesson here is that the past once existed, but that our historical knowledge of it is semiotically transmitted.

I do not mean to suggest that this is a radical, new insight. In 1910 Carl Becker wrote that 'the facts of history do not exist for any historian until he creates them' (525), that representations of the past are selected to signify whatever the historian intends. It is this very difference between events (which have no meaning in themselves) and facts (which are given meaning) that postmodernism obsessively foregrounds. Even documents are selected as a function of a certain problem or point of view (Ricoeur 1984a, 108). Historiographic metafiction often points to this fact by using the paratextual conventions of historiography (especially footnotes) to both inscribe and undermine the authority and objectivity of historical sources and explanations. Unlike the documentary novel as defined by Barbara Foley, what I have been calling postmodern fiction does not 'aspire to tell the truth' (Foley 1986a, 26) as much as to question *whose* truth gets told. It does not so much associate 'this truth with claims to empirical validation' as contest the ground of any claim to such validation. How can a historian (or a novelist) check any historical account against past empirical reality in order to test its validity? Facts are not given but are constructed by the kinds of questions we ask of events (H. White 1987b, 43). In the words of *Waterland*'s history teacher, the past is a 'thing which cannot be eradicated, which accumulates and impinges' (Swift 1983, 109). What postmodern discourses – fictive and historiographic – ask is: how do we know and come to terms with such a complex 'thing'?

5 British historiographic metafiction*

SUSANA ONEGA

Susana Onega's subject here is the 'eclosion of the historical novel in the late 1970s and 1980s'. Taking two generations of critically aware British novelists, Onega argues that British historiographic metafiction represents a specific and perhaps belated expression of a world-wide 'retreat into history' with its origins in North American 'fabulation' and Spanish-American 'magic realism'. For Onega, the scope of British historiographic metafiction in the last decade reflects a general subversion of Western rationality and its dualistic foundations, even if historiographic metafiction is obliged to resurrect certain forms of that dualism in the process of subversion. Onega acknowledges specific influences on historiographic metafiction from literary and cultural theory, notably the deconstructive contention that fiction and reality are not categorically distinct in the way that pre-modernist rationality demanded, and the Foucauldian or New Historicist idea that history has colluded with dualistic reason in suppressing or excluding mythical, esoteric and cabalistic elements with which rationality has always formed a union. This latter view leads Onega to argue that 'history' for historiographic metafiction is a pretext to enter a kind of time tunnel and rediscover suppressed histories in the process of redefining concepts of 'reality' and 'truth'. While much of the discussion here centres on the work of John Fowles, the value of Onega's piece is in surveying the scope of historiographic metafiction in contemporary British fiction.

Now that we are entering the decade of the 1990s it seems appropriate to look back at the novels published in the eighties in Britain in an attempt to find general characteristics, common traits, recurrent tendencies with which to impose order over chaos, unity over variety, thus paying due homage to the most deeply rooted myth of Western civilization, our unflinching faith in the power of rationality to pin down, arrange and classify the otherwise chaotic flood of phenomena of all kinds, incessantly taking place in the universe.

Perhaps the best way to approach the novels written in the 1980s would

---

*This paper is a synthesis of a plenary lecture read during the 14th AEDEAN Conference that took place in Vitoria in December 1990 and published in the conference proceedings.

be to listen to what the writers have to say about themselves. We can, then, attempt a first approximation by synthesizing the classification of contemporary British fiction recently carried out by Maureen Duffy, novelist, poet, playwright and critic, who gave a lecture on 'New Trends in British Fiction' during the 12th National Conference of The Spanish Association for Anglo-American Studies, that took place in Alicante in December 1988.

Maureen Duffy selected two kinds of novels as representative of very recent British fiction. The first kind, which included *Nice Work* (1988) by David Lodge and *The Radiant Way* (1987) by Margaret Drabble, she mentioned as examples of what she called 'the resurgence of middle class realism'. What Duffy calls a revival is perhaps better described as a continuation of the old realistic trend traceable to the Amis–Larkin–Wain troika in the late forties and fifties and even going further back to the Varsity novel of the 1930s. Although the ascription of Lodge to this neo-realistic trend would be somewhat problematic, we may agree with Maureen Duffy that Margaret Drabble occupies here a central position.

The other novels she mentioned, written by novelists belonging to a more recent generation, were Bruce Chatwin's *The Songlines*, Jeanette Winterson's *The Passion*, Jim Crace's, *A Gift of Stones* and the novels of Peter Ackroyd, *Hawksmoor* and *Chatterton*. For Maureen Duffy these were the best examples of what she called 'the most notable current in recent English fiction', characterized in general terms by the 'retreat into history', a retreat, however, which, as she explained, is not carried out 'in order to illuminate the present, but to dazzle, like entering a kind of Aladdin's cave of glittering objects'.

Maureen Duffy's description of this new kind of dazzling historical novel as the most important trend in recent British fiction is really striking, for it reaches in one intuitive stroke the same conclusion that Linda Hutcheon reached by much more erudite and sophisticated means in her book, *A Poetics of Postmodernism*, first published in 1988.

Throughout the 268 pages of her book, Linda Hutcheon very insistently argues that the specific poetics of postmodernism is exclusively realized in a particular kind of novel she calls 'historiographic metafiction', which she describes as 'those well-known and popular novels which are both intensely self-reflexive and yet paradoxically also lay claim to historical events and personages' (1988: 5).

According to Hutcheon, the unique combination of history and fiction that takes place in 'historiographic metafiction' perfectly expresses what is for her the defining characteristic of the Postmodernist ethos: its basic contradictory nature, for

> it does not deny [the liberal humanist dominant], as some have asserted.... Instead, it contests it from within its own assumptions.

[...] What this means is that the familiar humanist separation of art and life (or human imagination and order *versus* chaos and disorder) no longer holds. Postmodernist contradictory art still installs that order, but it then uses it to demystify our everyday processes of structuring chaos, of imparting or assigning meaning.

(1988: 6–7)

How new and how important is this new historical trend? What are its basic characteristics? It is my purpose in the rest of this paper to try to answer these basic questions. The first one, 'how new is this trend?', I will try to answer obliquely by relating an anecdote.

In 1983 I wrote a letter to David Lodge in which I asked him for his advice and help in carrying out a research project on such pseudo-historical novels as *The French Lieutenant's Woman*. The project, which I was just starting, was to analyse novels of this sort, in order to establish the points of divergence between real Victorian novels and these modern imitations. David Lodge's answer ran as follows: 'If you are interested specifically in deliberate anachronism of narrative technique and verbal allusion in a modern novel about the Victorian age, then *The French Lieutenant's Woman* is the only text I can think of that does this very elaborately' (personal communication 12 October 1983). Of course, Lodge's answer referred only to imitations of a concrete historical period, the Victoria era, and not to historical novels in general, but I think this does not invalidate Lodge's implicit acknowledgement that historiographic metafiction was an extreme rarity in British fiction as late as October 1983.

Today, the panorama has completely changed. Maureen Duffy herself, has written one historical novel, *Capital* (1975). Other historiographic metafictions include John Fowles' *A Maggot* (1986), William Golding's trilogy *Rites of Passage* (1980), *Close Quarters* (1987) and *Fire Down Below* (1989); Lawrence Durrell's *Avignon Quintet* (*Monsieur*, 1974, *Livia*, 1978, *Constance*, 1982, *Sebastian, or Ruling Passions*, 1983 and *Quinx, or The Ripper's Tale*, 1985, Graham Swift's *Shuttlecock* (1981) and *Waterland* (1983), Julian Barnes' *Flaubert's Parrot* (1984), *Staring at the Sun* (1986) and *A History of the World in 10½ Chapters* (1989), Peter Ackroyd's *The Great Fire of London* (1982), *The Last Testament of Oscar Wilde* (1983), *Hawksmoor* (1985), *Chatterton* (1987) and *First Light* (1989), Rose Tremain's *Restoration* (1989), A.S. Byatt's *Possession: A Romance* (1990), Charles Palliser's *The Quincunx: The Inheritance of John Huffam* (1989), and Jeanette Winterson's *Boating for Beginners* (1985) and *Sexing the Cherry* (1988), besides Winterson's *The Passion* (1987) and Jim Crace's *A Gift of Stones* (1988) mentioned by Duffy and the 'science' tetralogy by the Irish John Banville: *Dr Copernicus* (1976), *Kepler* (1981), *The Newton Letter* (1983) and *Mefisto* (1986).

A first distinction we may draw is that, broadly speaking, these writers belong to two literary generations. The older one including Golding,

Fowles, Durrell and Byatt, goes back to the 1950s and 1960s and provides the link between modernism and postmodernism. The younger generation can be divided into two: those novelists whose literary careers started in the sixties or seventies with Maureen Duffy, John Banville and Jim Crace, and the generation of the eighties *stricto sensu*, with Graham Swift, Jeanette Winterson, Julian Barnes, Peter Ackroyd, Rose Tremain, and Charles Palliser.

If we concentrate on this last group, we will find that they interestingly combine in themselves artistic creativity with the critical awareness provided by university trainings in Oxford or Cambridge and, with the only exception of Jeanette Winterson, by their experience as literary critics.

They have therefore, a thorough, specialist, knowledge of the literary tradition to which they belong, but also of literary theory. They have all won several prizes and awards and seem to conform very well to Maureen Duffy's description of the successful novelist fighting in the 'leisure industry' for recognition by the media. The novels they write are very different in range, scope, interest and sensibility and yet all of them share what we can describe as a relish in irony and paradox, besides what Duffy defined as a dazzling 'retreat into history'.

Why this eclosion of the historical novel in the late 1970s and 1980s? Is this, as Linda Hutcheon maintains, the only kind of fiction that fulfills the poetics of Postmodernism? These are the basic questions we should ask ourselves when confronted with this phenomenon. In order to answer them I will have to go back to the point where David Lodge's letter left the discussion.

When *The French Lieutenant's Woman* appeared in 1969 it was welcomed by its first reviewers as an extraordinary example of the revival of the historical novel in England, while at the same time they completely misunderstood Fowles' aim in writing it. Critics like Walter Allen (1970: 660) and Prescott Evarts, Jr. (1972: 57) implicitly accused John Fowles of openly and shamelessly imitating old conventions, and of trying to cheat us into accepting them as new, insisting on viewing *The French Lieutenant's Woman* primarily as a historical novel on which futile attempts at experimentation had been made at random.

Analysing the games of frame breaks in the novel, however, it is easy to see that Fowles' real aim in writing it was not so much to write a Victorian novel out of time, but rather, in line with contemporary metafictional practice, to build an illusion only to destroy it, to show us its provisionality, its intrinsic fictional character, thus making us reflect on the Victorian literary conventions of realism and recognize it for what it is: a provisional frame created by the combined work of the author and the 'willing suspension of disbelief' of the reader.

Similarly, when Fowles blurs the boundaries between the narrative levels within which the narrator and the characters respectively move, and between these and the level of the flesh-and-blood writer, he is pointing to a basic deconstructive contention; the advisability of seeing everyday reality as a construction similar to that of fiction, and as such, similarly 'written' and 'writable'.

This contention that reality is subjective and polymorphous, is taken up and developed seriously in *Daniel Martin* (1977) and in a wild satiric vein in *Mantissa* (1982), where we find Miles Green, a ludicrously naïve contemporary writer, boastfully and chauvinistically trying to assert omniscient control over his Muse and over his created world, only to find himself secluded in the domed and quilted room of his own brain and exhausted and trapped within the monothematic sexist world of his own imagination.

If there is one common feature shared by the writers of historiographic metafiction it may be said to be precisely the concern to transcend the *cul de sac* in which Miles Green finds himself, incapable as he is of getting out of the prisonhouse of his own brain, where he has been locked up since existentialism and deconstruction took the Modernist contention of the split of world and self to its logical consequences. The solution, as Daniel Martin intuits, is to write a literature capable of telling the 'real'. But in order to do so, concepts like 'reality' and 'truth', and the position of man in the universe would have to be redefined.

Traditionally, art has been seen as autonomous and unrelated to the truth of external reality, art creating its own reality, within which beautiful or ugly are all important, false or true negligible. History, on the other hand, has traditionally been defined as an empirical search for external truths, so that, in Aristotle's terms (1982, 1, 451 a–b), the historian could speak only of what has happened, while the poet spoke of what could or might happen according to the laws of probability and possibility, not truth.

New historicists like Hayden White and Paul Veyne, however, are now ready to question the capacity of history to reveal absolute truths, so that, in Jacques Ehrman's extreme formulation, 'history and literature have no existence in and of themselves. It is we who constitute them as the objects of our understanding' (in Hutcheon, 1988: 111).

By depriving history of its pretensions to absolute truth, the New historicists and the postmodernist creative writers after them have negotiated the reunification of self and world, but have apparently simultaneously deprived this reunification of ultimate significance. Levelled to the plane of human construct, history, like literature, appears in principle incapable of offering ultimate answers about the basic human questions. However, before we decide that historiographic metafiction does not really bridge the modernist gap between world and self but rather deepens it by adding history to the list of subjective human constructs, we should bear Linda Hutcheon's warning in mind that historiographic metafiction, like all postmodernist art, is 'a contradictory phenomenon, one that uses and abuses, installs and then subverts, the very concepts it challenges' (1988: 4).

In order to grasp the import of this statement we should suspend our judgement for a moment in order to turn our attention to *A Maggot*, John Fowles' latest novel to date and his most powerful historiographic metafiction.

A Maggot was published in 1986, seven years after *The French Lieutenant's Woman*. The plot is situated in 1736, that is, in the England of Swift, Pope, and Walpole. Paid by an anonymous Duke, a cunning and efficient barrister called Henry Ayscough has accumulated all kinds of evidence about the journey from London to Devon undertaken by the Duke's son, called Mr B, in the company of four other travellers, a middle aged 'uncle', a Sergeant, a manservant, and a maid, which ended in the disappearance of the Duke's son and the death of the manservant. As the novel progresses Henry Ayscough discovers that none of the travellers is what he seems to be, they all use diverse false names and Mr B has put about different versions with regard to the purpose of their journey. On top of that, when Rebecca, the maid, and David Jones, the Sergeant, are questioned by Ayscough about what really happened both at the neolithic circle of Stonehenge and in the cave where Mr B disappeared, each gives a contradictory version, Jones describing them as satanic experiences, Rebecca as encounters with celestial beings.

Confronted with this fog of alternative names, plots and interpretations, critics like Julian Moynahan (1985) and Katherine Tarbox (1988) would typically lament the novel's 'evasiveness' (Moynahan, ibid., p. 47) and absence of 'controlling plot', 'consistent protagonist' or 'narrative focus' (Tarbox, ibid., p. 136), concluding that 'Ayscough never does reach truth incontestable, *nor does the reader*' (Tarbox, ibid., p. 138 my italics). For Tarbox the novel has no structure or coherent significance: 'Nearly all the characters are actual historical personages, and Fowles uses them to demonstrate that human lives do not necessarily have definite beginnings and ends' (p. 143), while Moynahan becomes 'convinced that Fowles has failed to write a serious book. As he says, it is a maggot' (ibid., p. 49).

However, although these versions seem logically contradictory, once it is realized that both the versions about the real aim of the journey and about Mr B's identity are simply more or less fanciful literary 'variations' on one unique theme – some form of disobedience or frustration – it is possible to interpret the journey in psychological terms, as a hero's quest for individuation that, as I have shown elsewhere (Onega, 1989: 137–63), neatly follows Jung's scheme of the quaternity (Jung, 1959 (1980): 175).

Thus, from a psychological perspective, the journey becomes a hero's quest for a new totality of the self, which must be achieved through Mr B's acceptance of the *coincidentia oppositorum*, the reconciliation of his conscious, his *shadow* and his *anima* potentialities in the global perception of the self as such. Similarly, from a psychological point of view, the contradictory versions given by Rebecca and David Jones about the events that took place at Stonehenge and in the cave acquire overall meaning, for, as Walter Miller Jr. unfailingly detects, 'the equivalence of the infernal and the celestial versions of the scene in the cave conform to Jung's psychology, and both versions of the cave scene are true' (1985: 11).

At the same time, however, the novel offers another, strikingly opposed, interpretation. Literally, Mr B selected two players and a prostitute reputed for her acting ability, removed them from the London theatre and the brothel were they respectively worked, and hired them to interpret the roles of uncle, bodyguard and main during the journey. After that Mr B once and again tested the credulity of his fellow travellers by telling them a series of tales about the real aim of the journey, insisting that he had been offered 'a part in a history and is not forgiven for refusing to play it' and that he, like the rest, is made of imperfect words and ideas, and to serve other ends' (p. 150).

The fact that Mr B is capable of creating these literary variations himself while at the same time he sees himself and his fellow travellers as hired actors interpreting their allotted roles in the *comoedia vitae* (p. 22) qualifies the previous interpretations of his journey, adding to them a further perspective, according to which the revolt of the Son against the Father becomes the character's refusal to play the role allotted to him by the author. No matter whether we consider Mr B as the son of a Duke who has disappeared, or as a Cambridge scholar involved in alchemical research, or as a mythical hero undertaking his heroic quest, or as a psychologically split ego who must cure his neurosis and find a new totality of the self – what he primarily is, is a literary character who has been asked to play all these roles within a fictional universe and who, for all the apparent freedom he seemed to have in devising the roles of the other characters, was conscious at heart of his radical bondage and of the fact that, for all his rebelliousness, he must comply and 'serve other ends', John Fowles' ends, no doubt.

Taking to its logical consequences the modernist split of self and world, Fowles reached an absurdist *cul de sac* in *Mantissa*, unable as he was to free Miles Green from the prisonhouse of his own mind. After this, in *A Maggot*, Fowles intuitively responded to his need for transcendence in archetypal terms, that is, by a return to dualistic thinking.

So, in *A Maggot*, Fowles creates a maze-like set of false tracks that as far as Henry Ayscough and the rationalist reader alike are concerned, lead nowhere, while he simultaneously offers the more intuitive reader a perfectly coherent reading, following the kind of dualistic, archetypal symbolism that Jung presented as the contemporary equivalent of pre-rationalist myth and religion.

The archetypal quality of Mr B's journey is what confers on him his representative character. Mr B's essential transformation is applicable to every man, and so may be interpreted as evidence that Man has finally achieved his reunification with the universe in the figure of Cosmic Man. However, as the interpretation that reduces Mr B to an unfree literary character paradoxically indicates, this reunification of Man and Cosmos is only temporarily achieved within the boundaries of the paper walls of Fowles' novel. So, in accordance with the puzzling contradictory nature of historiographic metafiction, Fowles simultaneously affirms and negates the validity of this reunification.

In *A Maggot*, Ayscough's rationality and logic are set in opposition to Mr B's white magic which he has acquired at Cambridge, has a numerologic and alchemical origin, and is related to the ancestral pre-rationalist rituals of Stonehenge.

In Peter Ackroyd's *Hawksmoor* a basic dual opposition is likewise set between the antagonistic and yet complementary beliefs of the rationalist architect and member of The Royal Society, Sir Christopher Wren, and those of his assistant, architect Nicholas Dyer, a convinced black magician and satanist. This basic duality is expressed at every possible level. Structurally, in the fact that two different plots are simultaneously developed: one appears in the odd chapters, is set in the eighteenth century, and narrates the story of Nicholas Dyer, who was commissioned to build seven churches in the City of London and Westminster after the Great Fire of 1666; the other, narrated in the even chapters, is set in contemporary England, and deals with the story of detective Nicholas Hawksmoor, who was commissioned to investigate a series of murders committed near the churches built by Dyer. But the odd and even chapters are structurally and thematically interrelated with each other: the last words of each odd chapter are also the opening words of the next chapter and the cases Hawksmoor investigates are in fact Nicholas Dyer's murders.

Furthermore, detective and architect share a striking complementarity, so striking that, from a Jungian point of view they can be seen as split facets of a single individual, the conscious and unconscious aspects of the flesh-and-blood Augustan architect, Nicholas Hawksmoor, who worked for Sir Christopher Wren in the historical past.

Unlike Henry Ayscough, and unlike the rationalists of The Royal Society, architect Nicholas Dyer believes, like Mr B, that the world cannot be explained by rational means and that true knowledge does not lie in logical deduction but rather in the acquisition of forbidden knowledge through occult practices. Dyer believes in the Hermetic Principle of Correspondence synthesized in the dictum 'as above, so below'. So, he

reproduces with his seven churches the pattern cast by the Seven Orders
of the seven planets in heaven, a magic Septilateral Figure, through which
he eventually puts an end to his successive reincarnations and brings
about the reunification of himself with detective Hawksmoor, thus
transcending mortality and achieving, like Mr B in *A Maggot*, his sought-
for essential transformation into the *Anthropos*, Cosmic man (Jung, 1980:
113–47).

The Augustan Age, with its well-known polarities of reason and
passion, order and chaos, logic and magic, expresses like no other the
age's specific contradiction between the official culture of rationalism and
Enlightenment and actual taste that, as *A Maggot* and *Hawksmoor* suggest,
was much more ancestral, obscurantist and irrational. Indeed the basic
dualism that suffuses the age of the Enlightenment, expressed, for
example, in the co-existence of the sentimental novel and the Gothic
romance, helps explain the attraction that the Augustan Age, and also the
Restoration and the early nineteenth century seem to have for writers of
historiographic metafiction like Rose Tremain, Peter Ackroyd, Charles
Palliser, John Banville and John Fowles.

Describing recent British historiographic metafiction, Maureen Duffy
said that these historical novels retreated into the past, but not 'in order to
illuminate the present, but to dazzle, like entering a kind of Aladdin's cave
of glittering objects' and it is true that in novels like Peter Ackroyd's
Hawkmoor and *First Light*, John Banville's *Dr Copernicus*, *Kepler*, *The Newton
Letter* and *Mefisto*, or John Fowles' *A Maggot* the attempt to recreate a
concrete historical period in traditional terms is only a pretext for a much
more interesting and disturbing aim, which is to enter the tunnel of time
in order to recover the other, suppressed, half of Western civilisation and
history: the mythical, esoteric, gnostic and cabalistic elements which once
formed an inextricable unity with reason and logic, and which have been
progressively repressed and muffled since the Middle Ages by the
mainstream of rationalism.

By so doing these writers hope to find alternative patterns of meaning
capable of giving sense to the human condition. Incapable of reconciling
self and world by rational means, they try to transcend the limits of the
self in symbolic and archetypal terms. Mr B in *A Maggot*, as we have seen,
achieves his individuation by using his occult knowledge to guide him
along the stages of his hero's quest, reproducing with his hired actors and
servant the archetypal figure of the *quaternario*. Likewise, in Peter
Ackroyd's novel, Nicholas Dyer uses his black magic in order to transcend
his human condition, creating with his Septilateral Figure a ladder that
literally opens the gates of heaven for him.

With their painful and prolonged studies of the occult Mr B and
Nicholas Dyer are trying to recover, like archaeologist Mark Clare in
Ackroyd's *First Light*, something the Mint family had always managed to

preserve: the lost wisdom of their neolithic forefathers, prior to the Aristotelian either-or dichotomy best symbolized in the mythic circle of Stonehenge.

Mr B's *quaternario*, like Dyer's Septilateral Figure and like the *quincunx* in Lawrence Durrell's *Avignon Quintet* or, explicitly, in Charles Palliser's *The Quincunx*, or again like the elliptical circle of white stones enclosing the ancient tumulus in Dorset that appears in *First Light*, and which strikingly recalls the New Physicists' concept of the parabolic curve on whose vertex opposites are integrated, are all archetypal figurations of mandalic totality, and they express the achievement of the symbolic reconciliation of world and self in the figure of Cosmic Man, memorably drawn by Leonardo da Vinci as a star-man with arms and legs outstretched. Even if, as often happens in these novels, this reunification is shown as fictional and ephemeral, the comfort its achievement conveys is the knowledge that, in Mark Clare's words:

> [...] nothing really dies. Just because we are trapped in time, we assume that there is only one direction to go. But when we are dead, when we are out of time, everything returns [...] our bodies are made out of dead stars. We carry their light inside us. So everything goes back. Everything is part of the pattern. We carry our origin within us, and we can never rest until we have returned.
>
> (Ackroyd, 1989: 318)

In 1981 Robert Nadeau convincingly argued for the existence of a close cause-effect relationship between contemporary fiction and the collapse of Western rationalism in terms of the discoveries of the New Science, and he used as examples of this the writings of John Barth, John Updike, Kurt Vonnegut Jr., Thomas Pynchon, Tom Robbins, Don Delillo and John Fowles. Nadeau's book then, concentrates on American writers and presents John Fowles as a somewhat isolated case in the general panorama of contemporary British fiction.

We have seen how this panorama has now completely changed. Although realism-biased Oxbridge scholars like Valentine Cunningham, still insist on speaking about 'The Englishness of English Fiction' (Cunningham, 1990) and on picturing contemporary creative writing as 'very enclosed' and 'resisting with ironic weapons the pressures that appear to come from the outside' (ibid) the truth is that the eclosion of British historiographic metafiction in the 1980s shows British novelists catching up with a worldwide phenomenon, which goes back not only to North American experimental 'fabulation' but also to Spanish-American 'magic-realism' and to Gabriel García Marquez and Jorge Luis Borges in particular. García Marquez' *Cien Años de Soledad* (1967) may be seen as one of the first historiographic metafictions in which fantasy, myth and archetype are consistently used as a richer alternative to realistic rationalism for the means of recovering a people's lost identity, while Borges' *Ficciones*, with their archetyal labyrinths, Babel towers of printed matter and magical mirrors of ink, clearly foreshadow the metafictional and fantasy elements in the writings of novelists like Peter Ackroyd, Jeannette Winterson, John Fowles and Salman Rushdie.

We can, then, visualize the eclosion of historiographic metafiction in Britain in the 1980s as part of a worldwide development related to Spanish-American 'magic realism' and North American 'fabulation' that includes writers from all over the world, like Milan Kundera, Heinrich Böll, Christa Wolf, Italo Calvino, Umberto Eco, E.L. Doctorow, Ian Watson, William Kennedy, Susan Daitch, Chris Scott, Rudy Wiebe, Timothy Findley, Margaret Atwood, J. Michael Coetzee and Salman Rushdie.

Even if we refuse to accept Linda Hutcheon's contention that historiographic metafiction is *the only kind* of fiction that really fulfills the poetics of postmodernism we would have to admit that this trend very richly and powerfully catches and expresses the deepest concerns of contemporary man.

Bibliography and References

ACKROYD, PETER, *First Light* (London: Abacus, 1989).

ALLEN, WALTER, 'The Achievement of John Fowles', *Encounter*, XXV, 2, August, 64–7.

ARISTOTLE, *Poetics*, James Hutton trans. (London and New York:Norton, 1982).

BARTHES, ROLAND, *The Pleasure of the Text*, Richard Miller trans. (New York: Hill and Wang, 1975 (1973).

CUNNINGHAM, VALENTINE 'The Englishness of English Fiction', 5th Oxford Conference of Literature Teaching Overseas (April) (unpublished conference, 1990).

DUFFY, MAUREEN, 'New Trends in British Fiction', Proceedings of the 12th National Conference of AEDEAN, University of Alicante (December) (19880.

EVARTS, PRESCOTT, JR., 'Fowles's *The French Lieutenant's Woman* as Tragedy', *Critique*, XIII, 3, (1972), 57–69.

FOWLES, JOHN *The French Lieutenant's Woman* (Bungay, Suffolk: Triad/Granada, 1969 (1983).

FOWLES, JOHN, *Daniel Martin* (London: Jonathan Cape, 1977).

FOWLES, JOHN, *Mantissa* (London: Jonathan Cape, 1982).

FOWLES, JOHN, *A Maggot* (London: Jonathan Cape, 1986).

HUTCHEON, LINDA, *A Poetics of Postmodernism: History, Theory, Fiction* (New York & London: Routledge, 1988).

JUNG, CARL G. 'Concerning Rebirth', in *The Archetypes and the Collective Unconscious. The Collected works*, Vol. IX (part I). Sir Herbert, Read *et al.* (eds) (London & Henley: Routledge & Kegan Paul (1980)), pp. 113–47.

MILLER, WALTER, JR., 'Chariots or Goddesses, or What?' *The New York Times Book Review* 8 September 1985.

MOYNAHAN, JULIAN 1985 'Fly Casting', *New Republic*, 193 (7 October), 47–9.

NADEAU, ROBERT, *Readings from the New Book on Nature* (Amherst: University of Massachusetts Press, 1981).

ONEGA, SUSANA, *Form and Meaning in the Novels of John Fowles* (Ann Arbor and London: UMI Research Press, 1989).

TARBOX, KATHERINE, *The Art of John Fowles* (Athens, Georgia: University of Georgia Press, 1988).

Notes

1. The research carried out for the writing of this paper has been financed by the Spanish Ministry of Education (DGICYT, Programa Sectorial de Promoción del Conocimiento, 1991).

6 The Question of narrative in contemporary historical theory*

HAYDEN WHITE

Historiographic metafiction characteristically questions the distinction between history and fiction, and articulates historiographical issues in narrative form. But just as historical theory finds its way into narrative, so too does narrative find its way into history, and narrative theory into historical theory. Only in recent decades has the co-implication of narrative and historical theory been the subject of rigorous thought, particularly in the application of structuralist narratology to historical narrative. Here, Hayden White discusses the recent influence of narrative theory on historical theory in four areas represented by Anglo-American analytical philosophers, socially scientific historians, semiologically orientated literary theorists and hermeneutic philosophers. Concerned respectively with the epistemic status of history as a kind of explanation, the ideology of narrative as a representational strategy, the idea of history as one code of discourse among others, and of narrative as a kind of time-consciousness, these groups have taken the co-implication of narrative and history, and of narrative theory and historical theory, as a central philosophical problem. In particular, White is interested in the process of narrativising real events, the way in which events are transformed by the formal demands of narrative, and this particular interest brings him into contact with the more general issue of the 'truth' of literature.

I

In contemporary historical theory the topic of narrative has been the subject of extraordinarily intense debate. Looked at from one perspective, this is surprising; for on the face of it there should be very little to debate about narrative. Narration is a manner of speaking as universal as language itself, and narrative is a mode of verbal representation so seemingly natural to human consciousness that to suggest it is a problem might well appear pedantic.[1] But it is precisely because the narrative mode of representation is so natural to human consciousness, so much an aspect

*Reprinted from *History and Theory*, 23, 1, (1984), 1–33.

of everyday speech and ordinary discourse, that its use in any field of study aspiring to the status of a science must be suspect. For whatever else a science may be, it is also a practice which must be as critical about the way it *describes* its objects of study as it is about the way if *explains* their structures and processes. Viewed from this perspective, we can trace the development of modern sciences in terms of their progressive demotion of the narrative mode of representation in their descriptions of the phenomena which comprise their specific objects of study. And this explains in part why the humble subject of narrative should be so widely debated by historical theorists in our time; for to many of those who would transform historical studies into a science, the continued use by historians of a narrative mode of representation is an index of a failure at once methodological and theoretical. A discipline that produces narrative accounts of its subject matter as an end in itself seems methodologically unsound; one that investigates its data in the interest of telling a story about them appears theoretically deficient.[2]

Within professional historical studies, however, the narrative has been viewed for the most part neither as a product of a theory nor as the basis for a method, but rather as a *form of discourse* which may or may not be used for the representation of historical events, depending upon whether the primary aim is to *describe* a situation, *analyze* an historical process, or *tell* a story.[3] On this view, the amount of narrative in a given history will vary and its function will change depending upon whether it is conceived as an end in itself or only a means to some other end. Obviously, the amount of narrative will be greatest in accounts designed to tell a story, least in those intended to provide an analysis of the events of which it treats. Where the aim in view is the telling of a story, the problem of narrativity turns on the issue of whether historical events can be truthfully represented as manifesting the structures and processes of those met with more commonly in certain kinds of 'imaginative' discourses, that is, such fictions as the epic, the folk tale, myth, romance, tragedy, comedy, farce, and the like. This means that what distinguishes 'historical' from 'fictional' stories is first and foremost their *contents*, rather than their *form*. The content of historical stories is real events, events that really happened, rather than imaginary events, events invented by the narrator. This implies that the form in which historical events present themselves to a prospective narrator is *found* rather than *constructed*.

For the narrative historian, the historical method consists in the investigation of the documents in order to determine what is the true or most plausible story that can be told about the events of which they are evidence. A true narrative account, on this view, is not so much a product of the historian's poetic talents, as the narrative account of imaginary events is conceived to be, as a necessary result of a proper application of historical 'method'. The form of the discourse, the narrative, adds nothing to the content of the representation, but is rather a simulacrum of the structure and processes of real events. And insofar as this representation *resembles* the events of which it is a representation, it can be taken as a true account. The story told in the narrative is a 'mimesis' of the story *lived* in some region of historical reality, and insofar as it is an accurate imitation it is to be considered a truthful account thereof.

In traditional historical theory, at least since the middle of the nineteenth century, the story told about the past was distinguished from whatever *explanation* might be offered of why the events related in the story occurred when, where, and how they did. After the historian had discovered the true story of 'what happened' and accurately represented it in a narrative, he might abandon the narrational manner of speaking and, addressing the reader directly, speaking in his own voice, and representing his considered opinion as a student of human affairs, dilate on what the story he had told indicated about the nature of the period, place, agents, agencies, and processes (social, political, cultural, and so forth) that he had studied. This aspect of the historical discourse was called by some theorists the *dissertative* mode of address and was considered to comprise a form as well as a content different from those of the narrative.[4] Its form was that of the logical demonstration and its content of historian's own thought about the events, regarding either their causes or their significance for the understanding of the *types* of events of which the lived story was an instantiation. This meant, among other things, that the dissertative aspect of an historical discourse was to be assessed on grounds different from those used to assess the narrative aspect. The historian's dissertation was an *interpretation* of what he took to be the true story, while his narration was a *representation* of what he took to be the real story. A given historical discourse might be factually accurate and as veracious in its narrative aspect as the evidence permitted and still be assessed as mistaken, invalid, or inadequate in its dissertative aspect. The facts might be truthfully set forth and the interpretation of them misguided. Or conversely a given interpretation of events might be suggestive, brilliant, perspicuous, and so on and still not be justified by the facts or square with the story related in the narrative aspect of the discourse. But whatever the relative merits of the narrative and the dissertative aspects of a given historical discourse, the former was fundamental, the latter secondary. As Croce put it in a famous dictum, 'Where there is no narrative, there is no history.[5] Until the real story had been determined and the true story told, there was nothing of a specifically *historical* nature to interpret.

But this nineteenth-century view of the nature and function of narrative in historical discourse was based on an ambiguity. On the one hand, narrative was regarded as only a form of discourse, a form which featured the story as its content. On the other hand, this form was itself a content insofar as historical events were conceived to *manifest themselves* in reality as elements and aspects of stories. The form of the story told was supposed to be necessitated by the form of the story enacted by historical agents. But what about those events and processes attested by the documentary record which did not lend themselves to representation in a story but which could be represented as objects of reflection only in some other discursive mode, such as the encyclopedia, the epitome, the tableau, the statistical table or series, and so on? Did this mean that such objects were 'unhistorical,' did not belong to history, or did the possibility of representing them in a non-narrative mode of discourse indicate a limitation of the narrative mode and even a prejudice regarding what could be said to *have* a history?

Hegel had insisted that a specifically historical mode of being was linked to a specifically narrative mode of representation by a shared 'internal vital principle'.[6] This principle was, for him, nothing other than politics, which was both the precondition of the kind of interest in the past which informed historical consciousness and the pragmatic basis for the production and preservation of the kind of records that made historical inquiry possible:

> We must suppose historical narrations to have appeared contemporaneously with historical deeds and events. Family memorials, patriarchal traditions, have an interest confined to the family and the clan. The uniform course of events which such a condition implies is no subject of serious remembrance ... It is the state which first presents a subject-matter that is not only *adapted* to the prose of History, but involves the production of such History in the very progress of its own being.

In other words, for Hegel, the content (or referent) of the specifically historical discourse was not the real *story* of what happened, but the peculiar relation between a public present and a past which a state endowed with a constitution made possible.

> Profound sentiments generally, such as that of love, as also religious intuition and its conceptions, are in themselves complete – constantly present and satisfying; but that outward existence of a political constitution which is enshrined in its rational laws and customs, is an *imperfect* Present; and cannot be thoroughly understood without a knowledge of the past.[8]

Hence, the ambiguity of the term 'history'; it 'unites the objective with the subjective side, and denotes quite as much the *historia rerum gestarum*, as the *res gestae* themselves' and 'comprehends not less what has *happened*, than the *narration* of what has happened'. This ambiguity, Hegel said, reflects 'a higher order than mere outward accident'.[9] It was neither narrative per se that distinguished historiography from other kinds of discourses nor the reality of the events recounted that distinguished historical from other kinds of narrative. It was the interest in a specifically political mode of human community that made a specifically historical mode of inquiry possible; and the political nature of this mode of community that necessitated a narrative mode for its representation. As thus considered, historical studies had their own proper subject-matter, which is 'those momentous collisions between existing, acknowledged duties, laws, and rights, and those contingencies which are adverse to this fixed system'[10]; their own proper aim, which is to depict these kinds of conflicts; and their own proper mode of representation, which is the (prose) narrative. When either the subject-matter, the aim, or the mode of representation is lacking in a discourse, it may still be a contribution to knowledge but it is something less than a full contribution to *historical* knowledge.

Hegel's views on the nature of historical discourse had the merit of making explicit what was acknowledged in the dominant practice of historical scholarship in the nineteenth century, namely, an interest in the study of political history, but which was often hidden behind vague professions of an interest in narration as an end in itself. The *doxa* of the profession, in other words, took the form of the historical discourse, what it called the true story, for the content of the discourse, while the real content, politics, was represented as being primarily only a vehicle for or occasion of storytelling. This is why most professional historians of the nineteenth century, although they specialized in political history, tended to regard their work as a contribution less to a science of politics than to the political lore of national communities. The narrative form in which their discourses were cast was fully commensurate with this latter aim. But it reflects both an unwillingness to make historical studies into a science, and, more importantly, a resistance to the idea that politics should be an object of scientific study to which historiography might contribute.[11] It is in this respect, rather than in any overt espousal of a specific political program or cause, that nineteenth-century professional historiography can be regarded as ideological. For if ideology is the treatment of the form of a thing as a content or essence, nineteenth-century historiography is ideological precisely insofar as it takes the characteristic form of its discourse, the narrative, as a content, that is, narrativity, and treats 'narrativity' as an essence shared by both discourses and sets of events alike.

It is within the context of considerations such as these that we may attempt a characterization of the discussions of narrative in historical theory that have taken place in the West over the last two or three decades. We can discern four principal strains in these discussions: first, that represented by certain Anglo-American analytical philosophers

(Walsh, Gardiner, Dray, Gallie, Morton White, Danto, Mink) who have
sought to establish the epistemic status of narrativity, considered as a *kind
of explanation* especially appropriate to the explanation of historical, as
against natural, events and processes.[12] Second, that of certain social-
scientifically oriented historians, of whom the members of the French
Annales group may be considered exemplary. This group (Braudel, Furet,
Le Goff, LeRoy Ladurie) regarded narrative historiography as a non-
scientific, even *ideological representational strategy*, the extirpation of which
was necessary for the transformation of historical studies into a genuine
science.[13] Third, that of certain semiologically oriented literary theorists
and philosophers (Barthes, Foucault, Derrida, Todorov, Julia Kristeva,
Benveniste, Genette, Eco), who have studied narrative in all of its
manifestations and viewed it as simply one discursive 'code' among
others, which might or might not be appropriate for the representation of
'reality', depending only on the *pragmatic* aim in view of the speaker of the
discourse.[14] And finally, that of certain hermeneutically oriented
philosophers, such as Gadamer and Ricoeur, who have viewed narrative
as *the manifestation in discourse* of a specific kind of time-consciousness or
structure of time.[15]

We might have added a fifth category to this list, namely that of certain
historians who can be said to belong to no particular philosophical or
methodological persuasion, but speak rather from the standpoint of the
doxa of the profession, as defenders of a *craft* notion of historical studies,
and who view narrative as a respectable way of 'doing' history (as J.H.
Hexter puts it) or 'practising' it (as Geoffrey Elton would have it).[16] But
this group does not so much represent a theoretical position as incarnate a
traditional attitude of eclecticism in historical studies – an eclecticism
which is a manifestation of a certain suspicion of theory itself as an
impediment to the proper practice of historical inquiry, conceived as
empirical inquiry.[17] For this group, narrative representation poses no
significant theoretical problem. We need therefore only register this
position as the *doxa* against which a genuinely theoretical inquiry must
take its rise – and pass on to a consideration of those for whom narrative is
a problem and an occasion for theoretical reflection.

II

The *Annales* group have been most critical of narrative history, but in a
rather more polemical than a distinctively theoretical way. For them,
narrative history was simply the history of past politics and, moreover,
political history conceived as short-term, 'dramatic' conflicts and crises
which lend themselves to 'novelistic' representations, of a more 'literary'
than a properly 'scientific' kind. As Braudel put it in a well-known essay:

> [T]he narrative history so dear to the heart of Ranke offer[s] us ... [a] gleam but no illumination; facts but no humanity. Note that this narrative history always claims to relate 'things just as they really happened.' ... In fact, though, in its own covert way, narrative history consists of an interpretation, an authentic philosophy of history. To the narrative historians, the life of men is dominated by dramatic accidents, by the actions of those exceptional beings who occasionally emerge, and who often are the masters of their own fate and even more of ours. And when they speak of 'general history,' what they are really speaking of is the intercrossing of such exceptional destinies, for obviously each hero must be matched against another. A delusive fallacy, as we all know.[18]

This position was taken up rather uniformly by other members of the *Annales* group, but more as a justification for their promotion of an historiography devoted to the analysis of 'long-term trends in demography, economics, and ethnology, that is, 'impersonal' processes, than as an incentive to analyze what 'narrative' itself consisted of and the basis of its millennial popularity as the 'proper' mode of historical representation.[19]

It should be stressed that the rejection of narrative history by the *Annalistes* was due as much to their distaste for its conventional subject-matter, that is, past politics, as to their conviction that its form was inherently 'novelistic' and 'dramatizing' rather than 'scientific'.[20] Their professed conviction that political affairs did not lend themselves to scientific study, because of their evanescent nature and status as epiphenomena of processes deemed to be more basic to history, was consistent with the failure of modern politology (I thank J. Topolski for this useful word) to create a genuine science of politics. But the rejection of politics as a fit object of study for a scientific historiography is curiously complementary to the prejudice of nineteenth-century professional historians regarding the undesirability of a scientific politics. To hold that a science of politics is impossible is, of course, as much of an ideological position as to hold that such a science is undesirable.

But what has *narrative* to do with all this? The charge leveled by the *Annalistes* is that narrativity is inherently 'dramatizing' or 'novelizing' of its subject-matter, as if dramatic events either did not exist in history or, if they do exist, are by virtue of their dramatic nature not fit objects of historical study.[21]

It is difficult to know what to make of this strange congeries of opinions. One can narrativize without dramatizing, as the whole of modernist literature demonstrates, and dramatize without 'theatricalizing', as the modern theatre since Pirandello and Brecht makes eminently clear. So, how can one condemn narrative on grounds of its 'novelizing' effects?

One suspects that it is not the 'dramatic' nature of novels that is at issue but a distaste for a genre of literature that puts human agents rather than impersonal processes at the center of interest and suggests that such agents have some significant control over their own destinies.[22] But novels are not necessarily humanistic any more than they are necessarily 'dramatic'. In any case, the free will-determinism question is quite as much an ideological issue as that of the possibility or impossibility of a science of politics. Therefore, without presuming to judge the positive achievement of the *Annalistes* in their effort to reform historical studies, we must conclude that the reasons they adduce for their dissatisfaction with 'narrative history' are jejune.

It may be, however, that what some of them have to say about this topic is only a stenographic reproduction of a much more extensive analysis and deconstruction of narrativity that was carried out in the 1960s by structuralists and post-structuralists, who claimed to demonstrate that narrative was not only an instrument of ideology, but the very paradigm of ideologizing discourse in general.

III

This is not the place for yet another exposition of structuralism and post-structuralism, of which there are more than enough already.[23] But the significance of these two movements for the discussion of 'narrative history' can be briefly indicated. This significance, as I see it, is threefold: anthropological, psychological, and semiological. From the anthropological perspective, as represented above all by Claude Lévi-Strauss, it was not 'narrative' so much as 'history' itself that was the problem.[24] In a famous polemic, directed against Sartre's *Critique de la raison dialectique*, Lévi-Strauss denied the validity of the distinction between 'historical' (or 'civilized') and 'pre-historical' (or 'primitive') societies, and therewith the legitimacy of the notion of a specific 'method' of study and mode of representing the structures and processes of the former. The kind of knowledge which the so-called historical method was supposed to provide, that is to say, 'historical knowledge', was, in Lévi-Strauss's view, hardly distinguishable from the mythic lore of 'savage' communities. Indeed, historiography – by which Lévi-Strauss understood traditional, 'narrative' historiography – was nothing but the myth of Western and especially modern, bourgeois, industrial, and imperialistic societies. The substance of this myth consisted of the mistaking of a method of representation, narrative, for a content, that is, the notion of a humanity uniquely identified with those societies capable of believing that they had *lived* the kinds of stories that Western historians had *told* about them. The historical, which is to say, the diachronic, representation of events *is* a method of analysis, Lévi-Strauss granted, but 'it is a method with no distinct object corresponding to it', much less a method peculiarly adequate to the understanding of 'humanity' or 'civilized societies'.[25] The representation of events in terms of their chronological order of occurrence, which Lévi-Strauss identified as the putative 'method' of historical studies, is for him nothing but a heuristic *procedure* common to every field of scientific study, whether of nature or of culture, *prior* to the application of whatever analytical techniques are necessary for the identification of those events' common properties as elements of a *structure*.[26]

The specific chronological scale used for this ordering procedure is always culture-specific and adventitious, a purely heuristic device, the validity of which depends upon the specific aims and interests of the scientific discipline in which it is used. The important point is that, in Lévi-Strauss's view of the matter, there is no such thing as *a* single scale for the ordering of events, but rather as many chronologies as there are culture-specific ways of representing the passage of time. Far from being a science or even a basis for a science, the narrative representation of any set of events was at best a proto-scientific exercise and at worst a basis for a kind of cultural self-delusion. 'The progress of knowledge and the creation of new sciences,' he concluded, 'take place through the generation of anti-histories which show that a certain order which is possible only on one [chronological] plane ceases to be so on another.'[27]

Not that Lévi-Strauss was opposed to narrative as such. Indeed, his monumental *Mythologiques* was intended to demonstrate the centrality of narrativity to the production of cultural life in all its forms.[28] What he objected to was the expropriation of narrativity as the 'method' of a 'science' purporting to have as its object of study a 'humanity' more fully realized in its 'historical' than in its 'pre-historical' manifestations. The import of his criticism was therefore directed at that 'humanism' in which Western civilization took so much pride but the ethical principles of which it seemed to honor more in the breach than in the observance. This was the same 'humanism' which Jacques Lacan sought to undermine in his revision of psychoanalytical theory, Louis Althusser wished to expunge from modern Marxism, and Michel Foucault had simply dismissed as the ideology of Western civilization in its most repressive and decadent phase.[29] For all of these – as well as for Jacques Derrida and Julia Kristeva – not only 'history' in general but 'narrativity' specifically were merely representational practices by which society produced a human 'subject' peculiarly adapted to the conditions of life in the modern *Rechtsstaat*.[30] Their arguments on behalf of this view are too complex to be represented here, but the nature of their kind of hostility to the notion of 'narrative history' can be suggested by a brief consideration of Roland Barthes's essay of 1967 on 'The Discourse of History'.

In this essay, Barthes challenged the distinction, basic to historicism in all its forms, between 'historical' and 'fictional' discourse. The point of attack chosen for this argument was the kind of historiography that favored a narrative representation of past events and processes. Barthes asked:

> Does the narration of past events, which, in our culture from the time of the Greeks onwards, has generally been subject to the sanction of historical 'science,' bound to the underlying standard of the 'real,' and justified by the principles of 'rational' exposition – does this form of narration really differ, in some specific trait, in some indubitably distinctive feature, from imaginary narration, as we find it in the epic, the novel, and the drama?[31]

It is obvious from the manner in which he posed this question – with the placement of the words 'science', 'real', and 'rational' between inverted commas – that Barthes's principal aim was to attack the vaunted objectivity of traditional historiography. And this is precisely what he did – by exposing the ideological function of the narrative mode of representation with which it has been associated.

As in his theoretical appendix to *Mythologies* (1957), Barthes did not so much oppose science to ideology as distinguish between progressive and reactionary, liberating and oppressive ideologies.[32] In the 'Discourse of History' he indicated that history could be represented in a number of different modes, some of which were less 'mythological' than others inasmuch as they overtly called attention to their own process of production and indicated the 'constituted,' rather than 'found' nature of their referents. But, in his view, traditional historical discourse was more retrograde than either modern science or modern art, both of which – in his view – signaled the *invented* nature of their 'contents'. Historical studies, alone among the disciplines pretending to the status of scientificity, remained a victim of what he called 'the fallacy of referentiality'.

Barthes purported to demonstrate that '[a]s we can see, simply from looking at its structure, and without having to invoke the substance of its content, historical discourse is in its essence a form of ideological elaboration,' or to put it more precisely, an imaginary elaboration, by which he meant a 'speech-act,' that was 'performative' in nature, 'through which the utterer of the discourse (a purely linguistic entity) "fills out" the place of the subject of the utterance (a psychological or ideological entity).'[33] It should be observed that, although Barthes here refers to historical discourse in general, it is historical discourse endowed with 'narrative structure' that is his principal object of interest; and this for two reasons. First, he finds it paradoxical that 'narrative structure, which was originally developed within the cauldron of fiction (in myths and the first epics)', should have become, in traditional historiography, 'at once the sign and the proof of reality',[34] But second, and more importantly, narrative was, for Barthes, following Lacan, the principal instrumentality by which society fashions the narcissistic, infantile consciousness into a 'subjectivity' capable of bearing the 'responsibilities' of an 'object' of the law in all its forms.

In the acquisition of language, Lacan had suggested, the child also acquires the very paradigm of orderly, rule-governed behaviour. In the development of the capacity to assimilate 'stories' and to tell them, however, Barthes adds, the child also learns what it is to be that creature which, in Nietzsche's phrase, is capable of making promises, of 'remembering forward' as well as backward, and of linking his end to his beginning in such a way as to attest to an 'integrity' which every individual must be supposed to possess if he is to become a 'subject' of (any) system of law, morality, or propriety. What is 'imaginary' about any *narrative* representation is the illusion of a centered consciousness capable of looking out on the world, apprehending its structure and processes, and representing them to itself as having all of the formal coherency of narrativity itself. But, in Barthes's view, this is to mistake a 'meaning' (which is always constituted rather than found) for 'reality' (which is always found rather than constituted).[35]

Behind this formulation lay a vast mass of highly problematical theories of language, discourse, consciousness, and ideology, with which the names of both Lacan and Althusser especially were associated. Barthes drew upon these for his own purpose. This purpose was nothing less than the dismantling of the whole heritage of nineteenth-century 'realism' – which he viewed as the pseudo-scientific content of that ideology which appeared as 'humanism' in its sublimated form.

It was no accident, for Barthes, that 'realism' in the nineteenth-century novel and 'objectivity' in nineteenth-century historiography had developed *pied-à-pied*. What they had in common was a dependency on a specifically narrative mode of discourse, the principal purpose of which was to substitute surreptitiously a conceptual content (a *signified*) for a *referent* that it pretended merely to describe. As he had written, in the seminal 'Introduction to the Structural Analysis of Narrative' (1966):

> Claims concerning the 'realism' of narrative are therefore to be discounted ... The function of narrative is not to 'represent,' it is to constitute a spectacle ... Narrative does not show, does not imitate ... 'What takes place' in a narrative is from the referential (reality) point

of view literally *nothing*; 'what happens' is language alone, the adventure of language, the unceasing celebration of its coming.[36]

This passage refers to narrative in general, to be sure, but the principles enunciated were extendable to historical narrative as well. Whence his insistence, at the end of 'The Discourse of History,' that 'in objective history, the real is never more than an unformulated signified, sheltering behind the apparently all-powerful referent. This situation characterizes what might be called the *realistic effect* [*effet du réel*].'[37]

Much could be said about this conception of narrative and its supposed ideological function, not least about the psychology on which it is based and the ontology which it presupposes. It is – obviously – reminiscent of Nietzsche's thought about language, literature, and historiography and, insofar as it bears upon the problem of historical consciousness, it does not say much that goes beyond 'The Uses and Abuses of History for Life' and *The Genealogy of Morals*. This Nietzschean affiliation is openly admitted by such post-structuralists as Derrida, Kristeva, and Foucault, and it is this Nietzschean turn in French thought over the last twenty years or so that serves to distinguish the post-structuralists from their more 'scientistic' structuralist predecessors, as represented by Lévi-Strauss, Roman Jakobson, and the early Barthes. Post-structuralism has little in common with the aspiration of those historians among the *Annales* group who dreamed of transforming historical studies into a kind of science. But the 'de-construction' of narrativity carried out by Barthes and the post-structuralists is consistent with the objections which the *Annalistes* raised against the narrative mode of representation in historiography.

IV

Barthes's formulation of the problematics of 'narrative history' points up a significant difference, however, between discussions of this subject which developed in France in the 1960s and those which had taken place in the previous two decades in the Anglophone philosophical community, dominated at that time by analytical philosophy. The most apparent difference lies in the consistency with which narrative was defended by the analytical philosophers, both as a mode of representation and as a mode of explanation, in contrast to the attacks upon it emanating from France. Different accounts were given by different philosophers of the bases for the conviction that narrative was a perfectly valid mode of representing historical events and even of providing an explanation of them. But in contrast to the French discussion, in the Anglophone world narrative historiography was viewed for the most part not as an ideology, but rather as an antidote for the nefarious 'philosophy of history' à la Hegel and Marx, the presumed ideological linchpin of 'totalitarian' political systems.

Here, too, however, the lines of debate were muddied by the issue of history's status as a science and discussion of the kind of epistemic authority that historical knowledge could claim in comparison with the kind of knowledge provided by the physical sciences. There was even a vigorous debate within Marxist circles, a debate which reached a culmination in the 1970s, over the extent to which a Marxist, 'scientific' historiography should be cast in a narrativist, as against a more properly analytical, mode of discourse. And in this debate issues similar to those which divided the *Annalistes* from their more conventional co-professionals had to be addressed. But here narrativity was much less a matter of concern than the issue of 'materialism *versus* idealism'.[38] On the whole, among both historians and philosophers and among both Marxist and non-Marxist practitioners of these disciplines, no one seriously questioned the legitimacy of distinctively 'historical' studies, as Lévi-Strauss had done in France, or the adequacy, at some level, of the narrative to represent veraciously and objectively the 'truths' discovered by whatever methods the individual historian happened to have used in his research, as Barthes and Foucault did in France. Some social scientists raised such questions, but given the tenuousness of their own claims to methodological rigor and the exiguousness of their 'science,' they bore little theoretical fruit with respect to the question of 'narrative history'.[39]

The differences between these two strains of discussions of historical narrative also reflected fundamentally different conceptions of the nature of discourse in general. In literary and linguistic theory, the discourse is conventionally thought of as any unit of utterance larger than the (complex) sentence. What are the principles of discourse-formation, corresponding to those rules of grammar which preside over the formation of the sentence? These principles are obviously not grammatical themselves, since one can construct chains of grammatically correct sentences that do not aggregate or coalesce into a recognizable discourse.

Obviously, one candidate for the role or organon of discourse-formation is logic, the protocols of which preside over the formation of all 'scientific' discourses. But logic yields place to other principles in poetic discourse, principles such as phonetics, rhyme, meter, and so on, the exigencies of which may authorize violations of logical protocols in the interest of producing formal coherencies of another kind. And then there is rhetoric, which may be regarded as a principle of discourse-formation in those speech events which aim at persuasion or impulsion to action rather than description, demonstration, or explication. In both poetic and rhetorical speech, the communication of a *message* about some extrinsic referent may be involved, but the functions of 'expression' on the one side and of 'conation' of the other may be given a higher order of importance. Therefore, the distinctions among 'communication,' 'expression,' and 'conation' permit the differentiation, in terms of function, among different kinds of rules of discourse-formation, of which logic is only one and by no means the most privileged.

Everything depends, as Roman Jakobson put it, on the 'set' (*Einstellung*) toward the 'message' contained in the discourse in question.[40] If the conveyance of a message about an extrinsic referent is the primary aim of the discourse, we can say that the communication function predominates; and the discourse in question is to be assessed in terms of the clarity of its formulation and its truth-value (the validity of the information it provides) with respect to the referent. If, on the other hand, the message is treated as being primarily an occasion for expressing an emotional condition of the speaker of the discourse (as in most lyrics) or for engendering an attitude in the recipient of the message, conducing to an action of a particular kind (as in hortatory speeches), then the discourse in question is to be assessed less in terms of its clarity or its truth-value with respect to its referent than in terms of its performative force – a purely pragmatic consideration.

This functional model of discourse relegates logic, poetic, and rhetoric alike to the status of 'codes' in which different kinds of 'messages' can be cast and transmitted with quite different aims in view: communicative, expressive, or conative, as the case may be.[41] These aims are by no means mutually exclusive; indeed, every discourse can be shown to possess aspects of all three of these functions. And this goes for 'factual' as well as 'fictional' discourse. But considered as a basis for a general theory of discourse this model permits us to ask how *narrative* discourse in particular utilizes these three functions. And more relevantly to our purpose in this essay, it permits us to see how contemporary discussions of the nature of the narrative history have tended to ignore one or another of these functions in order either to save narrative history for 'science,' on the one side, or consign it to the category of 'ideology,' on the other.

Most of those who would defend narrative as a legitimate mode of historical representation and even as a valid mode of explanation (at least, for history) stress the communicative function. On this view, a history is conceived to be a 'message' about a 'referent' (the past, historical events, and so on) the content of which is *both* 'information' (the 'facts'), on the one side, and an 'explanation' (the 'narrative' account), on the other. Both the facts in their particularity and the narrative account in its generality must meet a correspondence, as well as a coherence, criterion of truth-value. The coherence criterion invoked is of course that of logic, rather than those of poetic or rhetoric. Individual propositions must be logically consistent with one another and the principles conceived to govern the process of syntagmatic combination must be consistently applied. Thus, for example, although an earlier event can be represented as a cause of a later event, the reverse is not the case. By contrast, however, a later event can serve to illuminate the 'significance' of an earlier event, but not the reverse (for example, the birth of Diderot does not illuminate the significance of the composition of *Rameau's Nephew*, but the composition of *Rameau's Nephew* illuminates, retrospectively, as it were, the 'significance' of the birth of Diderot). And so on...[42]

The correspondence criterion is another matter, however. Not only must the singular existential statements that comprise the 'chronicle' of the historical account 'correspond' to the events of which they are predications, the narrative as a whole must 'correspond' to the general configuration of the sequence of events of which it is an account. Which is to say that the sequence of 'facts' *as they are emplotted* in order to make a 'story' out of what would otherwise be only a 'chronicle,' must correspond to the general configuration of the 'events' of which the 'facts' are propositional indicators.

For those theorists who stress the communication function of narrative historical discourse, the correspondence of the 'story' to the events it relates is established at the level of the conceptual content of the 'message'. This conceptual content may be thought to consist either of the factors which link events in chains of causes and effects or of the 'reasons' (or 'intentions') motivating the human agents of the events in question. The causes (necessary if not sufficient) or reasons (conscious or unconscious) for events taking place[43] as they in fact did are set forth in the narrative in the *form* of the story it tells.

On this view, the narrative form of the discourse is only a *medium* for the message, having no more truth-value or informational content than any other formal structure, such as a logical syllogism, a metaphorical figure, or a mathematical equation. Considered as a code, the narrative is a vehicle rather in the way that the Morse code serves as the vehicle for the transmission of messages by a telegraphical apparatus. Which means, among other things, that as thus envisaged the narrative code adds nothing in the way of information or knowledge that could not be conveyed by some other system of discursive encodation. This is proven by the fact that the *content* of any narrative account of real events can be extracted from the account, represented in a dissertative format, and subjected to the same criteria of logical consistency and factual accuracy as a scientific demonstration. The narrative actually composed by a given historian may be more or less 'thick' in content and more or less 'artistic' in its execution; it may be more or less elegantly elaborated – in the way that the 'touch' of different telegraphers is conceived to be. But this, the proponents of this view would have it, is more a matter of individual 'style' than of 'content'. In the historical narrative, it is the 'content' alone that has 'truth-value'. All else is 'ornament'.

This notion of narrative discourse fails, however, to take account of the enormous number of *kinds* of narratives that every culture disposes for those of its members who might wish to draw upon them for the encodation and transmission of messages. Moreover, every narrative discourse consists, not of one single code monolithically utilized, but rather of a complex set of codes, the interweaving of which by the author – for the production of a story infinitely rich in suggestion and variety of affect, not to mention attitude toward and subliminal evaluation of its subject-matter – attests to his talents as an artist, as master rather than as the servant of the codes available for his use. Whence the 'density' of such relatively informal discourses as those of 'literature' and 'poetry' as against those of 'science'. As the Russian textologist J. Lotman has remarked,[44] the artistic text carries much more 'information' than does the scientific text, because the former disposes more codes and more levels of encodation than does the latter. At the same time, however, the artistic as against the scientific text directs attention as much to the virtuosity involved in its production as it does to the 'information' conveyed in the various codes employed in its composition.

It is this complex multilayeredness of discourse and its consequent capacity to bear a wide variety of interpretations of its meaning that the *performance model of discourse* seeks to illuminate. From the perspective provided by this model, a discourse is regarded as an apparatus for the *production of meaning*, rather than as only a vehicle for the transmission of information about an extrinsic referent. As thus envisaged, the 'content' of the discourse consists as much of its form as it does of whatever information might be extracted from a reading of it.[45] It follows that to change the form of the discourse might not be to change the information about its explicit referent, but it would certainly change the meaning produced by it.

For example, a set of events simply listed in the chronological order of their original occurrence is not, *pace* Lévi-Strauss, devoid of meaning. Its meaning is precisely the kind which any list is capable of producing – as Rabelais's and Joyce's use of the genre of the list amply attests. A list of events may be only a 'thin' chronicle (if the items in the list are presented chronologically) or a 'slim' encyclopedia (if organized topically). In both cases the same information may be conveyed, but different meanings are produced.

A chronicle, however, is not a narrative, even if it contains the same set of facts as its informational content. And this because a narrative discourse *performs* differently from a chronicle. 'Chronology' is no doubt a 'code' shared by both chronicle and narrative, but narrative utilizes other codes as well and produces a meaning quite different from that of any chronicle.

It is not that the code of narrative is more 'literary' than that of chronicle – as many historians of historical writing have suggested. And it is not that the narrative 'explains' more or even explains more fully than does the chronicle. The point is that narrativization produces a meaning quite different from that produced by chronicalization. And it does this by imposing a discursive form on the events which comprise its own chronicle by means that are poetic in nature. Which is to say that the narrative code is drawn from the performative domain of poiesis rather than that of noesis. This is what Barthes meant when he said: 'Narrative does not *show*, does not *imitate* ... [Its] function is not to "*represent*," it is to *constitute* a spectacle' (my italics).

It is generally recognized that one way of distinguishing poetic from prosaic discourse is by the prominence given in the former to patterning – of sounds, rhythms, meter, and so on – which draws attention to the form of the discourse quite apart from (or in excess of) whatever 'message' it may contain on the level of its literal verbal enunciation. The form of the poetic text produces a 'meaning' quite other than whatever might be represented in any prose paraphrase of its literal verbal content. But the same can be said of the various genres of *Kunstprosa* (oratorical declamation, legal brief, prose romance, novel, and so on), of which the historical narrative is undeniably a species; only here, the patterning in question is not that of sound and meter so much as that of the rhythms and repetitions of motific structures which aggregate into themes, and of themes which aggregate into plot-structures. This is not to say, of course, that such genres do not also utilize the various codes of logical argumentation and scientific demonstration; for indeed they do. But these codes have nothing to do with the production of the kind of meaning that is effected by narrativization.

Certain narrative discourses may have arguments embedded within them, in the form of 'explanations' of *why* things happened as they did, set forth in the mode of direct address to the reader, in the author's own voice, and perceivable as such. But such arguments are more properly considered as a 'commentary' on, rather than a part of, the narrative. In historical discourse, the narrative serves to transform a list of historical events that would otherwise be only a chronicle into a story. In order to effect this transformation, the events, agents, and agencies represented in the chronicle must be encoded as 'story-elements,' that is to say, characterized as the kinds of events, agents, and agencies that can be apprehended as elements of specific 'story-types'. On this level of encodation, the historical discourse directs the reader's attention to a secondary referent, different in kind from the events that make up the primary referent, namely, the 'plot-structures' of the various story-types cultivated in a given culture.[46] When the reader recognizes the story being told in an historical narrative as a specific kind of story, for example, as an epic, romance, tragedy, comedy, or farce, he can be said to have 'comprehended' the 'meaning' produced by the discourse. This 'comprehension' is nothing other than the recognition of the 'form' of the narrative.

The production of meaning, in this case, can be regarded as a performance, because any given set of real events can be emplotted in a number of ways, can bear the weight of being told as any number of different kinds of stories. Since no given set or sequence of real events is *intrinsically* 'tragic,' 'comic,' or 'farcical,' but can be constructed as such only by the imposition of the structure of a given story-type on the events, it is the choice of the story-type and its imposition upon the events which endow them with meaning. The effect of such emplotment may be regarded as an 'explanation' if one chooses so to view it, but in this case it would have to be recognized that the generalizations that serve the function of universals in any version of a nomological-deductive argument are the *topoi* of literary 'plots', rather than the causal laws of science.

This is why a narrative history can legitimately be regarded as something other than a scientific account of the events of which it speaks – as the *Annalistes* have rightly argued. But it is not sufficient reason to deny to narrative history substantial 'truth-value'. Narrative historiography may very well, as Furet indicates, 'dramatize' historical events and 'novelize' historical processes, but this only indicates that the truths in which narrative history deals are of an order different from those of its social-scientific counterpart. In the historical narrative the systems of meaning-production peculiar to a culture or society are tested against the capacity of any set of 'real' events to yield to such systems. If these systems have their purest, most fully developed, and formally most coherent representations in the 'literary' or 'poetic' endowment of modern, secularized cultures, this is no reason to rule them out as *merely* imaginary constructions. To do so would entail the denial that literature and poetry have anything valid to teach us about 'reality'.

V

The relationship between historiography and literature is, of course, as tenuous and difficult to define as that between historiography and science. In part, no doubt, this is because historiography in the West arises against the background of a distinctively 'literary' (or rather 'fictional') discourse which itself had taken shape against the even more archaic discourse of 'myth'. In its origins, historical discourse differentiates itself from literary discourse by virtue of its subject-matter ('real' rather than 'imaginary' events), rather than by its form. But form here is ambiguous, for it refers not only to the manifest appearance of historical discourses (their appearance *as* stories) but also to the systems of meaning-production (the modes of emplotment) which historiography shared with 'literature' and 'myth'. This affiliation of narrative historiography with literature and myth should provide no reason for embarrassment, however, because the systems of meaning-production shared by all three are distillates of the historical experience of a people, a group, a culture. And the knowledge provided by narrative history is that which results from the testing of the systems of meaning-production originally elaborated in myth and refined in the alembic of the hypothetical mode of fictional articulation. In the historical narrative, experiences distilled into fiction as *typifications* are subjects to the test of their capacity to endow 'real' events with meaning. And it would take a *Kulturphilistinismus* of a very high order to deny to the results of this testing procedure the status of genuine knowledge.

In other words, just as the contents of myth are tested by fiction, so too the forms of fiction are tested by (narrative) historiography. If in similar manner the content of narrative historiography is subjected to tests of adequacy to the representation and explanation of another order of 'reality' than that presupposed by traditional historians, this should be seen less as an opposition of 'science' to 'ideology,' as the *Annalistes* often seem to view it, than as a continuation of the process of mapping the limit between the imaginary and the real which begins with the invention of 'fiction' itself.

The historical narrative does not, as narrative, dispel false beliefs about the past, human life, the nature of the community, and so on; what it does is test the capacity of a culture's fictions to endow real events with the kinds of meaning that literature displays to consciousness through its fashioning of patterns of 'imaginary' events. Precisely insofar as the historical narrative endows sets of real events with the kinds of meaning found otherwise only in myth and literature, we are justified in regarding it as a product of *allegoresis*. Therefore, rather than regarding every historical narrative as 'mythic' or 'ideological' in nature, it is more correct to regard it as allegorical, which is to say: it says one thing and means another.

As thus envisaged, the narrative figurates the body of events that serves as its primary referent and transforms these 'events' into intimations of patterns of meaning that any *literal* representation of them as 'facts' could never produce. This is not to say that an historical discourse is not properly assessed in terms of the truth-value of its factual (singular existential) statements taken individually and the logical conjunction of the whole set of such statements taken distributively. For unless an historical discourse acceded to assessment in these terms, it would lose all justification for its claim to represent and provide explanations of specifically 'real' events. But such assessment touches only that aspect of the historical discourse which is conventionally called its 'chronicle'. It does not provide us with any way of assessing the content of the narrative itself.

This point has been made most tellingly by Louis O. Mink, who has written:

> One can regard any text in direct discourse as a logical conjunction of assertions. The truth-value of the text is then simply a logical function of the truth or falsity of the individual assertions taken separately: the conjunction is true if and only if each of the propositions is true. Narrative has in fact been analyzed, especially by philosophers intent on comparing the form of the narrative with the form of theories, as if it were nothing but a logical-conjunction of past-referring statements; and on such an analysis there is no problem of *narrative truth*. The difficulty with the model of logical conjunction, however, is that it is not a model of narrative at all. It is rather a model of a chronicle. Logical conjunction serves well enough as a representation of the only ordering relation of chronicles, which is '... and then ... and then ... and then ... and then ...' Narratives, however, contain indefinitely many order relations, and indefinitely many ways of *combining* these relations. It is such a combination that we mean when we speak of the coherence of a narrative, or lack of it. It is an unsolved task of literary theory to classify the ordering relations of narrative form; but whatever the classification, it should be clear that a historical narrative claims truth not merely for each of its individual statements taken distributively, but for the complex form of the narrative itself.[47]

But the 'truth' of 'narrative form' can display itself only indirectly, that is to say, by means of *allegoresis*. What else could be involved in the representation of a set of real events as a tragedy, comedy, farce, and so on? Is there, for example, any test, logical or empirical, that could be applied to determine the truth value of the assertion by Marx that the events of 'the 18th Brumaire of Louis Buonaparte' constitute a 'farcical' re-enactment of the 'tragedy' of 1789?[48] Marx's discourse is certainly assessable by the criteria of factual accuracy in his representation of particular events and the logical consistency of his explanation of why they occurred as they did. But what is the truth-value of his figuration of the whole set of events, achieved by narrative means, as a farce? Are we intended to take this as only a figure of speech, a metaphorical expression, and therefore not subject to assessment on grounds of its 'truth–value'? To do so would require that we dismiss the narrative aspect of Marx's discourse, the story he tells about the events, as mere ornament and not an essential aspect of the discourse as a whole.

Marx's assertion of the farcical nature of the events he describes is made only indirectly (by means of the aphorism that opens his discourse and by his narrativization of the events, the story he makes of them), which is to say, allegorically. This does not mean that we would be justified in assuming that Marx did not intend us to take this assertion 'seriously' and to regard it as 'truthful' in its content. But what is the relation between the assertion of the farcical nature of the events and the 'facts' registered in the discourse, on the one side, and the dialectical analysis of them given in the passages in which Marx, speaking in his own voice and as a putative 'scientist' of society, purports to 'explain' them, on the other? Do the facts confirm the characterization of the events as a farce? Is the logic of Marx's explanation consistent with the logic of the narrative? What 'logic' governs this narrativizing aspect of Marx's discourse?

The logic of Marx's explicit argument about the events, his explanation of the facts, is manifestly 'dialectical,' that is, his own version of Hegel's logic. Is there another 'logic' presiding over the representation of the events as a 'farce'? This is the question which the threefold distinction among the chronicle of events, the explanation of them given in direct discourse as commentary, and the narrativization of the events provided by *allegoresis* helps us to answer. And the answer is given at the moment we recognize the allegorical aspect of the characterization of the events of 'the 18th Brumaire' as a 'farce'. It is not 'fact' that legitimates the representation of the events as a 'farce,' and it is not 'logic' that permits the projection of the fact as a 'farce'. There is no way in which one could conclude on logical grounds that any set of 'real' events is a farce. This is a judgment, not a conclusion; and it is a judgment that can be justified only on the basis of a poetic troping of the 'facts' so as to give them, in the very process of their initial description, the aspect of the elements of the story-form known as 'farce' in the literary code of our culture.

If there is any logic presiding over the transition from the level of fact or event in the discourse to that of narrative, it is the logic of figuration itself, which is to say, tropology. This transition is effected by a displacement of the facts onto the ground of literary fictions or, what amounts to the same thing, the projection onto the facts of the plot-structure of one or another of the genres of literary figuration. Or, to put it yet another way, the transition is effected by a process of transcodation, in which events originally transcribed in the code of chronicle are re-transcribed in the literary code of the farce.

To present the question of narrativization in historiography in these terms, of course, is to raise the more general question of the 'truth' of literature itself. On the whole, this question has been ignored by the analytical philosophers concerned to analyze the logic of narrative explanations in historiography. And this because, it seems to me at least, the notion of explanation which they brought to their investigation ruled out the consideration of figurative discourse as productive of genuine knowledge. Since historical narratives refer to 'real' rather than 'imaginary' events, it was assumed that their 'truth-value' resided either in the literal statements of fact contained within them or in a combination of these and a literalist paraphrase of statements made in figurative language. It being generally given that figurative expressions are either false, ambiguous, or logically inconsistent (consisting as they do of what some philosophers call 'category mistakes'), it followed that whatever explanations might be contained in an historical narrative should be expressible only in literal language. Thus in their summaries of explanations contained in historical narratives, these analysts of the form tended to reduce the narrative in question to sets of discrete propositions, for which the simple declarative sentence served as a model. When an element of figurative language turned up in such sentences, it was treated as only a figure of speech, the content of which was either its literal meaning or a literalist paraphrase of what appeared to be its grammatically 'correct' formulation. But in this process of literalization, what gets left out is precisely those elements of figuration, tropes and figures of thought, as the rhetoricians call them, without which the narrativization of real events, the transformation of a chronicle into a story, could never be effected. If there is any 'category mistake' involved in this literalizing procedure, it is that of mistaking a narrative account of real events for a literal account thereof. A narrative account is always a figurative account, an allegory. To leave this figurative element out of consideration in the analysis of a narrative is not only to miss its aspect as allegory; it is also to miss the performance in language by which a chronicle is transformed into a narrative. And it is only a modern prejudice against allegory or, what amounts to the same thing, a scientistic prejudice in favor of literalism, that obscures this fact to many modern analysts of historical narrative. In any event, the dual conviction that, on the one hand, truth must be represented in literal statements of fact and, on the other, that explanation must conform to the scientific model or its commonsensical counterpart, has led most analysts to ignore the specifically 'literary' aspect of historical narrative and therewith whatever 'truth' it may convey in figurative terms.

VI

Needless to say, the notion of literary, even mythical, truth is not alien to those philosophers who continue to work in a tradition of thought that has its modern origin in Hegelian idealism, its continuator in Dilthey, and its recent, existentialist-phenomenological avatar in Heideggerian hermeneutics. For thinkers in this line, 'history' has always been less an object of study, something to be explained, than a mode of being-in-the-world which both makes possible 'understanding' and invokes it as a condition of its own deconcealment. This means that historical knowledge can be produced only on the basis of a kind of inquiry fundamentally different from those cultivated in the (nomological-deductive) physical sciences and the (structural-functional) social sciences. According to Gadamer and Ricoeur, the 'method' of the historico-genetic sciences is hermeneutics, conceived less as decipherment than as 'inter-pretation,' literally 'translation,' a 'carrying over' of meanings from one discursive community to another. Both Gadamer and Ricoeur stress the 'traditionalist' aspect of the hermeneutical enterprise, or what amounts to the same thing, the 'translational' aspect of tradition. It is tradition which unites the interpreter with the *interpretandum*, apprehended in all the strangeness that marks it as coming from a 'past,' in an activity productive of the establishment of the individuality and communality of both. When this individuality-in-communality is established across a temporal distance, the kind of knowledge-as-understanding produced is a specifically historical knowledge.[49]

So much is familiar to any reader of this tradition of philosophical discourse and utterly foreign to traditional historians as well as to those who wish to transform historiography into a science. And why not? The terminology is figurative, the tone pious, the epistemology mystical – all of the things that traditional historians and their more modern, social scientifically oriented counterparts wish to expunge from historical studies. Yet this tradition of thought has a special relevance for the consideration of our topic, for it has been left to one of its representatives, Paul Ricoeur, to attempt nothing less than a metaphysics of narrativity.

Ricoeur has confronted all of the principal conceptions of discourse, textuality, and reading on the current theoretical scene. He has, moreover, surveyed exhaustively contemporary theories of historiography and the notions of narrative advanced in both contemporary philosophy of history and social science. On the whole, he finds much to commend in the analytical philosophers' arguments, especially as represented by Mink, Danto, Gallie, and Dray, who view narrative as providing a kind of explanation different from, though not antithetical to, 'nomological-deductive' explanations. Ricoeur, however, holds that narrativity in historiography conduces more to the attainment of an 'understanding' of the events of which it speaks than to an 'explanation' that is only a softer version of the kind found in the physical and social sciences. Not that he opposed understanding to explanation. These two modes of cognition are related 'dialectically,' he maintains, as the 'unmethodical' and 'methodical' aspects of all knowledge that deals with (human) actions rather than with (natural) events.[50]

The 'reading' of an action, according to Ricoeur, resembles the reading of a text; the same kind of hermeneutic principles are required for the comprehension of both. Since 'history is about the *actions* of men in the past,' it follows that the study of the past has as its proper aim the hermeneutic 'understanding' of human actions.[51] In the process of attaining this understanding, explanations of various sorts are called for, in much the same way that explanations of 'what happened' in any story are called for on the way to the story's full elaboration. But these explanations serve as a means for understanding 'what happened,' rather than as ends in themselves. Thus, in the writing of the historical text, the aim in view should be to represent (human) events in such a way that their status as parts of meaningful wholes will be made manifest.[52]

To grasp the meaning of a complex sequence of human events is not the same as being able to explain why or even how the particular events that comprise the sequence occurred. One might be able to explain why and how every event in a sequence occurred and still not have understood the meaning of the sequence considered as a whole. Carrying over the analogy of reading to the process of understanding, one can see how one might understand every sentence in a story and still not have grasped its 'point'. It is the same, Ricoeur maintains, in our efforts to grasp the meaning of human actions. Just as texts *have* meanings that are not reducible to the specific words and sentences used in their composition, so too do actions. Actions *produce* meanings by their consequences, whether foreseen and intended or unforeseen and unintended, which become embodied in the institutions and conventions of given social formations.[53] To understand historical actions, then, is to 'grasp together,' as parts of wholes that are 'meaningful,' the intentions motivating actions, the actions themselves, and their consequences as reflected in social and cultural contexts.[54]

In historiography, Ricoeur argues, this 'grasping together' of the elements of situations in which 'meaningful action' has occurred is effected by the 'configuration' of them through the instrumentality of 'plot.' For him, unlike many commentators on historical narrative, 'plot' is not a structural component of fictional or mythical stories alone, but is crucial to the historical representations of events as well. Thus he writes:

> Every narrative combines two dimensions in various proportions, one chronological and the other nonchronological. The first may be called the episodic dimension, which characterizes the story made out of events. The second is the configurational dimension, according to which the plot construes significant wholes out of scattered events.[55]

But this 'plot' is not imposed by the historian on the events; nor is it a code drawn from the repertoire of literary models and used 'pragmatically' to endow what would otherwise be a mere collection of facts with a certain rhetorical form. It is 'plot,' he says, which figures forth the 'historicality' of events. Thus, he writes, '[t]he plot ... places us at the crossing point of temporality and narrativity: to be historical, an event must be more than a singular occurrence, a unique happening. It receives its definition from its contribution to the development of a plot.'[56]

On this view, a specifically historical event is not one that can be inserted into a 'story' wherever the writer wishes; it is rather a kind of event that can 'contribute' to 'the development of a plot'. It is as if the plot were an entity in process of development prior to the occurrence of any given event, and any given event could be endowed with 'historicality' only in the extent to which it could be shown to contribute to this process. And, indeed, such seems to be the case, because for Ricoeur, 'historicality' is a structural mode or level of 'temporality' itself.

Time, it would appear, is possessed of three 'degrees of organization': 'within-time-ness,' 'historicality,' and 'deep temporality'. These 'degrees of organization' are reflected in turn in three kinds of experiences or representations of time in consciousness: 'ordinary representations of time ... as that "in" which events take place'; those in which 'emphasis is placed on the weight of the past and, even more ... the power of recovering the "extension" between birth and death in the work of "repetition"'; and, finally, those which seek to grasp 'the plural unity of future, past, and present'.[57] In the historical narrative – indeed, in *any* narrative, even the most humble – it is narrativity which 'brings us back from within-time-ness to historicality, from "reckoning with" time to "recollecting" it'. In short, 'the narrative function provides a transition from within-time-ness to historicality,' and it does this by revealing what must be called the 'plot-like' nature of temporality itself.[58]

As thus envisaged, the narrative level of any historical account has a referent quite different from that of its 'chronicle' level. While the chronicle represents events as existing 'within time,' the narrative represents the aspect of time in which endings can be seen as linked to beginnings to form a continuity within a difference. The 'sense of an ending' which links a terminus of a process with its origin in such a way as to endow whatever had happened in between with a significance that can only be gained by 'retrospection,' is achieved by the peculiarly human capacity of what Heidegger called 'repetition'. This 'repetition' is the specific modality of the existence of events in 'historicality,' as against their existence 'in time'. In 'historicality' conceived as 'repetition,' we grasp the possiblity of 'the retrieval of our most basic potentialities inherited from our past in the form of personal fate and collective destiny.'[59] And this is why, among other reasons, to be sure, Ricoeur feels justified in holding 'temporality to be that structure of existence that reaches language in narrativity and narrativity to be the language structure that has temporarility as its ultimate referent.'[60] It is this contention which justifies, I think, speaking of Ricoeur's contribution to historical theory as an attempt to contrive a 'metaphysics of narrativity'.

The significance of this metaphysics of narrativity for historiographical theory lies in Ricoeur's suggestion that the historical narrative must, by virtue of its narrativity, have as its 'ultimate referent' nothing other than 'temporality' itself. Placed within the wider context of Ricoeur's *oeuvre*, what this means is that he has assigned historical narrative to the category of symbolic discourse, which is to say, a discourse whose principal force derives neither from its informational content nor from its rhetorical effect, but rather from its imagistic function.[61] A narrative, for him, is neither an icon of the events of which it speaks, an explanation of these events, nor a rhetorical refashioning of 'facts' for a specifically persuasive effect. It is rather a symbol, which mediates between different universes of meaning 'configuring' the dialectic of their relationship in an image. This image is nothing other than the narrative itself, that 'configuration' of events reported in the chronicle by the revelation of their 'plot-like' nature.

Thus, in telling a story, the historian necessarily reveals a plot. This plot 'symbolizes' events by mediating between their status as existants 'within time' and their status as indicators of the 'historicality' in which these events participate. Since this historicality can only be indicated, never represented directly, this means that the historical narrative, like all symbolic structures, 'says something other than what it says and ... consequently, grasps me because it has in its meaning created a new meaning'.[62]

Ricoeur grants that in characterizing symbolic language in this way, he has all but identified it with 'allegory,' but this is not to say that it is only fantasy. This is because, for Ricoeur, allegory is a way of expressing that 'excess of meaning' present in those apprehensions of 'reality' as a dialectic of 'human desire', on the one side, and 'cosmic appearance,' on the other.[63] An historical narrative, then, can be said to be an allegorization of the experience of 'within-time-ness', the figurative meaning of which is the structure of temporality. The narrative expresses a meaning 'other' than that expressed in the chronicle, which is an 'ordinary representation of time ... as that "in" which events take place'. This secondary or figurative meaning is not so much 'constructed' as 'found' in the universal human experience of a 'recollection' that promises a *future* because it finds a 'sense' in every relationship between a past and a present. In the plot of the historical story, we apprehend a 'figure' of the 'power of recovering the "extension" between birth and death in the work of "repetition"'.[64]

For Ricoeur, then, narrative is more than a mode of explanation, more than a code, and much more than a vehicle for conveying information. It is not a discursive strategy or tactic that the historian may or may not use, according to some pragmatic aim or purpose. It is a means of symbolizing events without which their 'historicality' cannot be indicated. One can make true statements about events without symbolizing them – as in chronicle. One can even explain these events without symbolizing them – as is done all the time in the (structural-functional) social sciences. But one cannot represent the *meaning* of historical events without symbolizing them, and this because 'historicality' itself is both a reality *and* a mystery. All narratives display this mystery and at the same time foreclose any inclination to despair over the failure to solve it by revealing what might be called its form in 'plot' and its content in the meaning with which the plot endows what would otherwise be *mere event*. Insofar as events and their aspects can be 'explained' by the methods of the sciences, they are, it would seem, thereby shown to be neither 'mysterious' nor particularly 'historical'. What can be explained about historical events is precisely what constitutes their non- or a-historical aspect. What remains after events have been explained is both 'historical' and 'meaningful' insofar as it can be understood. And this remainder is understandable insofar as it can be 'grasped' in a symbolization, that is, shown to have the kind of meaning with which plots endow stories.

It is the success of narrative in revealing the meaning, coherence, or significance of events that attests to the legitimacy of its practice in historiography. And it is the success of historiography in narrativizing sets of historical events that attests to the 'realism' of narrative itself. In the kind of symbolization embodied in the historical narrative, human beings have a discursive instrument by which to assert (meaningfully) that the world of human actions is both real and mysterious, that is to say, is mysteriously real (which is not the same thing as saying that it is a real mystery); that what cannot be *explained* is in principle capable of being *understood*; and that, finally, this understanding is nothing other than its representation in the form of a narrative.

There is, then, a certain necessity in the relationship between the narrative, conceived as a symbolic or symbolizing discursive structure, and the representation of specifically historical events. This necessity arises from the fact that human events are or were products of human actions and these actions have produced consequences that have the structures of texts – more specifically, the structure of narrative texts. The understanding of these texts, considered as the products of actions, depends upon our being able to reproduce the processes by which they were produced, that is to say, our ability to narrativize these actions. Since these actions are in effect *lived* narrativizations, it follows that the only way to represent them is by narrative itself. Here the form of discourse is perfectly adequate to its content, since the one is narrative, the other what has been narrativized. The wedding of form with content produces the symbol, 'which says more than what it says,' but in historical discourse always says the same thing: 'historicality'.

Ricoeur's is surely the strongest claim for the adequacy of narrative to the realization of the aims of historical studies made by any recent theorist of historiography. He purports to solve the problem of the relationship between narrative and historiography by identifying the content of the former (narrativity) with the 'ultimate referent' of the latter (historicality). In his subsequent identification of the content of 'historicality' with a 'structure of time' that cannot be represented except in a narrative mode, however, he confirms the suspicions of those who regard narrative representations of historical phenomena as being inherently 'mythical' in nature. Nonetheless, in his attempt to demonstrate that historicality is a content of which narrativity is the form, he suggests that the real subject of any discussion of the *proper form* of historical discourse ultimately turns on a theory of the *true content* of 'history' itself.[65]

VII

My own view is that all theoretical discussions of historiography become enmeshed in the ambiguity contained in the notion of 'history' itself. This ambiguity does not derive from the fact that the term 'history' refers both to an object of study and to an account of this object, but rather from the fact that the object of study itself can be conceived only on the basis of an equivocation. I refer of course to the equivocation contained in the notion of a general *human* past that is split into two parts, one that is supposed to be 'historical', the other 'unhistorical'. This distinction is not of the same order as that between 'human events' and 'natural events,' on the basis of which historical studies constitute an order of facts different from those studied in the natural sciences. The differences between a life lived in nature and one lived in culture are sufficient grounds for honoring the distinction between natural events and human events on the basis of which historical studies and the human sciences in general can proceed to work out methods adequate to the investigation of the latter kind of events. And once an order of generally human events is conceptualized, and this order is further divided into human events past and human events present, it is surely legitimate to inquire to what extent different methods of study may be called for in the investigation of those designated as past as against those called for in the investigation of events designated as present (in whatever sense 'present' is construed).

But it is quite another matter, once this human past is postulated, to further divide *it* into an order of events that is 'historical' and another that is 'non-historical'. For this is to suggest that there are two orders of humanity, one of which is more human, *because it is more historical*, than the other.

The distinction between a humanity, or kind of culture, or kind of society that is historical and another that is nonhistorical is not of the same order as the distinction between two periods of time in the development of the human species: pre-historical and historical. For this distinction does not hinge on the belief that human culture was not developing prior to the beginning of 'history' or that this development was not 'historical' in nature. It hinges rather on the belief that there is a point in the evolution of human culture after which its development can be represented in a discourse different from that in which this evolution in its earlier phase can be represented. As is well-known and generally conceded, the possibility of representing the development of certain cultures in a specifically 'historical' kind of discourse is based on the circumstance that these cultures produced, preserved, and used a certain kind of record, written records. But the possibility of representing the development of certain cultures in a specifically historical discourse is not sufficient grounds for regarding cultures whose development cannot be similarly represented, because of their failure to produce these kinds of records, as continuing to persist in the condition of 'prehistory'.

And this for at least two reasons: one is that the human species does not enter into 'history' only 'in part'. The very notion of 'human species' implies that if any part of its exists 'in history' the whole of it does. Second, the notion of the entrance 'into history' of any part of the human species could not properly be conceived as a purely intramural operation, a transformation that certain cultures or societies undergo that is merely internal to themselves. On the contrary, what the entrance into history of certain cultures implies is that their relationships to those cultures that remained 'outside' of history have undergone radical transformations, so that what had formerly been a process of relatively autonomous or autochthonous relationships now becomes a process of progressive interaction and integration between the so-called 'historical' cultures and those 'non-historical'. This is that panorama of the domination of the so-called 'higher' civilizations over their 'neolithic' subject cultures and the 'expansion' of Western civilization over the globe that is the subject of the standard narrative of the world-history written from the point of view of 'historical' cultures. But this 'history' of 'historical' cultures is by its very nature, as a panorama or domination and expansion, at the same time the *documentation* of the 'history' of those supposedly 'non-historical' cultures and peoples who are the victims of this process. So that, we could conclude, the very records that make possible the writing of a history of historical cultures are also the records that make possible the writing of a history of the so-called 'non-historical' cultures. It follows that the distinction between historical and non-historical fractions of the human past, based on the distinction between the kinds of records available for their study, is as tenuous as the notion that there are two kinds of a specifically human past, the one that can be investigated by 'historical' methods, the other investigatable by some 'non-historical'method, such as anthropology, ethnology, ethnomethodology, or the like.

Insofar, then, as any notion of 'history' presupposes a distinction within the common human past between a segment or order of events that is specifically 'historical' and another order that is 'non-historical' this notion contains an equivocation, because insofar as the notion of 'history' indicates a generally human past, it cannot gain in specificity by dividing this past into an 'historical history' on the one side and a 'non-historical history' on the other. In this formulation, the notion of 'history' simply replicates the ambiguity contained in the failure to distinguish adequately between an object of study (the human past) on the one side and discourse about this object on the other.

Does the recognition of the tissue of ambiguities and equivocations contained in the notion of 'history' provide a basis for understanding recent discussions of the question of narrative in historical theory? I noted earlier that the notion of narrative itself contains an ambiguity of the same kind as that typically found in the use of the term 'history'. Narrative is at once a mode of discourse, a manner of speaking, and the product produced by the adoption of this mode of discourse. When this mode of discourse is used to represent 'real' events, as in 'historical narrative', the result is a kind of discourse with specific linguistic, grammatical, and rhetorical features, that is, 'narrative history'. Both the felt adequacy of this mode of discourse for the representation of specifically 'historical' events and its inadequacy as perceived by those who impute to narrativity the status of an 'ideology' derive from the difficulty of conceptualizing the difference between a manner of speaking and the mode of representation produced by its enactment.

The fact that narrative is the mode of discourse common to both 'historical' and 'non-historical' cultures and that it predominates in both mythic and fictional discourse makes it suspect as a manner of speaking about 'real' events. The non-narrative manner of speaking common to the physical sciences seems more appropriate for the representation of 'real' events. But here the notion of what constitutes a 'real' event turns, not on the distinction between 'true' and 'false' (which is a distinction that belongs to the order of discourses, not to the order of events), but rather on the distinction between 'real' and 'imaginary' (which belongs both to the order of events and to the order of discourses). One can produce an imaginary discourse about real events that may not be less 'true' for being 'imaginary'. It all depends upon how one construes the function of the faculty of imagination in human nature.

So, too, with respect to narrative representations of reality, especially when, as in historical discourses, these representations are of 'the human past'. How else can any 'past,' which is by definition comprised of events, processes, structures, and so forth that are considered to be no longer perceivable, be represented in either consciousness or discourse except in an 'imaginary' way? Is it not possible that the question of narrative in any discussion of historical theory is always finally about the function of imagination in the production of a specifically human truth?

Notes

1. As R. Barthes remarkes: 'narrative is international, transhistorical, transcultural: it is simply there, like life itself'. See his essay, 'Introduction to the Structural Analysis of Narrative' in *Image, Music, Text*, transl. S. Heath (New York, 1977), 79. The narrative mode of representation is, of course, no more 'natural' than any other mode of discourse, although whether it is a *primary* mode, against which other discursive modes are to be contrasted, is a matter of interest to historical linguistics. See E. Benveniste, *Problèmes de linguistique générale* (Paris, 1966); and G. Ginette, 'Frontières du récit,' *Figures II* (Paris, 1969), 49–69. E.H. Gombrich has suggested the importance of the relationship between the narrative mode of representation, a distinctively historical (as against a mythical) consciousness, and 'realism' in Western art. See *Art and Illusion: A Study in the Psychology of Pictorial Representation* (New York, 1960), 116–146.

2. Thus, for example, M. Mandelbaum denies the propriety of calling the kinds of accounts produced by historians 'narratives,' if this term is to be regarded as synonymous with 'stories'. See *The Anatomy of Historical Knowledge* (Baltimore, 1977), 25–26. In the physical sciences, narratives have no place at all, except as prefatory anecdotes to the presentation of findings; a physicist or biologist would find it strange to tell a story about his data *rather than* to analyze them. Biology became a science when it ceased to be practised as 'natural history,' that is, when scientists of organic nature ceased trying to construct the 'true story' of 'what happened' and began looking for the laws, purely causal and nonteleological, that could account for the evidence given by the fossil record, results of breeding practices, and so on. To be sure, as Mandelbaum stresses, a *sequential* account of a set of events is not the same as a *'narrative'* account thereof; the difference between them is the absence of any interest in teleology as an explanatory principle in the former. Any narrative account of anything whatsoever is a teleological account, and it is for this reason as much as any other that narrativity is suspect in the physical sciences. But Mandelbaum's remarks miss the point of the conventional distinction between a chronicle and a history based on the difference between a *merely* sequential account and a narrative account. The difference is reflected in the extent to which the history, as thus conceived, approaches to the formal coherence of a 'story'. See my essay, 'The Value of Narrativity in the Representation of Reality,' *Critical Inquiry* 7 (1980), 5–27.

3. See the remarks of G. Elton. *The Practice of History* (New York, 1967) 118–141; and J.H. Hexter, *Reappraisals in History* (New York, 1961), 8ff. These two works may be taken as indicative of the view of the profession in the 1960s, on the matter of the adequacy of 'story-telling' to the aims and purposes of historical studies. For both, narrative representations are an option of the historian, which he may choose or not according to his purposes. The same view was expressed by G. Lefebvre in *La Naissance de l'historiographie moderne* [lectures delivered originally in 1945–1946] (Paris, 1971), 321–326.

4. The distinction between dissertation and narrative was a commonplace of eighteenth-century rhetorical theories of historical composition. See Hugh Blair, *Lectures on Rhetoric and Belles Lettres* [1783], ed. H.F. Harding (Carbondale, Illinois, 1965), 259–310. See also J.G. Droysen, *Historik*, ed. Peter Leyh (Stuttgart, 1977), 222–280. For a more recent statement of the distinction, see Peter Gay, who writes: 'Historical narration without analysis is trivial, historical analysis without narration is incomplete.' *Style in History* (New York, 1974) 189. See also the recent survey by S. Bann, 'Towards a Critical Historiography,' *Philosophy* 56 (1981), 365–385.

5. This was Croce's earliest position on the matter. See 'La storia ridotta sotto il concetto generale dell'arte [1893], in *Primi saggi* Bari, 1951), 3–41. Croce wrote: 'Prima condixione per avere storia vera (e insième opera d'arte) è che sia possibile costruire una narrazioni (38). And: 'Ma si può, in conclusione, negare che tutto il lavoro di preparazione tenda a produrre narrazioni di cio ch'è accaduto?' (40), which was not to say, in Croce's view, that narration was in itself history. Obviously, it was the connection with facts attested by 'documenti viv' that made an historical narrative 'historical'. See the discussion in *Teoria e storia della storiografia* (1917) (Bari, 1966), 3–17, wherein Croce dilates on the diffeence between 'chronicle' and 'history.' Here the distinction is between a 'dead' and a 'living' account of the past that is stressed, rather than the absence or presence of 'narrative' in the account. Here, too, Croce stresses that one cannot write a genuine history on the basis of 'narrations' *about* 'documents' that no longer exist, and defines 'chronicle' as 'narrazione vuota' (11–15).

6. '[E]s ist eine innerliche gemeinsame Grundlage, welche sie zusammen hervortreibt.' Hegel, *Vorlesungen über die Philosophie der Geschichte* (Frankfurt am Main, 1970), 83.

7. *Idem.*

8. *Ibid.*, 83–84.

9. [M]üssen wir für höhere Art als für eine bloβ äusserliche Zufälligkeit ansehen. *Ibid.*, 83.

10. *Ibid.*, 44–45.

11. Which is not to say, of course, that certain historians were not averse to the notion of a scientific politics to which historiography might contribute, as the example of Tocqueville and the whole 'Machiavellian' tradition, which includes Treitschke and Weber, make clear enough. But it is important to recognize that the notion of the science to which historiography was to always distinguished from the kind of science cultivated in the study of natural phenomena. Whence the long debate over the presumed differences between the *Geisteswissenschaften* and *Naturwissenschaften* throughout the nineteenth century, in which 'historical studies' played the role of paradigm of the former kind of science. Insofar as certain thinkers, such as Comte and Marx, envisioned a science of politics based on a science of history, they were regarded less as historians than as philosophers of history and therefore not as contributors to historical studies at all.

   As for the 'science of politics' itself, it has generally been held by professional historians that attempts to construct such a science on the basis of historical studies gives rise to 'totalitarian' ideologies of the sort represented by Nazism and Stalinism. The literature on this topic is vast, but the gist of the argument that sustains it is admirably articulated in the work of the late Hannah Arendt. For example, she wrote:

   In any consideration of the modern concept of history one of the crucial problems is to explain its sudden rise during the last third of the eighteenth century and the concomitant decrease of interest in purely political thinking ... Where a genuine interest in political theory still survived it ended in despair, as in Tocqueville, or in the confusion of politics with history, as in Marx. For what else but despair could have inspired Tocqueville's assertion that 'since the past has ceased to throw its light upon the future the mind of man wanders in obscurity'? This is actually the conclusion of the great work in which he had 'delineated the society of the modern world' and in the introduction to which he had proclaimed that 'a new science of politics is needed for a new world'. And what else but confusion ... could have led to Marx's identification of action with 'the making of history'?

'The Concept of History' in *Between Past and Future* (London, 1961), 77

Obviously, Arendt was not lamenting the dissociation of historical studies from political thinking, but rather the degradation of historical studies into 'philosophy of history'. Since, in her view, political thinking moves in the domain of human wisdom, a knowledge of history was certainly necessary for its 'realistic' cultivation. It followed that both political thinking and historical studies ceased to be 'realistic' when they began to aspire to the status of (positive) sciences.

The view was given another formulation in Karl R. Popper's influential *The Poverty of Historicism* [1944–1945] (London, 1957); Popper concludes:

I wish to defend the view, so often attacked as old-fashioned by historicists, that *history is characterized by its interest in actual, singular, or specific events, rather than in laws or generalizations* ... In the sense of this analysis, *all* causal explanations of a singular event can be said to be historical in so far as 'cause' is always described by singular initial conditions. And this agrees entirely with the popular idea that to explain a thing causally is to explain how and why it happened, that is to say, to tell its 'story'. But it is only in history that we are really interested in the causal explanation of a singular event. In the theoretical sciences, such causal explanations are mainly means to a different end – the testing of universal laws. (143–144)

Popper's work was directed against all forms of social planning based on the pretension of a discovery of laws of history or, what amounted to the same thing in his view, laws of society. I have no quarrel with this point of view. My point here is merely that Popper's defense of 'old-fashioned' historiography, which equates an 'explanation' with the telling of a story, is a conventional way of both asserting the cognitive authority of this 'old-fashioned' historiography and denying the possibility of any productive relationship between the study of history and a prospective 'science of politics'. See also *Theorien in der Geschichtswissenschaft*, ed. J. Rüsen and H. Süssmith (Düsseldorf, 1980), 29–31.

12. The arguments set forth by this group are varied in detail, insofar as different philosophers give different accounts of the grounds on which a narrative account can be *considered* to be an explanation at all; and they run in diversity from the position that narrative is a 'porous,' 'partial,' or 'sketchy' version of the nomological-deductive explanations given in the sciences (this is Carl Hempel's later view) to the notion that narratives 'explain' by techniques, such as 'colligation' or 'configuration', for which there are no counterparts in scientific explanations. See the anthologies of writings on the subject in *Theories of History*, ed. Patrick Gardiner (London, 1959); and *Philosophical Analysis and History*, ed. William H. Dray (New York, 1966). See, in addition, the surveys of the subject

by William H. Dray, *Philosophy of History* (Englewood Cliffs, N.J., 1964); and, more recently, R.F. Atkinson, *Knowledge and Explanation in History* (Ithaca, 1978). For an early response in France to the Anglo-American debate, see Paul Veyne, *Comment on écrit l'histoire: Essai d'épistémologie* (Paris, 1971), 194–209. And in Germany, *Geschichte-Ereignis und Erzählung*, ed. Reinhart Koselleck and Wolf-Dieter Stempel (Munich, 1973).

13. The basic text is by Fernand Braudel, *Écrits sur l'histoire* (Paris, 1969). But see also, among many other words in a similarly polemical vein, Francois Furet, 'Quantitative History' in *Historical Studies Today*, ed. F. Gilbert and S.R. Graubard (New York, 1972), 54–60; *The Historian between the Ethnologist and the Futurologist*, ed. J. Dumoulin and D. Moisi (Paris/The Hague, 1973), proceedings of a congress held in Venice in 1971, in which the statements of Furet and Le Goff especially should be noted.

14. I stress the term 'semiological' as a way of gathering under a single label a group of thinkers who, whatever their differences, have had a special interest in narrative, narration, and narrativity, have addressed the problem of historical narrative from the standpoint of a more general interest in theory of discourse, and who have in common only a tendency to depart from a *semiological theory of language* in their analyses. A basic, explicative text is R. Barthes, *Éléments de Sémiologie* (Paris, 1964); but see also: 'Tel Quel', *Théorie d'ensemble* (Paris, 1968). And for a comprehensive theory of 'semiohistory', see Paolo Valesio, *The Practice of Literary Semiotics: A Theoretical Proposal* (Urbino, 1978); and *Novantiqua: Rhetorics as a Contemporary Theory* (Bloomington, Indiana, 1980).

    A generally semiological approach to the study of narrative has engendered a new field of studies, called 'narratology'. The current state and interests of scholars working in this field can be glimpsed by a perusal of three volumes of papers collected in *Poetics Today: Narratology I, II, III* (Tel-Aviv, 1980–1981), I and II. See also two volumes devoted to contemporary theories of 'Narrative and Narratives' in *New Literary History* 6 (1975), and 11 (1980); and the special edition of *Critical Inquiry*, 'On Narrative,' 7 (1980).

15. The positions are set forth in Hans-Georg Gadamer, *Le problème de la conscience historique* (Louvain, 1963); and Paul Ricoeur, *History and Truth*, transl. C.A. Kelbley (Evanston, Illinois, 1965); 'The Model of the Text: Meaningful Action Considered as a Text,' *Social Research* 38 (1971); 'Expliquer et comprendre,' *Revue philosophique de Louvain* 55 (1977); and 'Narrative Time,' *Critical Inquiry* 7 (1980).

16. J.H. Hexter, *Doing History* (Bloomington, Indiana, 1971), 1–14, 77–106. A philosopher who holds a similarly 'craft' notion of historical studies is Isaiah Berlin, 'The Concept of Scientific History,' *History and Theory* 1 (1960), 11.

17. The defense of historiography as an empirical enterprise continues and is often manifested in an open suspicion of 'theory'. See, for example, E.P. Thompson, *The Poverty of Theory* (London, 1978); and the discussion of this work by Perry Anderson, *Arguments within English Marxism* (London, 1980).

18. F. Braudel, 'The Situation of History in 1950', transl. S. Matthews, in *On History* (Chicago, 1980), 11.

19. Furet's position varies according to occasion. In his essay, 'Quantitative History,' he criticizes *histoire événementielle*, not because it is concerned with 'political facts' or because it is 'made up of a mere narrative of certain selected

"events" along the time axis,' but rather because 'it is based on the idea that these events are unique and cannot be set out statistically, and that the unique is the material par excellence of history.' He concludes: 'That is why this kind of history paradoxically deals at one and the same time in the short term and in a finalistic ideology.' (*Historical Studies Today*, ed Gilbert and Graubard, 54).

20. Cf. Jacques Le Goff: 'The *Annales* school loathed the trio formed by political history, narrative history, and chronicle or episodic (événementielle) history. All this, for them, was mere pseudohistory, history on the cheap, a superficial affair.' 'Is Politics Still the Backbone of History?' in *Historical Studies Today*, 340.

21. In a recent article, Furet indicates that 'l'explication historique traditionnelle obéit à la logique du récit,' which he glosses as 'l'avant explique l'après.' The selection of the facts is governed, he continues, by 'cette logique implicite, qui privilégie la période par rapport à l'objet, et choisit les èvénements par rapport à leur place dans une narration, défine par un début et une fin.' He goes on to characterize 'l'histoire politique' as 'le modèle de ce type d'histoire' because politics 'au sens large, constitue le répertoire privilégié du changment' and this in turn allows the representation of history in terms of the categories of human freedom ('la liberté des hommes'). It is 'la politique' which 'constitute l'histoire selon la structure d'un roman.' F. Furet, 'I metodi delle sicenze sociali nella recerca storica e la "storia totale"' in *La teoria della storiografia oggi*, ed. Pietro Rossi (Milan, 1983), 127. I quote from the French of the original typescript for the convenience of English readers, but the page references are to the Italian version.

22. Thus, Furet holds that 'le langage des sciences sociales est fondé sur la recherche des déterminations et des limites de l'action,' *Idem*, and concludes that it is necessary, in order for history to become an object of social scientific investigation, 'à renoncer non seulement à la forme principale de la discipline: le récit, mais également à sa matière préférée: la politique.' *Ibid.*, 128.

23. Among which, some of the better ones are: O. Ducrot, T. Todorov, *et alia*, *Qu'est-ce que le structuralisme?* (Paris, 1968); *The Languages of Criticism and the Sciences of Man: The Structuralist Controversy*, ed. R. Macksey and E. Donato (Baltimore, 1970); *Textual Strategies: Perspectives in Post-Structuralist Criticism*, ed. J.V. Harari (Ithaca, 1979); and *Structuralism and Since*, ed. John Sturrock (Oxford, 1979). On structuralism and historical theory, see Alfred Schmidt, *Geschichte und Struktur: Fragen einer marxistischen Historik* (Munich, 1971). I have dealt with some of the issues in two books: *Metahistory: The Historical Imagination in Nineteenth-Century Europe* (Baltimore, 1973); and *Tropics of Discourse* (Baltimore, 1978). For a fascinating example of the application of structuralist-post-structuralist ideas to problems of historical inquiry and exposition, see T. Todorov, *La conquête de l'Amérique: La question de l'autre* (Paris, 1982).

24. C. Lévi-Strauss, *The Savage Mind* (London, 1966), ch. 9. Lévi-Strauss writes: '[I]n Sartre's system, history plays exactly the part of myth' (254–255). Again: 'It suffices for history to move away from us in time or for us to move away from it in thought, for it to cease to be internalizable and to lose its intelligibility, a spurious intelligibility attaching to a temporary internality' (255). And again: 'As we say of certain careers, history may lead to anything, provided you get out of it' (262).

25. 'We need only recognize that history is a method with no distinct object corresponding to it to reject the equivalence between the notion of history and the notion of humanity.' *Ibid.*, 262. See also 248–250, 254.

26. 'In fact history is tied neither to man nor to any particular object. It consists

wholly in its method, which experience proves to be indispensable for cataloguing the elements of any structure whatever, human or non-human, in their entirety.' *ibid.*, 262.

27. *Ibid.*, 261, n.

28. C. Lévi-Strauss, *L'Origine des manières de table* (Paris, 1968), part II, ch. 2.

29. See Rosaline Coward and John Ellis, *Language and Materialism: Developments in Semiology and the Theory of the Subject* (London, 1977), 81–82; H. White, 'Michel Foucault,' in Sturrock, ed., *Structuralism and Since*.

30. J. Derrida, 'The Law of Genre,' *Critical Inquiry* 7 (1980), 55–82; and 'Structure, Sign and Play in the Discourse of the Human Sciences' in *L'Écriture et la différance* (Paris, 1967), ch. 10. Julia Kristeva writes: 'In the narrative, the speaking subject constitutes itself as the subject of a family, a clan, or state group; it has been shown that the syntactically normative sentence develops within the context of prosaic and, later, historic narration. The simultaneous appearance of *narrative* genre and *sentence* limits the signifying process to an attitude of request and communication.' 'The Novel as Polylogue' in *Desire in Language* (New York, 1980), 174. See also Jean-François Lyotard, 'Petite économie libidinale d'un dispositif narratif ...' in *Des dispositifs pulsionnels* (Paris, 1973), 180–184.

31. R. Barthes, 'Le discours de l'histoire,' *Social Science Information* (Paris, 1967), English translation by Stephen Bann; 'The Discourse of History' in *Rhetoric and History: Comparative Criticism Yearbook*, ed. Elinor Shaffer (Cambridge, England, 1981), 7.

32. R. Barthes, *Mythologies*, transl. Annette Lavers (New York, 1972), 148–159.

33. Barthes, 'The Discourse of History,' 16–17.

34. *Ibid.*, 18.

35. '[B]eyond the narrational level begins the world,' R. Barthes, 'Introduction to the Structural Analysis of Narratives' in *Image, Music, Text*, 115.

36. *Ibid.*, 124.

37. Barthes, 'The Discourse of History,' 17.

38. Cf. Anderson, 14, 98, 162.

39. See the remarks of Daniel Bell and Peter Wiles in Dumoulin and Moisi, eds., 64–71, 89–90.

40. Roman Jakobson, 'Linguistics and Poetics' in *Style in Language*, ed. T. Sebeok (Cambridge, Mass., 1960), 352–358. This essay by Jakobson is absolutely essential for the understanding of theory of discourse as it has developed within a generally semiological orientation since the 1960s. It should be stressed that whereas many of the post-structuralists have taken their stand on the arbitrariness of the sign and a fortiori the arbitrariness of the constitution of discourses in general, Jakobson continued to insist on the possibility of intrinsic meaning residing even in the phoneme. Hence, whereas discursive 'referentiality' was regarded as an illusion by the more radical post-structuralists, such as Derrida, Kristeva, Sollers, and the later Barthes, it was not so regarded by Jakobson. Referentiality was simply one of the 'six basic functions of verbal communication'. *Ibid.*, 357.

41. As Jakobson's student, Paolo Valesio, puts it: 'every discourse in its functional aspect is based on a relatively limited set of mechanisms ... that reduce every

referential choice to a formal choice.' *Novantiqua*, 21. Hence, for Valesio,

> it is never a question … of pointing to referents in the 'real' world, of distinguishing true from false, right from wrong, beautiful from ugly, and so forth. The choice is only between what mechanisms to employ, and these mechanisms already condition every discourse since they are simplified representations of reality, inevitably and intrinsically slanted in a partisan direction. The mechanisms always appear … to be gnoseological, but in reality they are *eristic:* they give a positive or a negative connotation to the *image* of the entity they describe in the very moment in which they start describing it. *ibid.*, 21–22.

42. The example is that of Arthur C. Danto, *Analytical Philosophy of History* (Cambridge, England, 1965).

43. See Dray, *Philosophy of History*, 43–47, 19.

44. J. Lotman. *The Structure of the Artistic Text*, transl. R. Vroon (Ann Arbor, Michigan, 1977), 9–20, 280–284.

45. *Ibid.*, 35–38.

46. See my *Metahistory*, 'Introduction: The Poetics of History' 1–38; and *Tropics of Discourse*, chs. 2–5.

47. Louis O. Mink, 'Narrative Form as a Cognitive Instrument' in *The Writing of History: Literary Form and Historical Understanding*, ed. R.H. Canary and H. Kozicki (Madison, Wisconsin, 1978), 143–144.

48. 'Hegel remarks somewhere that all facts and personages of great importance in world history occur, as it were, twice. He forgot to add: the first time as tragedy, the second as farce. Causidière for Danton, Louis Blanc for Robespierre, the *Montagne* of 1848 to 1851 for the *Montagne* of 1793 to 1795, the Nephew for the Uncle. And the same caricature occurs in the circumstances attending the second edition of the eighteenth Brumaire.' Karl Marx, 'The Eighteenth Brumaire of Louis Buonaparte' in K. Marx and F. Engels, *Selected Works* (New York, 1969), 97. This is not merely an aphorism. The *whole work* is *composed* as a farce. Cf. White, *Metahistory*, 320–327; and H. White, 'The problem of Style in Realistic Representation: Marx and Flaubert' in *The Concept of Style*, ed. B. Lang (Philadelphia, 1979), pp. 213–229.

49. H.-G. Gadamer, 'The problem of Historical Consciousness' in *Interpretive Social Science: A Reader*, ed. P. Rabinow and W. Sullivan (Berkeley, 1979), 106–107, 134; and P. Ricoeur, 'Du conflit à la convergence de méthodes en exégèse biblique' in R. Barthes, P. Beauchamps, *et alia*, *Exégèse et hermeneutique* (Paris, 1971), 47–51.

50. P. Ricoeur, 'Explanation and Understanding: On Some Remarkable Connections among the Theory of the Text, Theory of Action, and Theory of History,' in *The Philosophy of Paul Ricoeur*, ed. C.E. Reagan and D. Stewart (Boston, 1978), 165.

51. *Ibid.*, 161.

52. *Ibid.*, 153–158.

53. P. Ricoeur, 'The Model of the Text: Meaningful Action Considered as a Text,' in Rabinow and Sullivan, eds., 83–85.

54. *Ibid.*, 77–79.

55. P. Ricoeur, 'Narrative Time,' *Critical Inquiry* 7 (1980), 178–179.

56. *Ibid.*, 171.

57. *Idem.*

58. *Ibid.*, 178

59. *Ibid.*, 183–184.

60. *Ibid.*, 169.

61. P. Ricoeur, 'Existence and Hermeneutics,' in Reagan and Stewart, eds., 98.

62. P. Ricoeur, 'The Language of Faith,' in *ibid.*, 233.

63. *Idem.*

64. Ricoeur, 'Narrative Time,' 178–184.

65. This essay was completed and in press before I had an opportunity to take account of Ricoeur's latest work, *Time and Narrative* (Chicago, 1983). This work, in my view, puts the whole problem of narrative, not to mention philosophy of history, on a new and higher plane of discussion.

Part Three

The Writer Critic

7   The Novel Now*

DAVID LODGE

David Lodge, as a novelist and professional academic critic who person-
ifies the boundary between fiction and criticism, turns his mind here to
the influence of recent criticism on his own and other contemporary
British fiction. Lodge is concerned with the way in which recent critical
attacks on ideas of the 'author' and 'reality' have been reflected in fiction
itself, in metafictional anti-realism and the incorporation of a surrogate
author into the novel as ways of addressing these issues in the theory of
fiction. There is obviously some scepticism on Lodge's part about the
idea of critical influence on fiction. Most poststructuralist criticism is, he
claims, unintelligible to most novelists; and when it is intelligible (as for
himself) it is counter-intuitive in the sense that attacks on the ideas of
authorship and the representation of reality rarely accord with the
novelist's own conception of fiction. To close the gap between what
Lodge calls 'humanist' and 'poststructuralist' accounts of fictional
meaning, and therefore the gap between novelists and their academic
commentators, he turns to the work of Mikhail Bakhtin, whose idea of
the novel as a composite of various discourses allows him to place it
somewhere between these polarities. Bakhtin also offers to Lodge an
'ideological' justification of the novel as a form of resistance to repressive, authoritarian and monologic ideologies of the kind that poststructuralism rejects, while maintaining some connection with humanist
notions such as the author and the represented external reality.

This essay began as a keynote address to a conference at Brown
University called 'Why the novel matters: a post-modern perplex' in
1987, subsequently published in Novel, 21 (1988) and included in Lodge's
collection of essays *After Bakhtin* in 1990.

When I began the twin careers of novelist and academic critic some thirty
years ago, the relationship between fiction and criticism was
comparatively unproblematical. Criticism was conceived of as a second-
order discourse dependent on the first-order discourse of fiction. Novelists
wrote novels and critics criticized them. This latter activity was usually

*Reprinted from LODGE, D. *After Bakhtin: Essays on Fiction and Criticism* (London:
Routledge, 1990), pp. 11–24.

described as a combination of description, interpretation and evaluation of texts, with different schools striking a different balance between the terms of this formula. The function of theory was to provide a more and more comprehensive and refined methodology for carrying out this work, and in the 1960s in England and America this task was seen as very much a matter of bringing novel criticism up to a level of formal sophistication comparable to that achieved by the New Criticism (from, say, William Empson to W.K. Wimsatt) in relation to poetry.

This critical activity also had an ideological function, seldom overtly acknowledged, namely, the maintenance of a canon. The storehouse of fiction has many floors, but it is shaped like a ziggurat, or pyramid. There is a lot of space on the ground floor for contemporary work, but much of it is speedily dumped in the trash cans outside the back door, without ever having been shelved upstairs in the storeys reserved for 'serious' writing. As authors are promoted higher and higher up the scale of value, and recede into the historical past, their number becomes fewer and fewer, the accommodation for them more limited. The top floor, reserved for the classics, is very small indeed. The English Victorian novel, for instance, is represented by the work of perhaps a dozen novelists, out of the thousand or more who actually wrote novels in that period. This is inevitable: the collective consciousness can store only a finite number of texts; when one is added, another must drop out to make room for it.

The higher you go up the storeys of the ziggurat, the more evident it is that the process of selection and exclusion is controlled by academic critics, rather than by reviewers, literary journalists and writers themselves. This is because the academic study of literature depends crucially on the existence of a canon. Without a common body of texts to refer to and compare, the subject would become impossible to teach or learn. Teachers who set out to subvert the idea of the literary canon are obliged to provide an alternative one, usually of theoretical texts. And if critics need a canon, novelists need a tradition. You cannot begin to write novels without having read at least one, and probably hundreds; without defining yourself in relationships of apprenticeship, discipleship, rivalry, and antagonism with precursors and peers. Sometimes, for instance in the hey-day of modernism, a realignment of writers in relation to tradition is carried over into a revision of the academic canon, which in turn affects the reading of the next generation of aspirant writers. The comparative rarity of such cross-fertilization in today's literary culture is one of its more worrying symptoms.

The traditional model of the relationship between fiction and criticism is not, then, entirely disinterested. It privileges the novelist in the sense that he or she is seen as the creative source without whom the critic would have nothing to criticize, but it is used to police the work of contemporary writing in a way that can be oppressive. It is an author-centred model –

the history of the English or American novel is seen as the story of exceptionally gifted writers who handed on the great tradition of fiction, each adding some distinctive contribution of their own. But it is also self-centred, since the process of sifting and evaluating and interpreting the classic or potentially classic texts serves the purpose of the academic institution. Academic critics have great respect for the canonical novelists, but not much for novelists who don't seem to be interested in getting into the canon. One gets the impression from a good deal of traditional academic criticism, certainly that associated with the name of F.R. Leavis, that it is a finer thing to be a critic working on a major novelist than to be oneself a good minor novelist. This is not generally true of reviewers, who are more generous in their reception of new fiction. Indeed, one of the functions academic critics have often seen themselves as performing is to counteract the inflated currency of journalistic reviewing. But both kinds of critic have, until recently, shared the same implied aesthetic, which a contemporary academic theorist, Catherine Belsey, has labelled 'expressive realism'.[1] That is to say, they have interpreted and evaluated novels as more or less powerful expressions of a unique sensibility or world-view – the author's – and as more or less truthful representations of reality.

This traditional, or as it is sometimes called, humanist model of the relationship between fiction and criticism is still widely subscribed to. However, in the last twenty years or so it has sustained a number of attacks from within the academic institution as the latter has become increasingly dominated by structuralist and post-structuralist theory. The effect has been to throw academic literary studies into a state of exciting intellectual ferment or terminal crisis, according to your point of view. But as far as I can see it has had little effect on the ground floor of the ziggurat, that is to say on the reception of new writing, at least in England and America. Whether it has had any effect on novelists themselves, and whether such an effect is or might be either liberating or inhibiting are questions worth considering.

It all started, of course, with the impact of structuralism on literary criticism in the 1960s. In its classic form, structuralism seeks to understand culture in terms of the systems of signification that underlie it: the emphasis is on the system, not individual realizations of the system. In this respect it modelled itself on the linguistics of Saussure, who maintained that linguistic science should concern itself with the finite system of *langue*, not the infinite variety of *parole*. Another of Saussure's seminal ideas, much misunderstood, and often vulgarized, was that the relationship between the two aspects of the verbal sign, the signifier and the signified, is arbitrary. It is not the relationship between words and things that allows language to signify, but the difference between elements of the linguistic system. Language, in the famous phrase, is a system of differences.

It is easy to see why this way of thinking, when applied to literature, diverted attention away from what was unique to texts and towards what they have in common: codes, conventions, rules; why it reduced the originating power of the author, and elevated the importance of the reader, in the production of meaning; why it subverted the privileged status of the literary canon, since the beauty of semiotic systems could be demonstrated as well, or better, by reference to anonymous folk tales and myths, or the products of popular culture like thrillers, advertising and fashion; why it subverted the notion of realism, exposing it as an art of bad faith because it seeks to disguise or deny its own conventionality. In short, although structuralism in its classical form was a rather conservative methodology, seeking to interpret rather than change the world (to invoke Marx's formula), it was capable of being co-opted, in the revolutionary atmosphere of the 1960s, to a radical intellectual critique of traditional humanistic ideas about literature and culture.

At that time there *was* some creative interaction between the new structuralist-influenced criticism and the production and reception of new writing. In France the *nouvelle critique* provided a basis for defending and interpreting the *nouveau roman*. In America and to a lesser extent in Britain, various kinds of post-modernist experiments in fiction seemed to derive from or at least could be explained in terms of the new critical attacks upon realism. But, as structuralism pursued its own premises and problems into a second phase of debate and speculation generally called 'post-structuralism', it became more and more scholastic, esoteric and inward-looking in its concerns, and had less and less to do with the encouragement or criticism of new imaginative writing – unless you regard it as a form of avant-garde literature in its own right. The tendency of post-structuralist theory has certainly been to abolish the conceptual boundary between creative and critical discourse which was one of the basic assumptions of the traditional humanist model. The most influential figures in this post-structuralist phase – Lacan, Derrida, Althusser, Foucault – were not literary critics by discipline. And although their theories have had a profound effect upon academic literary studies, it is not one which, at first glance, seems likely to inspire or encourage the writer who practises his art outside the academy.

Unfortunately, this discourse is so opaque and technical in its language that the first glance – baffled, angry, or derisive – is likely to be the last one. An unhappy consequence of recent developments has certainly been the loss of a common language of critical discourse which used to be shared between academic critics, practising writers, literary journalists and the educated common reader. Thirty or forty years ago, a reader of the book pages of the London *Observer* or the *New York Times Book Review* could pick up a copy of *Scrutiny* or the *Sewanee Review* and be able to take an intelligent interest in most of what he found in those university-based journals. If such a reader were to pick up their equivalents today – *Critical Inquiry*, say, or the *Oxford Review* – he would in all probability be totally baffled and bewildered, unable to make any sense at all of what purports to be literary criticism. Nor would he find there much comment on contemporary imaginative writing. Critics these days are too busy keeping up with each other's work.

Perhaps this discontinuity between the most advanced and innovative discourse about literature and the production and reception of new writing matters more to someone like me, who has a foot in both worlds, than it does to writers who have no connection with the academic world and are free to ignore its abstruse debates, or to academics who take for granted that the high ground of aesthetics will always be accessible only to a small minority. But I can't believe that this is a healthy situation, and I do believe that contemporary theory has something useful and important to say about what Poe called the philosophy of composition, alien as it may seem to the creative writer at first sight.

Let me try and illustrate the point by citing two statements by two eminent modern theorists, Roland Barthes and Paul de Man, on two issues, the idea of the author, and the relationship between fiction and reality, which have been central both to the practice of fiction writing and the reception and criticism of fiction in modern culture. The idea of the author as a uniquely constituted individual subject, the originator and in some sense owner of his work, is deeply implicated in the novel as a literary form and historically coincident with the rise of the novel; so is an emphasis on the mimetic function of verbal art, its ability to reflect or represent the world truthfully and in detail. Both these principles are called into question in the statements I wish to cite.

The first is from Roland Barthes's essay, 'The death of the author' (1968). He seeks to replace 'author' with the term 'scriptor':

> The Author, when believed in, is always conceived of as the past of his own book: book and author stand automatically on a single line divided into a *before* and an *after*. The Author is thought to *nourish* the book, which is to say that he exists before it, thinks, suffers, lives for it, is in the same relation of antecedence to his work as a father to his child. In complete contrast, the modern scriptor is born simultaneously with the text, is in no way equipped with a being preceding or exceeding the writing, is not the subject with the book as predicate; there is no other time than that of the enunciation and every text is eternally written *here and now* ...

We know now that a text is not a line of words releasing a single 'theological' meaning (the 'message' of the Author-God) but a multidimensional space in which a variety of writings, none of them original, blend and clash.[2]

The second quotation is from Paul de Man's essay, 'Criticism and crisis', in *Blindness and Insight* (1971):

> That sign and meaning can never coincide is what is precisely taken for granted in the kind of language we call literary. Literature, unlike everyday language, begins on the far side of this knowledge; it is the only form of language free from the fallacy of unmediated expression ... The self-reflecting mirror effect by means of which a work of fiction asserts, by its very existence, its separation from empirical reality, its divergence, as a sign, from a meaning that depends for its existence on the constitutive activity of this sign, characterises the work of literature in its essence. It is always against the explicit assertion of the writer that readers degrade the fiction by confusing it with a reality from which it has forever taken leave.[3]

Now my first reaction as a novelist is to contest these remarks – to say to Barthes that I *do* feel a kind of parental responsibility for the novels I write, that the composition of them *is*, in an important sense, my past, that I do think, suffer, live for a book while it is in progress; and to say to de Man that my fiction has not 'for ever taken leave of reality' but is in some significant sense a representation of the real world, and that if my readers did not recognize in my novels some truths about the real behaviour of, say, academics or Roman Catholics, I should feel I had failed, and so would my readers.

Certainly the way in which fiction is produced and circulated and received in our culture is totally at odds with the assertions of Barthes and de Man. The reception of new writing has in fact probably never been more obsessively author-centred than it is today, not only in reviewing, but in supplementary forms of exposure through the media – interviews and profiles in the press and on TV, prizes, public readings and book launches and so on. All this attention is focused on the author as a unique creative self, the mysterious, glamorous origin of the text; and the questions one is asked on these occasions invariably emphasize the mimetic connection between fiction and reality which de Man denies exists: what is your book *about*? Is it autobiographical? Is such and such a character based on a real person? Do academics/Catholics really behave like that? and so on. Let it not be supposed that such questions come only from naive or uneducated readers. Some of the most committed post-structuralists among my acquaintances are also the most determined to read my novels as *romans à clef*.

I suppose most novelists have had this experience, and found it an uncomfortable one. Then the extreme formulations of Barthes and de Man about the impersonality and fictiveness of literary discourse begin to look rather attractive, and one may appeal to something like them in order to discourage a reductively empiricist reading of one's work. For what is objectionable about such a reading is that it seems to treat the text as a sign of something more concrete, more authentic, more real, which the writer could, if he or she cared to, hand over in its raw and naked truth. Even much more sophisticated criticism based on the same assumptions can seem oppressive to the author, delving into the biographical origins of one's fiction, seeking to establish a perfect fit between the novelist's personal identity and his *oeuvre*. Graham Greene has a nice passage in *Ways of Escape* where he says that there comes a time when the established writer

> is more afraid to read his favourable critics than his unfavourable, for with terrible patience they unroll before his eyes the unchanging pattern of the carpet. If he has depended a great deal on his unconscious, and his ability to forget even his own books when they are once on the public shelves, his critics remind him – this theme originated ten years ago, that simile which came so unthinkingly to his pen a few weeks back was used nearly twenty years ago...[4]

Greene's insistence on the need of the novelist to forget his own books, and in a sense his own past, sounds surprisingly close to Barthes's concept of the modern scriptor who only exists at the moment of composition. But in the same book Greene claims a documentary truthfulness for his fiction that neither Barthes nor de Man would allow:

> Some critics have referred to a strange violent 'seedy' region of the mind ... which they call Greeneland, and I have sometimes wondered whether they go round the world blinkered. 'This is Indo-China,' I want to exclaim, 'This is Mexico, this is Sierra Leone carefully and accurately described.'[5]

The closer we come to the actual experience of writing, the more we encounter paradox and contradiction. Are books made out of the writer's observation and experience, or out of other books? Does the writer write his novel or does the novel 'write' the writer? Is the implied author of a novel – the creative mind to whom we attribute its existence, and whom we praise or blame for its successes and failures – the 'same' as the actual historical individual who sat at his desk and wrote it, and who has his own life before and after that activity, or an identity who exists only at the moment of composition? Can a novel be 'true to life' or does it merely create a 'reality effect'? Is reality itself such an effect? Is the absence of the writer from his own text that which spurs him to refine and polish his language so that his meaning will be effectively communicated without the supplementary aids of voice, gesture, physical presence, etc., which assist communication in ordinary speech? Or is the association of meaning with presence a fallacy which writing, through its inherent ambiguity and openness to a variety of interpretations, helps to expose?

Structuralists and post-structuralists will give one set of answers to these questions and humanist or expressive realist critics another set. Most writers, I suspect – certainly I myself – would be inclined to say in each case, 'Yes and no', or 'Both alternatives are true'. But the expressive realist theses (that novels arise out of their authors' experience and observation of life, that they are works of verbal mimesis, and so on) are based on common sense, the grounds for believing them are self-evident. The grounds for believing the antithetical propositions are not self-evident, and the value of contemporary literary theory may be that by articulating them it prevents – or would prevent if it were more accessible – the total dominance of our literary culture by expressive realism.

It is not fortuitous, I think, that the anxieties generated by modern critical theory weigh more heavily, or press more sharply, upon writers and critics of prose fiction than upon poets and dramatists and their critics. The novel came into existence under the sign of contradiction, as Lennard J. Davis has argued in his stimulating book, *Factual Fictions: The Origins of the English Novel*.[6] It emerged, he argued, from a new kind of writing which he calls 'news/novels discourse', the earliest manifestations of that journalistic, documentary reporting of recent or current events which we take for granted in the modern era, but which was virtually unknown before the Renaissance because it depended upon the invention of the printing press. As Davis points out (he is not of course the first to do so, but he gets more mileage out of the idea than earlier critics), most of the early English novelists had close connections with the world of printing and/or journalism, and framed their fictitious narratives with avowals that these were factual documents (letters, confessions, etc.) of which they were merely the editors. Novelists perceived that by imitating the form of documentary or historical writing they could exert an exciting new power over their readers, obtaining total faith in the reality of fictitious characters and events. (There was no way, Davis plausibly argues, by which an eighteenth-century reader could be sure whether *Robinson Crusoe* or *Pamela* were true stories or not.) By the same means they threw a defensive smoke screen around the contradictory demands made upon them as storytellers – on the one hand the traditional aesthetic imperative that literature should embody general truths about human nature, and on the other hand the audience's appetite for the truth-is-stranger-than-fiction particularity of journalistic reportage.

Like Ian Watt's, Davis's theory of the rise of the novel applies more obviously to Defoe and Richardson than it does to Fielding, who mocked the technique of pseudo-documentary reporting in *Shamela* and *Joseph Andrews*. But Davis points out that Fielding was a journalist before he was a novelist and that he integrated the facts of a real historical events (the Jacobite Rising of 1745) into his fictional *History of Tom Jones* with unprecedented care and attention to detail. He was also attacked (ironically enough by Richardson among others) for basing his characters transparently upon real people.

Davis's thesis may be overstated, but he is certainly on to something. The ambivalent and sometimes contradictory relationship between fact and fiction in the early novel persists into its classic and modern phases. Think for instance of Dickens's Preface to *Bleak House*, where he insists that 'everything set forth in these pages concerning the Court of Chancery is substantially true and within the truth', and assures his readers that there are 'about thirty cases on record' of spontaneous combustion, while at the same time saying, 'I have purposely dwelt on the romantic side of familiar things'. Or consider the work of James Joyce. Almost every incident and character in his novels and stories can be traced back to some fact of his own life and experience, and he boasted that if the city of Dublin were to be destroyed it could be reconstructed from his books, yet at the same time he made large implicit and explicit claims for the timeless and universal significance of those narratives. Novelists are and always have been split between, on the one hand, the desire to claim an imaginative and representative truth for their stories, and on the other the wish to guarantee and defend that truth-claim by reference to empirical facts: a contradiction they seek to disguise by elaborate mystifications and metafictional ploys such as framing narratives, parody and other kinds of intertextuality and self-reflexivity or what the Russian formalists called 'baring of the device'. These ploys are not, as is sometimes thought, absent from the classic realist novel – one finds examples in for instance, *The Heart of Midlothian*, *Northanger Abbey* and *Vanity Fair*; but they do seem to be particularly marked in contemporary fiction, as if in response to or defence against the epistemological scepticism of contemporary critical theory.

I recently taught, at the University of Birmingham, a short seminar course on contemporary British fiction. Taking Kingsley Amis's *Lucky Jim* as a benchmark to represent the kind of social realism typical of British fiction in the fifties, I selected seven texts to illustrate subsequent developments: *A Clockwork Orange* by Anthony Burgess; *The French Lieutenant's Woman* by John Fowles; *Not to Disturb* by Muriel Spark; *Briefing for a Descent into Hell* by Doris Lessing; *The White Hotel* by D.M. Thomas; *The History Man* by Malcolm Bradbury and *Money* by Martin Amis. Five of these texts introduce their author, or a thinly disguised surrogate for him or her, into the text itself in order to raise questions about the ethics and aesthetics of the novel form; and the other two (the

Lessing and the Thomas) incorporate documentary sources into their fictional stories in ways which transgress the conventional distinction between factual and fictional narrative. Martin Amis actually has his hero, or anti-hero, who is called John Self, meet *himself*, that is to say, a character called Martin Amis, a novelist. John Self asks the question that everybody asks novelists '"Hey," I said, "When you [write], do you sort of make it up, or is it just, you know, like what happens?"' The Martin Amis character answers: 'Neither'.[7]

In the passage I quoted earlier, Paul de Man referred to 'the self-reflecting mirror effect by means of which a work of fiction asserts, by its very existence, its separation from empirical reality, its divergence, as a sign, from a meaning that depends for its existence on the constitutive activity of [that] sign'. What is self-evidence to the deconstructionist critic is, in fact, by no means obvious to the average novel reader. But by arranging an encounter – indeed, several encounters – between himself and his character within the story he is writing, Martin Amis makes that 'self-reflecting mirror effect' concrete and explicit. So do, in different ways, the other writers I mentioned.

I do not mean to suggest that such metafictional devices are mandatory for the contemporary novelist. The vitality and viability of the realist tradition in fiction continues to surprise those who have pronounced obsequies over it. Indeed it would be false to oppose metafiction to realism; rather, metafiction makes explicit the implicit problematic of realism. The foregrounding of the act of authorship within the boundaries of the text which is such a common feature of contemporary fiction, is a defensive response, either conscious or intuitive, to the questioning of the idea of the author and of the mimetic function of fiction by modern critical theory.

Having mentioned Lennard Davis's *Factual Fictions*, I must take note of his latest book, *Resisting Novels*, which articulates a critique of the traditional humanist conception of the novel that comes from the ideological rather than the semiotic wing of post-structuralist theory. The book is in a sense the confessions of a justified sinner. Davis writes as a long-term addict of fiction who has come to the conclusion that novel-reading is bad for us. 'We can no longer smugly think of the novel as the culmination of the human spirit or the height of mimetic accomplishment,' he says.[8] 'Novels are not life, their situation of telling their stories is alienated from lived experience, their subject matter is heavily oriented towards the ideological, and their function is to help humans adapt to the fragmentation and isolation of the modern world' (p. 12). 'Novel reading as a social behaviour helps prevent change' (p. 17).

What Davis does is to draw out the ideological implications of the formal conventions of the novel. The novelistic handling of space encouraged the fetishization of objects and personal property. The complexity of characters in the classic novel is actually an illusion made possible by the very *few* traits of which they are composed and the codes of consistency and relevancy which bind them together. This novelistic concept of character has the ideological function of reconciling us to the alienation of modern existence. The novel cannot deal easily with group action, on which political change depends – or even group discussion. Dialogue in novels bears very little resemblance to real speech not only because it is grammatically well-formed but because it lacks the negotiated turn-taking of real conversation. And so on.

Davis's polemic in many ways resembles the critique of the classic realist text initiated by Roland Barthes and carried on by British critics of a left-wing political persuasion, for example Terry Eagleton, Catherine Belsey and Colin MacCabe. But whereas these critics usually bring forward the modernist or post-modernist text as a kind of fiction which avoids complicity with the ideology of bourgeois capitalism, Davis will make no such exceptions. His comment on modern fiction is that 'change is now removed even from the realm of the personal and psychological, as it had already been from the historical. Change becomes valenced by purely aesthetic categories – an aestheticism approved and promulgated by much of modern criticism' (p. 221).

Davis's book expresses a view antithetical to that put forward by D.H. Lawrence in his famous essay, 'Why the novel matters'. To Lawrence the novel mattered because of all forms of human discourse and cognition it was the only one which could embrace the totality of human experience, the whole of man alive:

> being a novelist, I consider myself superior to the saint, the scientist, the philosopher, and the poet, who are all greater masters of different bits of man alive, but never get the whole hog.
> The novel is the one bright book of life. Books are not life. They are only tremulations on the ether. But the novel as a tremulation can make the whole man alive tremble. Which is more than poetry, philosophy, science, or any other book-tremulation can do.[9]

Notice that Lawrence emphasizes that 'books are not life'. This is something Davis cannot forgive them for. He yearns nostalgically for a more primitive or organic culture in which narrative was not commodified in the form of a printed book, and consumed in silence and privacy, but exchanged orally in a real social encounter. The metaphysics of presence returns with a vengeance, not to bolster up the novel, but to sweep it away.

In one sense there is no answer to Davis's polemic. If you oppose life to art, acting to reading, rather than including the second term of these pairs in the first, if you think that the important thing is not to interpret the world but to change it, then the novel will seem at best an irrelevance, at worst an obstacle. But the logical conclusion of Davis's argument is that he should stop being a literary critic and become a political activist. His reluctance to do so leaves him floundering in his last chapter, hoping rather lamely that 'resisting the novel may in fact by a way of reforming the novel ...' (p. 239). One might argue that this is precisely what novelists themselves have always done, from Cervantes to Martin Amis: reformed the novel by building resistance to fictional stereotypes and conventions into the novel itself.

If we are looking for a theory of the novel that will transcend the opposition of humanist and post-structuralist viewpoints and provide an ideological justification for the novel that will apply to its entire history, the most likely candidate is the work of Mikhail Bakhtin. In their recent study of his life and work, Katerina Clark and Michael Holquist observe:

> Bakhtin's view of language differs from two other current conceptions of language ... Personalists [i.e. humanists] maintain that the source of meaning is the unique individual. Deconstructionists locate meaning in the structure of the general possibility of difference underlying all particular differences. Bakhtin roots meaning in the social, though the social is conceived in a special way.[10]

The special way is Bakhtin's concept of language as essentially dialogic: that is, the word is not, as in Saussure, a two-sided sign – signifier and signified – but a two-sided *act*. Bakhtin's linguistics is a linguistic of *parole*. The words we use come to us already imprinted with the meanings, intentions and accents or previous users, and any utterance we make is directed towards some real or hypothetical Other. 'The word in living conversation is directly, blatantly, oriented toward a future answer word,' says Bakhtin. 'It provokes an answer, anticipates it and structures itself in the answer's direction.'[11] According to Bakhtin, the canonic genres – tragedy, epic, lyric – suppressed this inherently dialogic quality of language in the interests of expressing a unified worldview. These genres, at least before they were 'novelized', are monologic. It as the destiny of the novel as a literary form to do justice to the inherent dialogism of language and culture by means of its discursive polyphony, its subtle and complex interweaving of various types of speech – direct, indirect and doubly-oriented (e.g. parody) – and its carnivalesque irreverence towards all kinds of authoritarian, repressive, monologic ideologies.

Davis is aware of the Bakhtinian defence of the novel, and tries to combat it in his chapter on 'Conversation and dialogue':

> conversation is truly 'dialogic,' to use Bakhtin's phrase – that is, including all voices. However, and here I would disagree with

Bakhtin, dialogue in novels lacks this crucial and democratic strand – everything that comes from the author is autocratically determined. The very basis of conversation – mutually negotiated turntaking – is replaced by order determined unilaterally by the author.

(pp. 177–8)

This, however, is based on a misunderstanding, or misrepresentation of what Bakhtin means by the dialogic in fiction. The dialogic includes, but is not restricted to, the quoted verbal speech of characters. It also includes the relationship between the characters' discourses and the author's discourse (if represented in the text) and between all these discourses and other discourses outside the text, which are imitated or evoked or alluded to by means of doubly-oriented speech. It is of course true that everything in a novel is put there by the novelist – in this sense the literary text is not, like a real conversation, a totally open system. But it is Bakhtin's point that the variety of discourses in the novel prevents the novelist from imposing a single world-view upon his readers even if he wanted to.

Bakhtin first formulated the idea of the polyphonic novel in his early monography, *Problems of Dostoevsky's Art*.[12] What then seemed to him to be a unique innovation of Dostoevsky's – the way in which the Russian novelist allowed different characters to articulate different ideological positions in a text without subordinating them to his own authorial speech – he later came to think was inherent in the novel as a literary form. In the revised and much expanded version of the Dostoevsky book, *Problems of Dostoevsky's Poetics* (1963), and in the essays collected in English under the title *The Dialogic Imagination*, he traced its genealogy back to the parodying-travestying genres of classical literature – the satyr play, the Socratic dialogue and the Menippean satire – and to that carnival folk-culture which kept the tradition alive through the Middle Ages and up to the Renaissance.

There is an indissoluble link in Bakhtin's theory between the linguistic variety of prose fiction, which he called heteroglossia, and its cultural function as the continuous critique of all repressive, authoritarian, one-eyed ideologies. As soon as you allow a variety of discourses into a textual space – vulgar discourses as well as polite ones, vernacular as well as literary, oral as well as written – you establish a resistance (to use Davis's word) to the dominance of any one discourse. Even in the classic realist novel and its modern descendants, in which, we are so often told by post-structuralist critics, the author's discourse is privileged and controls the proliferation of meaning by judging and interpreting the discourses of the characters, even there this control is only relative, and largely illusory. 'The possibility of employing on the plane of a single work discourses of various types, with all their expressive capacities, intact, without reducing them to a common denominator – this is one of the most characteristic

157

features of prose,' says Bakhtin.[13] To allow characters to speak with their own social, regional and individual accents, whether in quoted direct speech ('dialogue' in the ordinary sense of the term) or by allotting them the task of narrating itself, as in the epistolary novel, the confessional novel, and the colloquial vernacular narrative known to the Russians as *skaz*; or by means of free indirect style, a rhetorical technique discovered by novelists in the late eighteenth century and developed to stunning effect in the nineteenth and twentieth – to do all or any of these things in narrative is to make interpretive closure in the absolute sense impossible.

'The one grand literary form that is for Bakhtin capable of a kind of justice to the inherent polyphonies of life is the "novel"', says Wayne Booth, introducing the latest translation of *Problems of Dostoevsky's Poetics*, and echoing, consciously or unconsciously, Lawrence's definition of the novel as 'the one bright book of life'.[14] In another essay, called simply 'The Novel', first published in *Reflections on the Death of a Porcupine* (1925), Lawrence wrote:

> You can fool pretty nearly every other medium. You can make a
> poem pietistic, and still it will be a poem. You can write *Hamlet* in
> drama: if you wrote him in a novel, he'd be half comic, or a trifle
> suspicious; a suspicious character, like Dostoevsky's Idiot. Somehow,
> you sweep the ground a bit too clear in the poem or the drama, and
> you let the human Word fly a bit too freely. Now in a novel there's
> always a tom-cat, a black tom-cat that pounces on the white dove of
> the Word, if the dove doesn't watch it; and there is a banana-skin to
> trip on; and you know there is a water-closet on the premises. All
> these things help to keep the balance.[15]

This apologia for the novel was hardly likely to have been known to Bakhtin, yet it anticipates his theory in a remarkable way, especially in the polemical opposition it sets up between the novel and the canonized genres of tragedy and lyric poetry, in its invocation of Dostoevsky, and in the way it relates the novel's treatment of the human Word to its carnivalesque elements – represented here by the black tom-cat, the banana-skin and the water-closet. I have commented elsewhere on the carnivalesque in Lawrence's fiction, especially in *Mr Noon* and *The Lost Girl*, and on Dostoevskyean polyphony in *Women in Love*.[16] But the fact is that Bakhtin's theory of the novel applies equally well to all the other novelists I have mentioned in this essay.

To demonstrate this claim exhaustively here would obviously take too long. But recall that list of set texts I mentioned earlier, chosen to represent recent developments in British fiction, and consider how well they also answer to Bakhtin's theory of the novel: the carnival face-pulling, the parodying and travestying of academic discourse in *Lucky Jim*; the invented polyglossia, the *skaz* energy and vitality, the *Notes from Underground* subversiveness of *A Clockwork Orange*; the disconcerting hybridization of *The French Lieutenant's Woman*, its deliberately unresolved juxtaposition of nineteenth-century discourse with twentieth, and of two antithetical types of fiction categorized by Bakhtin as the existential adventure story and the social-psychological novel of everyday life; the parodying and travestying of literary genres in *Not to Disturb* – the whodunit, the Gothic novel, the Jacobean revenge tragedy; the violent clash of discourses – visionary, parodic, clinical, pornographic, documentary – in *Briefing for a Descent into Hell* and *The White Hotel*; the elaborate exploitation in *The History Man* of the social speech acts Bakhtin studied and classified under the heading of '*causerie*', especially the 'rejoinder' and the 'glance at someone else's word' – a feature of that particular text foregrounded by the author's refusal to make any authoritative judgement or interpretation of his characters, or to make us privy to their thoughts. Finally, *Money* is another *skaz* narrative in the *Notes from Underground* tradition, a demonic carnival, a suicide note from a character who indulges in every excess of the lower body, sexual and gastronomic, that the modern urban culture can provide, a repulsive character in many ways, yet one who retains an undeniable vitality by the sheer punk brilliance of his rhetoric; a hero or anti-hero who not only answers the author back, as Bakhtin said of Dostoevsky's heroes, but actually throws a punch at him.

As for my own contribution to contemporary British fiction, I must leave the Bakhtinian reading of that to others. I will only say that I have found Bakhtin's theory of the novel very useful when challenged to explain how I can write carnivalesque novels about academics while continuing to be one myself.

Notes

1. CATHERINE BELSEY, *Critical Practice* (1980), pp. 7ff.

2. ROLAND BARTHES, *Image, Music, Text*, in STEPHEN HEATH (trans. and ed.) (London: Fontana, 1977), pp. 145–6.

3. PAUL DE MAN, *Blindness and Insight*, 1983, p. 17.

4. GRAHAM GREENE, *Ways of Escape*, 1980, p. 134.

5. Ibid., p. 77.

6. LENNARD J. DAVIS, *Factual Fictions: The Origins of the English Novel* (New York, 1983), pp. 42ff.

7. MARTIN AMIS, *Money* (Harmondsworth: Penguin 1985), pp. 87–8.

8. LENNARD J. DAVIS, *Resisting Novels: Ideology and Fiction* (New York; 1987), p. 5. All page references are to this edition.

9. D.H. LAWRENCE, *Selected Literary Criticism* Anthony Beal (ed.) (1956), p. 105.

10. KATERINA CLARK and MICHAEL HOLQUIST, *Mikhail Bakhtin* (Cambridge, Mass: 1984), pp. 11–12.

11. MIKHAIL BAKHTIN, *The Dialogic Imagination* (Austin, Tx: 1981), p. 280.

12. MIKHAIL BAKHTIN, *Problemy tvorčestva Dostoevskogo* (Leningrad, 1929).

13. MIKHAIL BAKHTIN, *Problems of Dostoevsky's Poetics* (Manchester; 1984), p. 200.

14. Ibid., p. xxii.

15. D.H. LAWRENCE, *Reflections on the Death of a Porcupine* (Philadelphia, Pa; 1925), pp. 106–7.

16. See Ch. 4 of DAVID LODGE, *After Bakhtin: Essays on Fiction and Criticism* (London: Routledge, 1990).

8 The Literature of Exhaustion*

JOHN BARTH

Though he says so only in parenthesis, for Barth the novel's time is up as a major art form, and metafiction is one way that the novelist can respond to this predicament: the novelist becomes a kind of critic by writing a novel about the 'used-upness' of novelistic forms, or a novel which imitates a novel rather than the world. Barth was certainly right to proclaim in this essay that this state of exhaustion was no cause for despair, and recent literary history has vindicated the claim that the exhausted possibilities of the novel have proved a source of vitality in fiction. To explain the vitality that derives from novelistic exhaustion Barth surveys experimental techniques, particularly in the work of Borges and Beckett, which extend the horizons of the novel into philosophical realms, concerned with the representation of representation, the contamination of reality by dreams, the metaphysically disturbing effect of the *regressus in infinitum* produced by the story-within-a-story, and the process whereby characters in a novel become authors or readers within the fiction, reminding us of the fictitious aspect of our existence. This celebration of one writer/critic (Borges) by another became a seminal formulation of the case for the reciprocity between fiction and theory.

The fact is that every writer *creates* his own precursors. His work modifies our conception of the past, as it will modify the future.

Labyrinths Jorge Luis Borges

You who listen give me life in a manner of speaking. I won't hold you responsible. My first words weren't my first words. I wish I'd begun differently.

Lost in the Fun House John Barth

I want to discuss three things more or less together: first, some old questions raised by the new intermedia arts; second, some aspects of the Argentine writer Jorge Luis Borges, whom I greatly admire; third, some professional concerns of my own, related to these other matters and

---

*Reprinted from BRADBURY, M. (ed.), *The Novel Today* (London: Fontana, 1977), pp. 70–83. (Originally published in *Atlantic Monthly*, 220, 2, August (1967), 29–34.)

having to do with what I'm calling 'the literature of exhausted possibility'
– or, more chicly, 'the literature of exhaustion'.

By 'exhaustion' I don't mean anything so tired as the subject of physical,
moral, or intellectual decadence, only the used-upness of certain forms or
exhaustion of certain possibilities – by no means necessarily a cause for
despair. That a great many Western artists for a great many years have
quarrelled with received definitions of artistic media, genres, and forms
goes without saying: pop art, dramatic and musical 'happenings', the
whole range of 'intermedia' or 'mixed-means' art, bear recentest witness to
the tradition of rebelling against Tradition. A catalogue I received some
time ago in the mail, for example, advertises such items as Robert Filliou's
Ample Food for Stupid Thought, a box full of postcards on which are
inscribed 'apparently meaningless questions', to be mailed to whomever
the purchaser judges them suited for; Ray Johnson's *Paper Snake*, a
collection of whimsical writings, 'often pointed', once mailed to various
friends (what the catalogue describes as The New York Correspondence
School of Literature); and Daniel Spoerri's *Anecdoted Typography of Chance*,
'on the surface' a description of all the objects that happen to be on the
author's parlour table – 'in fact, however ... a cosmology of Spoerri's
existence'.

'On the surface', at least, the document listing these items is a catalogue
of The Something Else Press, a swinging outfit. 'In fact, however', it may
be one of their offerings, for all I know: The New York Direct-Mail
Advertising School of Literature. In any case, their wares are lively to read
about, and make for interesting conversation in fiction-writing classes, for
example, where we discuss Somebody-or-other's unbound, unpaginated,
randomly assembled novel-in-a-box and the desirability of printing
Finnegans Wake on a very long roller-towel. It's easier and sociabler to talk
technique than it is to make art, and the area of 'happenings' and their kin
is mainly a way of discussing aesthetics, really; illustrating 'dramatically'
more or less valid and interesting points about the nature of art and the
definition of its terms and genres.

One conspicuous thing, for example, about the 'intermedia' arts is their
tendency (noted even by *Life* magazine) to eliminate not only the
traditional audience – 'those who apprehend the artists' art (in
'happenings' the audience is often the 'cast', as in 'environments', and
some of the new music isn't intended to be performed at all) – but also the
most traditional notion of the artist: the Aristotelian conscious agent who
achieves with technique and cunning the artistic effect; in other words,
one endowed with uncommon talent, who has moreover developed and
disciplined that endowment into virtuosity. It's an aristocratic notion on
the face of it, which the democratic West seems eager to have done with;
not only the 'omniscient' author of older fiction, but the very idea of the

controlling artist, has been condemned as politically reactionary, even fascist.

Now, personally, being of the temper that chooses to 'rebel along traditional lines', I'm inclined to prefer the kind of art that not many people can *do*: the kind that requires expertise and artistry as well as bright aesthetic ideas and/or inspiration. I enjoy the pop art in the famous Albright-Knox collection, a few blocks from my house in Buffalo, like a lively conversation for the most part, but was on the whole more impressed by the jugglers and acrobats at Baltimore's old Hippodrome, where I used to go every time they changed shows: genuine *virtuosi* doing things that anyone can dream up and discuss but almost no one can do.

I suppose the distinction is between things worth remarking – preferably over beer, if one's of my generation – and things worth doing. 'Somebody ought to make a novel with scenes that pop up, like the old children's books,' one says, with the implication that one isn't going to bother doing it oneself.

However, art and its forms and techniques live in history and certainly do change. I sympathize with a remark attributed to Saul Bellow, that to be technically up to date is the least important attribute of a writer, though I would have to add that this least important attribute may be nevertheless essential. In any case, to be technically *out* of date is likely to be a genuine defect: Beethoven's Sixth Symphony or the Chartres Cathedral if executed today would be merely embarrassing. A good many current novelists write turn-of-the-century-type novels, only in more or less mid-twentieth-century language and about contemporary people and topics; this makes them considerably less interesting (to me) than excellent writers who are also technically contemporary: Joyce and Kafka, for instance, in their time, and in ours, Samuel Beckett and Jorge Luis Borges. The intermedia arts, I'd say, tend to be intermediary too, between the traditional realms of aesthetics on the one hand and artistic creation on the other; I think the wise artist and civilian will regard them with quite the kind and degree of seriousness with which he regards good shoptalk: he'll listen carefully, if non-committally, and keep an eye on his intermedia colleagues, if only the corner of his eye. They may very possibly suggest something usable in the making or understanding of genuine works of contemporary art.

The man I want to discuss a little here, Jorges Luis Borges, illustrates well the difference between a technically old-fashioned artist, a technically up-to-date civilian, and a technically up-to-date artist. In the first category I'd locate all those novelists who for better or worse write not as if the twentieth century didn't exist, but as if the great writers of the last sixty years or so hadn't existed (*nota bene* that our century's more than two-thirds done; it's dismaying to see so many of our writers following Dostoevsky or Tolstoy or Flaubert or Balzac, when the real technical question seems to me to be how to succeed not even Joyce and Kafka, but

those who've *succeeded* Joyce and Kafka and are now in the evenings of
their own careers). In the second category are such folk as an artist-
neighbour of mine in Buffalo who fashions dead Winnie-the-Poohs in
sometimes monumental scale out of oilcloth stuffed with sand and
impaled on stakes or hung by the neck. In the third belong the few people
whose artistic thinking is as hip as any French news-novelist's, but who
manage nonetheless to speak eloquently and memorably to our still-
human hearts and conditions, as the great artists have always done. Of
these, two of the finest living specimens that I know of are Beckett and
Borges, just about the only contemporaries of my reading acquaintance
mentionable with the 'old masters' of twentieth-century fiction. In the
unexciting history of literary awards, the 1961 International Publishers'
Prize, shared by Beckett and Borges, is a happy exception indeed.

One of the modern things about these two is that in an age of ultimacies
and 'final solutions' – at least *felt* ultimacies, in everything from weaponry
to theology, the celebrated dehumanization of society, and the history of
the novel – their work in separate ways reflects and deals with ultimacy,
both technically and thematically, as, for example, *Finnegans Wake* does in
its different manner. One notices, by the way, for whatever its
symptomatic worth, that Joyce was virtually blind at the end, Borges is
literally so, and Beckett has become virtually mute, musewise, having
progressed from marvellously constructed English sentences through
terser and terser French ones to the unsyntactical, unpunctuated prose of
Comment C'est and 'ultimately' to wordless mimes. One might extrapolate
a theoretical course for Beckett: language, after all, consists of silence as
well as sound, and the mime is still communication – 'that nineteenth-
century idea', a Yale student once snarled at me – but by the language of
action. But the language of action consists of rest as well as movement,
and so in the context of Beckett's progress, immobile, silent figures still
aren't altogether ultimate. How about an empty, silent stage, then, or
blank pages (an ultimacy already attained in the nineteenth century by
that *avant-gardist* of East Aurora, New York, Elbert Hubbard, in his *Essay
on Silence*) – a 'happening' here nothing happens, like Cage's 4'33"
performed in an empty hall? But dramatic communication consists of the
absence as well as the presence of the actors; 'we have our exits and our
entrances'; and so even that would be imperfectly ultimate in Beckett's
case. Nothing at all, then, I suppose: but Nothingness is necessarily and
inextricably the background against which Being et cetera; for Beckett, at
this point in his career, to cease to create altogether would be fairly
meaningful: his crowning work, his 'last word'. What a convenient corner
to paint yourself into! 'And now I shall finish,' the valet Arsene says in
Watt, 'and you will hear my voice no more.' Only the silence *Molloy*
speaks of, 'of which the universe is made'.

After which, I add on behalf of the rest of us, it might be conceivable to rediscover validly the artifices of language and literature – such far-out notions as grammar, punctuation ... even characterization! Even *plot*! – if one goes about it the right way, aware of what one's predecessors have been up to.

Now J.L. Borges is perfectly aware of all these things. Back in the great decades of literary experimentalism he was associated with *Prisma*, a 'muralist' magazine that published its pages on walls and billboards; his later *Labyrinths* and *Ficciones* not only anticipate the farthest-out ideas of The Something Else Press crowd – not a difficult thing to do – but being marvellous works of art as well, illustrate in a simple way the difference between the *fact* of aesthetic ultimacies and their artistic *use*. What it comes to is that an artist doesn't merely exemplify an ultimacy; he employs it.

Consider Borges's story 'Pierre Menard, Author of the Quixote': the hero, an utterly sophisticated turn-of-the-century French Symbolist, by an astounding effort of imagination, produces – not *copies* or *imitates*, mind, but *composes* – several chapters of Cervantes's novel.

> It is a revelation [Borges's narrator tells us] to compare Menard's *Don Quixote* with Cervantes's. The latter, for example, wrote (part one, chapter nine):
>
> > ... truth, whose mother is history, rival of time, depository of deeds, witness of the past, exemplar and adviser to the present, the future's counsellor.
>
> Written in the seventeenth century, written by the 'lay genius' Cervantes, this enumeration is a mere rhetorical praise of history. Menard, on the other hand, writes:
>
> > ... truth, whose mother is history, rival of time, depository of deeds, witness of the past, exemplar and adviser to the present, the future's counsellor.
>
> History, the *mother* of truth: the idea is astounding. Menard, a contemporary of William James, does not define history as an enquiry into reality but as its origin ...

Et cetera. Now, this is an interesting idea, of considerable intellectual validity. I mentioned earlier that if Beethoven's Sixth were composed today, it would be an embarrassment; but clearly it wouldn't be, necessarily, if done with ironic intent by a composer quite aware of where we've been and where we are. It would have then potentially, for better or worse, the kind of significance of Warhol's Campbell's Soup ads, the difference being that in the former case a work of art is being reproduced instead of a work of non-art, and the ironic comment would therefore be more directly on the genre and history of the art than on the state of the culture. In fact, of course, to make the valid intellectual point one needn't even re-compose the Sixth Symphony any more than Menard really needed to recreate the *Quixote*. It would've been sufficient for Menard to have *attributed* the novel to himself in order to have a new work of art, from the intellectual point of view. Indeed, in several stories Borges plays with this very idea, and I can readily imagine Beckett's next novel, for example, as *Tom Jones*, just as Nabokov's last was that multivolume annotated translation of Pushkin. I myself have always aspired to write Burton's version of *The 1001 Nights*, complete with appendices and the like, in twelve volumes, and for intellectual purposes I needn't even write it. What evenings we might spend (over beer) discussing Saarinen's Parthenon, D.H. Lawrence's *Wuthering Heights*, or the Johnson Administration by Robert Rauschenberg!

The idea, I say, is intellectually serious, as are Borges's other characteristic ideas, most of a metaphysical rather than an aesthetic nature. But the important thing to observe is that Borges doesn't attribute the *Quixote* to himself, much less re-compose it like Pierre Menard; instead, he writes a remarkable and original work of literature, the implicit theme of which is the difficulty, perhaps the unnecessity, of writing original works of literature. His artistic victory, if you like, is that he confronts an intellectual dead end and employs it against itself to accomplish new human work. If this corresponds to what mystics do – 'and every moment falling surely back into the finite' – it's only one more aspect of that old analogy. In homelier terms, it's a matter of every moment throwing out the bath water without for a moment losing the baby.

Another way of describing Borges's accomplishment is in a pair of his own favourite terms, *algebra* and *fire*. In his most often anthologized story, 'Tlön, Uqbar, Orbis Tertius', he imagines an entirely hypothetical world, the invention of a secret society of scholars who elaborate its every aspect in a surreptitious encyclopaedia. This *First Encyclopaedia of Tlön* (what fictionist would not wish to have dreamed up the *Britannica*?) describes a coherent alternative to this world complete in every aspect from its algebra to its fire, Borges tells us, and of such imaginative power that, once conceived, it begins to obtrude itself into and eventually to supplant our prior reality. My point is that neither the algebra nor the fire, metaphorically speaking, could achieve this result without the other. Borges's algebra is what I'm considering here – algebra is easier to talk about than fire – but any intellectual giant could equal it. The imaginary authors of the *First Encyclopaedia of Tlön* itself are not artists, though their work is in a manner of speaking fictional and would find a ready publisher in New York nowadays. The author of the story 'Tlön, Uqbar, Orbis Tertius', who merely *alludes* to the fascinating *Encyclopaedia*, is an artist; what makes him one of the first rank, like Kafka, is the combination of that intellectually profound vision with great human insight, poetic power, and consummate mastery of his means, a definition which would have gone without saying, I suppose, in any century but ours.

Not long ago, incidentally, in a footnote to a scholarly edition of Sir Thomas Browne (*The Urn Burial*, I believe it was), I came upon a perfect Borges datum, reminiscent of Tlön's self-realization: the actual case of a book called *The Three Impostors*, alluded to in Browne's *Religio Medici* among other places. *The Three Impostors* is a non-existent blasphemous treatise against Moses, Christ, and Mohammed, which in the seventeenth century was widely held to exist, or to have once existed. Commentators attributed it variously to Boccaccio, Pietro Aretino, Giordano Bruno, and Tommaso Campanella, and though no one, Browne included, had ever seen a copy of it, it was frequently cited, refuted, railed against, and generally discussed as if everyone had read it – until, sure enough, in the *eighteenth* century a spurious work appeared with a forged date of 1598 and the title *De Tribus Impostoribus*. It's a wonder that Borges doesn't mention this work, as he seems to have read absolutely everything, including all the books that don't exist, and Browne is a particular favourite of his. In fact, the narrator of 'Tlön, Uqbar, Orbis Tertius' declares at the end:

> ... English and French and mere Spanish will disappear from the globe. The world will be Tlön. I pay no attention to all this and go on revising, in the still days at the Adrogué hotel, an uncertain Quevedian translation (which I do not intend to publish) of Browne's *Urn Burial*.

(Moreover, on rereading 'Tlön', etc., I find now a remark I'd swear wasn't in it last year: that the eccentric American millionaire who endows the *Encyclopaedia* does so on condition that 'the work will make no pact with the impostor Jesus Christ'.)

This 'contamination of reality by dream', as Borges calls it, is one of his pet themes, and commenting upon such contaminations is one of his favourite fictional devices. Like many of the best such devices, it turns the artist's mode or form into a metaphor for his concerns, as does the diary-ending of *Portrait of the Artist as a Young Man* or the cyclical construction of *Finnegans Wake*. In Borges's case, the story 'Tlön', etc., for example, is a real piece of imagined reality in our world, analogous to those Tlönian artifacts called *hronir*, which imagine themselves into existence. In short, it's a paradigm of or metaphor for itself; not just the *form* of the story but the *fact* of the story is symbolic; 'the medium is the message'.

Moreover, like all of Borges's work, it illustrates in other of its aspects my subject: how an artist may paradoxically turn the felt ultimacies of our time into material and means for his work – *paradoxically* because by doing so he transcends what had appeared to be his refutation, in the same way that the mystic who transcends finitude is said to be enabled to live, spiritually and physically, in the finite world. Suppose you're a writer by vocation – a 'print-oriented bastard', as the McLuhanites call us – and you feel, for example, that the novel, if not narrative literature generally, if not the printed word altogether, has by this hour of the world just about shot its bolt, as Leslie Fiedler and others maintain (I'm inclined to agree, with reservations and hedges. Literary forms certainly have histories and historical contingencies, and it may well be that the novel's time as a major art form is up, as the 'times' of classical tragedy, grand opera, or the sonnet sequence came to be. No necessary cause for alarm in this at all, except perhaps to certain novelists, and one way to handle such a feeling might be to write a novel about it. Whether historically the novel expires or persists seems immaterial to me; if enough writers and critics *feel* apocalyptical about it, their feeling becomes a considerable cultural fact, like the feeling that Western civilization, or the world, is going to end rather soon. If you took a bunch of people out into the desert and the world didn't end, you'd come home shamefaced, I imagine; but the persistence of an art form doesn't invalidate work created in the comparable apocalyptic ambience. That's one of the fringe benefits of being an artist instead of a prophet. There are others.) If you happened to be Vladimir Nabokov you might address that felt ultimacy by writing *Pale Fire*: a fine novel by a learned pedant, in the form of a pedantic commentary on a poem invented for the purpose. If you were Borges you might write *Labyrinths*: fictions by a learned librarian in the form of footnotes, as he describes them, to imaginary or hypothetical books. And I'll add, since I believe Borges's idea is rather more interesting, that if you were the author of this paper, you'd have written something like *The Sot-Weed Factor* or *Giles Goat-Boy*: novels which imitate the form of the Novel, by an author who imitates the role of Author.

If this sort of thing sounds unpleasantly decadent, nevertheless it's about where the genre began, with *Quixote* imitating *Amadis of Gaul*, Cervantes pretending to be the Cid Hamete Benengeli (and Alonso Quijano pretending to be Don Quixote), of Fielding parodying Richardson. 'History repeats itself as farce' – meaning, of course, in the form or mode of farce, not that history is farcical. The imitation (like the Dadaist echoes in the work of the 'intermedia' types) is something new and *may be* quite serious and passionate despite its farcical aspect. This is the important difference between a proper novel and a deliberate imitation of a novel, or a novel imitative of other sorts of documents. The first attempts (has been historically inclined to attempt) to imitate actions more or less directly, and its conventional devices – cause and effect, linear anecdote, characterization, authorial selection, arrangement, and interpretation – can be and have long since been objected to as obsolete notions, or metaphors for obsolete notions: Robbe-Grillet's essays _For a New Novel_ come to mind. There are replies to these objections, not to the point here, but one can see that in any case they're obviated by imitations-of-novels, which attempt to represent not life directly but a representation of life. In fact such works are no more removed from 'life' than Richardson's or Goethe's epistolary novels are: both imitate 'real' documents, and the subject of both, ultimately, is life, not the documents. A novel is as much a piece of the real world as a letter, and the letters in _The Sorrows of Young Werther_ are, after all, fictitious.

One might imaginably compound this imitation, and though Borges doesn't he's fascinated with the idea: one of his frequenter literary allusions is to the 602nd night of _The 1001 Nights_, when, owing to a copyist's error, Scheherezade begins to tell the King the story of the 1001 nights, from the beginning. Happily, the King interrupts; if he didn't there'd be no 603rd night ever, and while this would solve Scheherezade's problem – which is every storyteller's problem: to publish or perish – it would put the 'outside' author in a bind. (I suspect that Borges dreamed this whole thing up: the business he mentions isn't in any edition of _The 1001 Nights_ I've been able to consult. Not _yet_, anyhow: after reading 'Tlön, Uqbar', etc., one is inclined to recheck every semester or so.)

Now Borges (whom someone once vexedly accused _me_ of inventing) is interested in the 602nd night because it's an instance of the story-within-the-story turned back upon itself, and his interest in such instances is threefold: first, as he himself declares, they disturb us metaphysically: when the characters in a work of fiction become readers or authors of the fiction they're in, we're reminded of the fictitious aspect of our own existence, one of Borges's cardinal themes, as it was of Shakespeare, Calderón, Unamuno, and other folk. Second, the 602nd night is a literary illustration of the _regressus in infinitum_, as are almost all Borges's principal images and motifs. Third, Scheherezade's accidental gambit, like Borges's other versions of the _regressus in infinitum_, is an image of the exhaustion, or attempted exhaustion, of possibilities – in this case literary possibilities – and so we return to our main subject.

What makes Borges's stance, if you like, more interesting to me than, say, Nabokov's or Beckett's is the premise with which he approaches literature; in the words of one of his editors: 'For [Borges] no one has claim to originality in literature; all writers are more or less faithful amanuenses of the spirit, translators and annotators of pre-existing archetypes.' Thus his inclination to write brief comments on imaginary books: for one to attempt to add overtly to the sum of 'original' literature by even so much as a conventional short story, not to mention a novel, would be too presumptuous, too naïve; literature has been done long since. A librarian's point of view! And it would itself be too presumptuous, if it weren't part of a lively, passionately relevant metaphysical vision and slyly employed against itself precisely, to make new and original literature. Borges defines the Baroque as 'that style which deliberately exhausted (or tries to exhaust) its possibilities and borders upon its on caricature'. While his own work is *not* Baroque, except intellectually (the Baroque was never so terse, laconic, economical), it suggests the view that intellectual and literary history has been Baroque, and has pretty well exhausted the possibilities of novelty. His *ficciones* are not only footnotes to imaginary texts, but postscripts to the real corpus of literature.

This premise gives resonance and relation to all his principal images. The facing mirrors that recur in his stories are a dual *regressus*. The doubles that his characters, like Nabokov's, run afoul of suggest dizzying multiples and remind one of Browne's remark that 'every man is not only himself ... men are lived over again'. (It would please Borges, and illustrate Browne's point, to call Browne a precursor of Borges. 'Every writer,' Borges says in his essay on Kafka, 'creates his on precursors.') Borges's favourite third-century heretical sect is the Histriones – I think and hope he invented them – who believe that repetition is impossible in history and therefore live viciously in order to purge the future of the vices they commit: in other words, to exhaust the possibilities of the world in order to bring its end nearer.

The writer he most often mentions, after Cervantes, is Shakespeare; in one piece he imagines the playwright on his deathbed asking God to permit him to be one and himself having been everyone and no one; God replies from the whirlwind that He is no one either; He has dreamed the world like Shakespeare, and including Shakespeare. Homer's story in Book IV of the *Odyssey*, of Menelaus on the beach at Pharos, tackling Proteus, appeals profoundly to Borges: Proteus is he who 'exhausts the guises of reality' while Menelaus – who, one recalls, disguised his own identity in order to ambush him – holds fast. Zeno's paradox of Achilles and the Tortoise embodies a *regressus in infinitum* which Borges carries through philosophical history, pointing out that Aristotle uses it to refute Plato's theory of forms, Hume to refute the possibility of cause and effect, Lewis Carroll to refute syllogistic deduction, William James to refute the notion of temporal passage, and Bradley to refute the general possibility of logical relations; Borges himself uses it, citing Schopenhauer, as evidence that the world is our dream, our idea, in which 'tenuous and eternal crevices of unreason' can be found to remind us that our creation is false, or at least fictive.

The infinite library of one of the most popular stories is an image particularly pertinent to the literature of exhaustion; the 'Library of Babel' houses every possible combination of alphabetical characters and spaces, and thus every possible book and statement, including your and my refutations and vindications, the history of the actual future, the history of every possible future, and, though he doesn't mention it, the encyclopaedias not only of Tlön but of every imaginable other world – since, as in Lucretius's universe, the number of elements, and so of combinations, is finite (though very large), and the number of instances of each element and combination of elements is infinite, like the library itself.

That brings us to his favourite image of all, the labyrinth, and to my point. *Labyrinths* is the name of his most substantial translated volume, and the only full-length study of Borges in English, by Ana Maria Barrenechea, is called *Borges the Labyrinth-Maker*. A labyrinth, after all, is a place in which, ideally, all the possibilities of choice (of direction, in this case) are embodied, and – barring special dispensation like Theseus's – must be exhausted before one reaches the heart. Where, mind, the Minotaur waits with two final possibilities: defeat and death, or victory and freedom. Now, in fact, the legendary Theseus is non-Baroque; thanks to Ariadne's thread he can take a shortcut through the labyrinth at Knossos. But Menelaus on the beach at Pharos, for example, is genuinely Baroque in the Borgesian spirit, and illustrates a positive artistic morality in the literature of exhaustion. He is not there, after all, for kicks (any more than Borges and Beckett are in the fiction racket for their health): Menelaus is *lost*, in the larger labyrinth of the world, and has got to hold fast while the Old Man of the Sea exhausts reality's frightening guises so that he may extort direction from him when Proteus returns to his 'true' self. It's a heroic enterprise, with salvation as its object – one recalls that the aim of the Histriones is to get history done with so that Jesus may come again the sooner, and that Shakespeare's heroic metamorphoses culminate not merely in a theophany but in an apotheosis.

Now, not just any old body is equipped for this labour, and Theseus in the Cretan labyrinth becomes in the end the aptest image of Borges after all. Distressing as the fact is to us liberal Democrats, the commonality, alas, will *always* lose their way and their souls; it's the chosen remnant, the virtuoso, the Thesean *hero*, who, confronted with Baroque reality, Baroque history, the Baroque state of his art, need *not* rehearse its possibilities to exhaustion, any more than Borges needs actually to *write* the *Encyclopaedia of Tlön* or the books in the Library of Babel. He need only be aware of their existence of possibility, acknowledge them, and with the aid of *very special* gifts – as extraordinary as saint- or hero-hood and not likely to be found in The New York Correspondence School of Literature – go straight through the maze to the accomplishment of his work.

9   From *Reflections on the Name of the Rose**

UMBERTO ECO

Umberto Eco is the writer/critic *par excellence*. In addition to his seminal work as a semiologist and critic, Eco is author of two major novels *The Name of the Rose* and *Foucault's Pendulum* which characterise the postmodern novel in two principal ways: they are written on the borderline on fiction and criticism by examining interpretive possibilities within the fiction; and they are both ironic revisitations of the past – historical novels concerned with the presentation and interpretation of history. In this extract from a work reflecting critically on the former of these novels, Eco begins with a consideration of the term 'postmodern' in relation to narrative, goes on to contemplate the place of the 'historical novel' in the postmodern age, and ends with a rather cryptic discussion of the possibility of a detective novel in which the murderer is identified as the external reader of the fiction. In this last point we see a formula for Eco's metafictional intention as a novelist, to transgress the conventional boundary between the fiction and the outside world by implicating the reader in fictional events, and therefore highlighting the role of the reader in the construction of intelligible meaning in fiction.

This extract forms the last three short chapters from *Reflections on the Name of the Rose* titled 'Postmodernism, Irony and the Enjoyable', 'The Historical Novel' and 'Ending', and provides an insight into the aesthetic values of a postmodern novelist aspiring to rise above the oppositions of realism and anti-realism, or what he calls 'formalism' and 'contentism'. It is particularly useful in relation to the idea of historiographic metafiction as an ideal form for the postmodern novel.

Between 1965 and today, two ideas have been definitively clarified: that plot could be found also in the form of quotation of other plots, and that the quotation could be less escapist than the plot quoted. In 1972 I edited the *Almanacco Bompiani*, celebrating 'The Return to the Plot,' though this return was via an ironic re-examination (not without admiration) of Ponson du Terrail and Eugène Sue, and admiration (with very little irony) of some of the great pages of Dumas. The real problem at stake then was,

---

*Reprinted from Eco, Umberto, *Reflections on the Name of the Rose*, trans. William Weaver (London: Secker & Warburg, 1985), pp. 65–81.

could there be a novel that was not escapist and, nevertheless, still enjoyable?

This link, and the rediscovery not only of plot but also of enjoyability, was to be realized by the American theorists of postmodernism.

Unfortunately, 'postmodern' is a term *bon à tout faire*. I have the impression that it is applied today to anything the user of the term happens to like. Further, there seems to be an attempt to make it increasingly retroactive: first it was apparently applied to certain writers or artists active in the last twenty years, then gradually it reached the beginning of the century, then still further back. And this reverse procedure continues; soon the postmodern category will include Homer.

Actually, I believe that postmodernism is not a trend to be chronologically defined, but, rather, an ideal category – or, better still, a *Kunstwollen*, a way of operating. We could say that every period has its own postmodernism, just as every period would have its own mannerism (and, in fact, I wonder if postmodernism is not the modern name for mannerism as metahistorical category). I believe that in every period there are moments of crisis like those described by Nietzsche in his *Thoughts Out of Season*, in which he wrote about the harm done by historical studies. The past conditions us, harries us, blackmails us. The historic avant-garde (but here I would also consider avant-grade a metahistorical category) tries to settle scores with the past, 'Down with moonlight' – a futurist slogan – is a platform typical of every avant-garde; you have only to replace 'moonlight' with whatever noun is suitable. The avant-garde destroys, defaces the past: *Les Demoiselles d'Avignon* is a typical avant-garde act. Then the avant-garde goes further, destroys the figure, cancels it, arrives at the abstract, the informal, the white canvas, the slashed canvas, the charred canvas. In architecture and the visual arts, it will be the curtain wall, the building as stele, pure parallelepiped, minimal art; in literature, the destruction of the flow of discourse, the Burroughs-like collage, silence, the white page; in music, the passage from atonality to noise to absolute silence (in this sense, the early Cage is modern).

But the moment comes when the avant-garde (the modern) can go no further, because it has produced a metalanguage that speaks of its impossible texts (conceptual art). The postmodern reply to the modern consists of recognizing that the past, since it cannot really be destroyed, because its destruction leads to silence, must be revisited: but with irony, not innocently. I think of the postmodern attitude as that of a man who loves a very cultivated woman and knows he cannot say to her, 'I love you madly,' because he knows that she knows (and that she knows that he knows) that these words have already been written by Barbara Cartland. Still, there is a solution. He can say, 'As Barbara Cartland would put it, I love you madly.' At this point, having avoided false innocence, having said clearly that it is no longer possible to speak innocently, he will nevertheless have said what he wanted to say to the woman: that he loves her, but he loves her in an age of lost innocence. If the woman goes along with this, she will have received a declaration of love all the same. Neither of the two speakers will feel innocent, both will have accepted the challenge of the past, of the already said, which cannot be eliminated; both will consciously and with pleasure play the game of irony ... But both will have succeeded, once again, in speaking of love.

Irony, metalinguistic play, enunciation squared. Thus, with the modern, anyone who does not understand the game can only reject it, but with the postmodern, it is possible not to understand the game and yet to take it seriously. Which is, after all, the quality (the risk) of irony. There is always someone who takes ironic discourse seriously. I think that the collages of Picasso, Juan Gris, and Braque were modern: this is why normal people would not accept them. On the other hand, the collages of Max Ernst, who pasted together bits of nineteenth-century engravings, were postmodern: they can be read as fantastic stories, as the telling of dreams, without any awareness that they amount to a discussion of the nature of engravings, and perhaps even of collage. If 'postmodern' means this, it is clear why Sterne and Rabelais were postmodern, why Borges surely is, and why in the same artist the modern moment and the postmodern moment can coexist, or alternate, or follow each other closely. Look at Joyce. The *Portrait* is the story of an attempt at the modern. *Dubliners*, even if it comes before, is more modern than *Portrait*. *Ulysses* is on the borderline. *Finnegans Wake* is already postmodern, or at least it initiates the postmodern discourse: it demands, in order to be understood, not the negation of the already said, but its ironic rethinking.

On the subject of the postmodern nearly everything has been said, from the very beginning (namely, in essays like 'The Literature of Exhaustion' by John Barth, which dates from 1967). Not that I am entirely in agreement with the grades that the theoreticians of postmodernism (Barth included) give to writers and artists, establishing who is postmodern and who has not yet made it. But I am interested in the theorem that the trend's theoreticians derive from their premises: 'My ideal postmodernist author neither merely repudiates nor merely imitates either his twentieth-century premodernist grandparents. He has the first half of our century under his belt, but not his back ... He may not hope to reach and move the devotees of James Michener and Irving Wallace – not to mention the lobotomized mass-media illiterates. But he *should* hope to reach and delight, at least part of the time, beyond the circle of what Mann used to call the Early Christians: professional devotees of high art ... The ideal postmodernist novel will somehow rise above the quarrel between realism and irrealism, formalism and 'contentism,' pure and committed literature, coterie fiction and junk fiction ... My own analogy would be with good jazz or classical music: one finds much on successive listenings or close examination of the score that one didn't catch the first time through; but the first time through should be so ravishing – and not just to specialists – that one delights in the replay.'

This is what Barth wrote in 1980, resuming the discussion, but this time under the title 'The Literature of Replenishment: Postmodernist Fiction.'[1] Naturally, the subject can be discussed further, with a greater taste for paradox; and this is what Leslie Fiedler does. In 1980 *Salmagundi* (no. 50– 51) published a debate between Fiedler and other American authors. Fiedler, obviously, is out to provoke. He praises *The Last of the Mohicans*, adventure stories, Gothic novels, junk scorned by critics that was nevertheless able to create myths and capture the imagination of more than one generation. He wonders if something like *Uncle Tom's Cabin* will ever appear again, a book that can be read with equal passion in the kitchen, the living room, and the nursery. He includes Shakespeare among those who knew how to amuse, along with *Gone with the Wind*. We all know he is too keen a critic to believe these things. He simply wants to break down the barrier that has been erected between art and enjoyability. He feels that today reaching a vast public and capturing its dreams perhaps means acting as the avant-garde, and he still leaves us free to say that capturing readers' dreams does not necessarily mean encouraging escape: it can also mean haunting them.

The Historical Novel

For two years I have refused to answer idle questions on the order of 'Is your novel an open work or not?' How should I know? That is your business, not mine. Or 'With which of your characters do you identify?' For God's sake, with whom does an author identify? With the adverbs, obviously.

Of all idle questions the most idle has been the one raised by those who suggest that writing about the past is a way of eluding the present. 'Is that true?' they ask me. It is quite likely, I answer: if Manzoni wrote about the seventeenth century, that means the nineteenth century did not interest him. Shakespeare rewrote medieval subjects and was not concerned with his own time, whereas *Love Story* is firmly committed to its own time, yet *La Chartreuse de Parme* told only of events that had occurred a good twenty-five years earlier ... It is no use saying that all the problems of modern Europe took the shape in which we still feel them during the Middle Ages: communal democracy and the banking economy, national monarchies and urban life, new technologies and rebellions of the poor. The Middle Ages are our infancy, to which we must always return, for anamnesis. But there is also the *Excalibur*-style Middle Ages. And so the problem is something else and cannot be skirted. What does writing a historical novel mean? I believe there are three ways of narrating the past. One is *romance*, and the examples range from the Breton cycle to Tolkien, also including the Gothic novel, which is not a novel but a romance. The past as scenery, pretext, fairy-tale construction, to allow the imagination to rove freely. In this sense, a romantic does not necessarily have to take place in the past; it must only not take place here and now, and the here and now must not be mentioned, not even as allegory. Much science fiction is pure romance. Romance is the story of an *elsewhere*.

Then comes the swashbuckling novel, the cloak-and-dagger stories, like the work of Dumas. This kind of novel chooses a 'real' and recognizable past, and, to make it recognizable, the novelist peoples it with characters already found in the encyclopedia (Richelieu, Mazarin), making them perform actions that the encyclopedia does not record (meeting Milady, consorting with a certain Bonacieux) but which the encyclopedia does not contradict. Naturally, to corroborate the illusion of reality, the historical characters will also do what (as historiography concurs) they actually did (besiege La Rochelle, have intimate relations with Anne of Austria, deal with the Fronde). In this ('real') picture the imaginary characters are introduced, though they display feelings that could also be attributed to characters of other periods. What d'Artagnan does, in recovering the Queen's jewels in London, he could have done as well in the fifteenth century or the eighteenth. It is not necessary to live in the seventeenth century to have the psychology of d'Artagnan.

In the historical novel, on the other hand, it is not necessary for characters recognizable in normal encyclopedias to appear. Take *The Betrothed*: the best-known real character is Cardinal Federigo, who, until Manzoni came along, was a name known only to a few people (the other Borromeo, Saint Charles, was the famous one). But everything that Renzo, Lucia, or Fra Cristoforo does could be done only in Lombardy in the seventeenth century. What the characters do serves to make history, what happened, more comprehensible. Events and characters are made up, yet they tell us things about the Italy of the period that history books have never told us so clearly.

In this sense, certainly, I wanted to write a historical novel, and not because Ubertino or Michael had really existed and had said more or less what they say, but because everything the fictitious characters like William say *ought* to have been said in that period.

I do not know how faithful I remained to this purpose. I do not believe I was neglecting it when I disguised quotations from later authors (such as Wittgenstein), passing them off as quotations from the period. In those instances I knew very well that it was not my medieval men who were being modern; if anything, it was the moderns who were thinking medievally. Rather, I ask myself if at times I did not endow my fictitious characters with a capacity for putting together, from the *disiecta membra* of totally medieval thoughts, some conceptual hircocervuses that, in this form, the Middle Ages would not have recognized as their own. But I believe a historical novel should do this, too: not only identify in the past the causes of what came later, but also trace the process through which those causes began slowly to produce their effects.

If a character of mine, comparing two medieval ideas, produces a third, more modern, idea, he is doing exactly what culture did; and if nobody has ever written what he says, someone, however confusedly, should surely have begun to think it (perhaps without saying it, blocked by countless fears and by shame).

In any case, there is one matter that has amused me greatly: every now and then a critic or a reader writes to say that some character of mine declares things that are too modern, and in every one of these instances, and only in these instances, I was actually quoting fourteenth-century texts.

And there are other pages in which readers appreciated the exquisite medieval quality whereas I felt those pages are illegitimately modern. The fact is that everyone has his own idea, usually corrupt, of the Middle Ages. Only we monks of the period know the truth, but saying it can sometimes lead to the stake.

Ending

I found again – two years after having written the novel – a note I made in 1953, when I was still a student at the university.

> Horatio and his friend call the Count of P. to solve the mystery of the ghost. The Court of P., eccentric and phlegmatic gentleman. Opposed to him, a young captain of the Danish guards, with FBI methods. Normal development of the action following the lines of the tragedy. In the last act the Court of P., having gathered the family together, explains the mystery; the murderer is Hamlet. Too late, Hamlet dies.

Years later I discovered that Chesterton has somewhere suggested an idea of the sort. It seems that the Parisian Oulipo group[2] has recently constructed a matrix of all possible murder-story situations and has found that there is still to be written a book in which the murderer is the reader.

Moral: there exist obsessive ideas, they are never personal; books talk among themselves, and any true detection should prove that we are the guilty party.

Notes

1. Both essays are reprinted in *The Literature of Exhaustion* (Northridge, Calif.: Lord John Press, 1982).
2. Ouvroir de Littérature Potentielle, organized by Queneau, Le Lyonnais, Peree, and others to produce literature by mathematical combinatory means.

Part Four

Readings of Metafiction

10 The Art of Metafiction*

LARRY MCCAFFERY

This study of William Gass's novel *Willie Masters' Lonesome Wife* establishes a definition of metafiction as 'a direct and immediate concern with
fiction-making' within a fiction and continues to show that the novel
represents a pure expression of this concern. Distinguishing the metafiction from the 'anti-novel', McCaffery argues that metafictions derive
from 'meta-theorems' being developed in the 1970s in other disciplines
which seek to contrive what Gass himself has called 'lingoes to converse
about lingoes'. It is reasonable to assume that Gass and McCaffery have
in mind here, among others, the disciplines of literary studies and
history, both of which experienced profound transformations during the
1970s, particularly in America, as a result of the impact of meta-
theorems, or discourses about discourses. McCaffery's point is that,
primarily, Gass is interested in the problems of metalingual and metafictional discourse as an extension of his formal training in the philosophy of language. The purity of Gass's metafiction for McCaffery lies in a
fascination with the idea that literature is made of words and only
words. The analysis therefore concentrates on the way that the novel
focuses on the materiality of words on a page, how they look, and how
we read them. Once again the idea of a metafiction as a confusion of what
lies within and outside of fiction becomes central as McCaffery analyses
the way in which words are foregrounded by Babs, Gass's central
character, who is herself conjured into existence only by words on the
page, as a kind of surrogate author who parallels Gass's own self-
conscious creation of a work from words.

As in every literary generation since Cervantes, the period since World
War II has produced considerable discussion about the 'anti-novel'. It is
most often regarded simply as any work of fiction whose intentions
include some sort of defiance of the current norms of fiction: 'the anti-
novel occurs whenever the novel loses faith in itself, becomes critical and
self-critical, wishes to break with the established norms of the medium'.[1]
Defined so broadly, the term may be applied to many innovative works;

*Reprinted from McCaffery, Larry, 'The Art of Metafiction: William Gass's *Willie
Masters' Lonesome Wife'*, *Critique: Studies in Modern Fiction*, XVIII, 1 (1976), 21–34.

Tristram Shandy would be an obvious example, so would *Madame Bovary*, *Ulysses*, *The Counterfeiters*, and even *Don Quixote* itself. Although we can recognize a fairly clear tradition within the anti-novel, the past fifteen years have seen anti-novels proliferate to an extent not previously experienced in the brief history of the novel. Indeed, recent critics have begun the task of defining and clarifying specific categories and tendencies within the form. Examining certain implications of form in fiction, William Gass has remarked that most critics are far too eager to label any unusual work of fiction as an 'anti-novel': 'many of the so-called anti-novels are really metafictions.'[2] Like other critics who have adopted the term 'metafiction,' Gass is making a subtle but much needed distinction between anti-novel and metafictions. The present essay will discuss some implications of the term 'metafiction' and then examine Gass's own work, *Willie Masters' Lonesome Wife*, a remarkably pure and interesting example of the genre.

By 1970, a certain type of work had begun to appear with insistent regularity, clearly belonging to the anti-novel tradition but maintaining a distinct unity of intention, approach, and subject matter. These works, represented by Donald Barthelme's *Snow White* (1967), John Barth's *Lost in the Funhouse* (1968), Robert Coover's *Pricksongs and Descants* (1969), and Ronald Sukenick's *Up* (1970), are all highly self-conscious works which deal directly with the inadequacies and problems of current fiction writing.[3] Akin to Beckett's self-ruminating narratives and owing even more to the cerebral, intensely literary creations of Borges and Nabokov, these works also derived from the meta-theorems being developed in many other disciplines. Like the meta-theorist, the metafictionist had seen that only by creating a new form with its own referential language could he deal effectively with his original subject – fiction-making; as Gass has noted, 'Everywhere lingoes to converse about lingoes are being contrived, and the case is no different in the novel.'[4]

Although most of its practitioners would cringe at being associated with genres and traditions of any sort, the metafictionist can be readily identified and certain of his conventions and idiosyncrasies pointed out. Obviously, many of the things we can say about the anti-novelist will apply to the metafictionist. Metafiction resembles anti-novels of the past, for example, in tending to appear unconventional and experimental – except in instances when it relies on familiar conventions for parodic purposes; the defining characteristic of metafiction, however, is its direct and immediate concern with fiction-making itself. To a certain extent any anti-novel is 'about' fiction-making; any experimental work of fiction suggests attitudes about the art of fiction by the very acts of subverting or ignoring specific conventions and of introducing others instead. By his own choice of forms, the anti-novelist indirectly criticizes past forms and suggests new perspectives on the relationship between fiction, the artist, and reality. When we examine a metafiction, however, we discover that fiction-making is not dealt with in such indirect fashion; instead, it takes as its main subject writers, writing, and anything else which has to do with the way books and stories are written. Not surprisingly, metafictions often present themselves as biographies of imaginary writers – as with many of Borges' tales, Nabokov's *Pale Fire* (1962), Alan Friedman's *Hermaphrodeity* (1972), Stephen Millhauser's *Edwin Mullhouse* (1972) – or even as autobiographical reflections of the authors themselves ('Ron Sukenick' is the main character in Sukenick's *Up*, Steve Katz appears as himself several times in *The Exaggerations of Peter Prince* (1968), and John Barth, balding and bespectacled, is by now a familiar element of many of his recent fictions). Metafictionists also frequently enjoy placing their readers in a situation once removed from the usual fictional stance by presenting and discussing the fictional work of an imaginary character (one immediately thinks of Gide's Edouard who is writing a book entitled *The Counterfeiters*); but contemporary fiction has produced an impressive variety of ingenious applications of the form – Nabokov's *Pale Fire*, Robert Coover's *The Universal Baseball Association* (1968), Raymond Federman's *Double or Nothing* (1971). These formal features, along with more blatant devices (such as having the narrator of a work engage the reader in a dialogue about the book he is reading), force us to consider the book we are reading *as an artifact*, undercutting the realistic impulses of the work and turning it into a 'self-reflexive' creation in that it not only takes art as its subject but tries to be its own subject.[5] To help clarify and illustrate the nature of the metafictionists' art, we will now examine an especially clear representative of the type.

Like all metafictions, *Willie Masters' Lonesome Wife* deals with writing and its own construction in a self-conscious manner.[6] The work proves to be especially complex and ambitious, however, because Gass brings to it not only a literary viewpoint, but a background in the philosophy of language (a subject in which Gass received his Ph.D. from Cornell). *Willie Masters'* deals with the building-blocks of fiction – words and concepts – in a more direct and sophisticated fashion than most other metafictions; it is more explicitly experimental than just about any other work of fiction which comes to mind and can serve as a virtual casebook of literary experimentalism, since it appropriates almost every experimental device used by writers in the past and suggests a good many possibilities for future development as well.

Interestingly enough, *Willie Masters'* is actually only one section of a much longer and more ambitious book which Gass worked on periodically during the 1960s. Before he abandoned the longer work as being impractical – it was originally to have dealt metafictionally with almost every Western narrative mode – two other short excerpts appeared, 'The Sugar Crock' and 'The Clairvoyant'. Like *Willie Masters'* these pieces are metafictional reflections on the nature of fiction-making, with self-conscious narrators pondering their relationship to their creations. They do not provide much background for *Willie Masters'*, although they introduce a few of the people who appear in the later work. Ella Bend, mentioned in passing in *Willie Masters'* (Red Section, 3), is the central character in both stories; we also meet Phil Gelvin, the unresponsive lover, as a rakish shoe salesman and 'Baby Babs' Masters herself, mentioned only in an unflattering comparison with another character ('fat in the belly like a sow, thick through his thighs like Willie Masters' Lonesome Wife'[8]).

Gass's basic intention in *Willie Masters'* is to build a work which will literally embody an idea he has elsewhere stated:

> It seems a country-headed thing to say that literature is language, that stories and the places and the people in them are merely made of words as chairs are made of smoothed sticks and sometimes of cloth or metal tubes. ... That novels should be made of words, and merely words, is shocking really. It's as thought you had discovered that your wife were made of rubber: the bliss of all those years, the fears ... from sponge.[9]

Gass never allows the reader to forget that literature is made of words and nothing else; here the words themselves are constantly called to our attention, their sensuous qualities emphasized in nearly every imaginable fashion. Indeed, the narrator of the work – the 'Lonesome Wife' of the title – is that lady language herself. Although the narrative has no real plot, the 'events' occur while Babs makes love to a particularly unresponsive lover named Gelvin – suggesting the central metaphor of the whole work: that a parallel exists – or should exist – between a woman and her lover, between the work of art and the artist, and between a book and its reader. The unifying metaphor is evident even before we open the book: on the front cover is a frontal photograph of a naked woman; on the back cover is a corresponding photograph of the back-side of the same woman. Gass, thus, invites one to enter his work of art – a woman made of words and paper – with the same sort of excitement, participation, and creative energy as one would enter a woman's body in sexual intercourse. The poet-narrator of Gass's short story, 'In the Heart of the Heart of the Country,' explains why the metaphor is appropriate when he says 'Poetry, like love, is – in and out – a physical caress'.[10] Babs puts it more bluntly: 'How close in the end is a cunt to a concept; we enter both with joy' (White Section, 4). Unfortunately, as we discover from Babs, all too frequently those who enter her do so without enthusiasm, often seemingly unaware that she is there at all.

As an appropriate extension of the metaphor, the central orderings of the work are very loosely the stages of sexual intercourse. In order to embody these parallels more closely, Gass uses the color and texture of the page to indicate subtle alterations in Babs' mind rather than relying on traditional chapter divisions and pagination. Even the page itself is not ordered in the usual linear fashion; instead, typographical variations establish a different visual order for each individual page. The first eight pages, for example, are printed on blue, thin paper with very little texture; these pages suggest the rather slow beginning of intercourse and Babs' playful, low-intensity thoughts and remembrances. The next twelve pages are thicker, more fully textured, and olive in color; this section, which is also the most varied in typography and graphics, corresponds to the rising stages of Babs' sexual excitement and her wildly divergent thoughts. Next follows eight red pages, with paper of the same texture as the first section, suggesting the climax of intercourse and the direct, intensely intellectual climax of Babs' thoughts about language. Finally, the fourth section uses a thick, high-gloss white paper like that of expensive magazines; these pages parallel Babs' empty, lonely feelings after intercourse when she realizes how inadequate the experience has been.

Reinforcing the feelings produced by color and texture are the photographs of Babs' nude body throughout the book. The first section opens with a picture of her upper torso and face, with her mouth eagerly awaiting the printer's phallic S-block. As the book continues, her face becomes less prominent and her body itself is emphasized. The photo at the beginning of the White Section (4) shows Babs curled up in fetal position, with her head resting upon her knees in a position indicating her sad, lonely feeling of resignation.

By far the most intricately developed device used by Babs to call attention to her slighted charms is the wide variety of type styles and other graphic devices with which she constructs herself.[11] One of the functions of the typographic changes – at least in the Blue and Red Sections (1 and 3) – is to indicate different levels of consciousness in Babs' mind. The opening Blue Section, for instance, is divided into three monologues printed mainly in separate, standard typefaces: roman, *italic*, and **boldface**. With these typographic aids, we can separate the strands of Babs' thoughts roughly as follows: the roman sections deal with her memories about the past and her concern with words; the *italic* sections indicate her memories of her first sexual encounter; and the **boldface** sections present her views about the nature of fundamental body processes and their relation to her aspirations for 'saintly love'. The Blue Section (1) can be read largely as an ordinary narrative, from top to bottom, left to right; the different typefaces, however, enable us to read each level of Babs' thought as a whole (by reading all the *italics* as a unit, then reading the **boldface** sections together). In the Olive and Red Sections (2 and 3), however, the graphics and typography destroy any linear response; Gass's aim in using such techniques is to achieve, like Joyce in

Ulysses, a freedom from many of the language's traditionally imposed rules of syntax, diction, and punctuation. To help emphasize the incredible versatility of human consciousness, Joyce relied (most notably in the 'Cyclops' and the 'Oxen of the Sun' episodes) on linguistic parody of earlier styles. Like his fellow Irishman, Laurence Sterne, Joyce was quite willing to use unusual typographic devices to help present his parodies. The devices – Sterne's blank and marbled pages, Joyce's headlines, question-and-answer format, the typographic formality of the 'Circe' episode – are foreign to the 'pure' storyteller but are available to a writer by the nature of books and print alone. Hugh Kenner has persuasively argued that Joyce hoped to liberate the narration of *Ulysses* from the typographical conventions of ordinary narratives and notes that the linear, one-dimensional method of presenting most books simply could not do justice to Joyce's expansive view of language: 'There is something mechanical, Joyce never lets us forget, about all reductions of speech to arrangement of 26 letters. We see him playing in every possible way with the spatial organization of printed marks.'[12] Kenner's remarks are perceptive, although he overstates his point when he says that Joyce experimented with printed marks 'in every possible way'. Gass's work, written fifty years later (in the Age of McLuhan – himself a Joyce scholar), carries the methods of typographic freedom to a much fuller development.

Gass's intentions in *Willie Masters'* can be compared to Joyce's in other ways. Like Joyce's presentation of a parodic history of English styles in the 'Oxen of the Sun' section, Gass's work is practically a history of typography. One of Gass's original intentions for *Willie Masters'* was to reproduce the first-edition typeface of any lines quoted from other works; this proved impractical, but type styles are found from nearly every period since Gutenberg, ranging from pre-printing-press calligraphy to old German gothic, Victorian typeface, and modern advertising boldface.

In addition to mimicking typefaces, Gass presents many other typographic conventions, often with parodic intent. One amusing example is found in the Olive Section (2) in which a one-act play is presented with all the rigid typographic formality usually found in a written transcription of a play. Babs provides asterisked comments and explanations about stage directions, costumes, and props. These remarks begin in very small type, but as the play progresses the typeface becomes larger and bolder. Gradually the number of asterisks before each aside becomes impossible to keep up with, and the comments themselves become so large that the text of the play is crowded off the page – to make room for a page containing only large, star-shaped asterisks. Gass thus pokes fun at a typographic convention in much the same way as John Barth did (with quotation marks) in 'The Menelaid'. Gass also uses the asterisks for reasons we do not usually expect – for their *visual appeal*. As Babs notes, 'these asterisks are the prettiest things in print' (Olive Section, 2).

Throughout the Olive and Red Sections (2 and 3) are examples of many other typographic variations: concrete poems, quoted dialogue inscribed in comic-book style, pages which resemble eye-charts, a Burroughs' newspaper 'cut-up,' and even the representations of coffee-stains.

In addition to drawing attention to how words look, Babs makes us examine the way we read words. In particular, she reminds us that the Western conventions of reading – left-to-right, top-to-bottom, from first page to last – are all merely conventions. Indeed, as Michael Butor has pointed out, even in Western cultures we are probably more familiar with books which do not rely on linear development (like dictionaries, manuals, or encyclopedias) than we realize: 'It is a misconception for us to think that the only kind of book are those which transcribe a discourse running from start to finish, a narrative or essay, in which it is natural to read by starting on the first page in order to finish on the last.'[13] In *Willie Masters'* especially in the Olive and Red Sections (2 and 3), Gass typographically makes ordinary reading impossible. In the Red Section (3), for example, Babs begins four or five narratives on a single page. In order to follow these largely unrelated narratives, each presented in a different typeface, we cannot begin at the top of the page and read down; instead, we are forced to follow one section from page to page and then go back to the beginning for the second narrative. Like Joyce who forces us to page backwards and forwards to check and cross-check references, Gass is taking advantage of what Kenner has termed 'the book as book',[14] the book's advantage lies in the fact that we can go backwards and forwards rather than being forced to move ever forward – as we are with a movie or a spoken narrative. The use of asterisks and marginal glosses indicates Gass's willingness to take advantage of the expressive possibilities of Babs' form as words on a printed page; he uses a typographical method to deflect the eye from its usual horizontal vertical network. Kenner has defined the effect in discussing the use of footnotes:

> The man who composes a footnote, and sends it to the printer along with his text, has discovered among the devices of printed language something analogous to counterpoint: a way of speaking in two voices at once, or of ballasting or modifying or even bombarding with exceptions his own discourse without interrupting it. It is a step in the direction of discontinuity: or organizing blocks of discourse simultaneously in space rather than consecutively in time.[15]

Especially in the Red Section (3) of *Willie Masters'*, our eye is never allowed to move easily on the page left-to-right and top-to-bottom; instead we turn from page to page, backwards and forwards, moving our eye up and down in response to footnotes or asterisks, from left to right to check marginal glosses, and occasionally 'standing back' to observe the organization of the page as a whole (as when we note that one is shaped like a Christmas tree, another like an eye-chart). The effect achieved here is remarkably close to Kenner's description of 'blocks of discourse' organized 'simultaneously in space rather than consecutively in time'.

The last – and most significant – method used by Babs to call attention to herself is also probably the least radical of her strategies. It is produced by the sensual, highly poetic quality of the language which she uses to create herself. This non-typographic method of focusing our attention on the words before us is often used by poets. In ordinary discourse and in the language of realistically motivated fiction, words do not usually call attention to themselves. The reason, as Valéry has explained, is that calling attention to words *as words* defeats the utility-function of ordinary language:

> Current, level language, the language that is used for a purpose, flies to its purpose, flies to its meaning, to its purely mental translation, and is lost in it ... Its form, its auditive aspect, is only a stage that the mind runs past without stopping. If pitch, if rhythm are present, they are there for the sake of sense, they occur only for the moment ... for meaning is its final aim.[16]

In ordinary discourse and in most fiction, words are used mainly as vehicles to refer us to a world (real or imaginary), and the words themselves remain invisible: as Babs says, 'The usual view is that you see through me, through what I am really – significant sound' (Red Section, 3). Babs, however, resembles the stereotyped woman in being vain about her physical qualities and resentful when she is used but not noticed. Babs shares with Valery (to whom Gass seems to owe much of his esthetics) the view that when words are placed in an esthetic context (as in a poem) their utility is sacrificed in favour of a unity of sound and sense:

> Again there is in every act of imagination a disdain of utility, and a glorious, free show of human strength; for the man of imagination dares to make things for no better reason than they please him – because he *lives*. And everywhere, again, he seeks out unity: in the world he unifies both sound and sense; ... between words and things he further makes a bond so that symbols seem to contain their objects.
> (Red Section, 3)

Like Barthelme's Snow White, who wishes 'there were some words in the world that were not the words, I always hear,'[17] Babs is bored with her own existence as she usually finds it: 'Why aren't there any decent words?' she exclaims at one point in the Blue Section (1); and in a footnote to the play in the Olive Section (2), she compares the 'dreary words' of ordinary

prose to ordinary action, which often loses all subtlety and beauty as it
strains to make itself understood to an audience 'all of whom are in the
second balcony.' Too often, claims Babs, writers – and readers – seem
unaware that words make up the body of all literature. At one point she
comments on the necessity of the writer accepting the medium in which
he works. The passage is typical of the lyrical, highly 'poetic' language
favored by Babs throughout her monologue:

> You are your body – you do not choose the feet you walk in – and the
> poet is his language. He sees the world, and words form in his eyes
> just like the streams and trees there. He feels everything verbally.
> Objects, passions, actions – I myself believe that the true kiss
> comprises a secret exchange of words, for the mouth was made by
> God to give form and sound to syllables; permit us to make, as our
> souls move, the magic music of names, for to say Cecilia, even in
> secret, is to make love.
>
> (Olive Section, 2)

These remarks not only direct our attention to the nature of the words on
the page but also reinforce the sexual parallels that have been suggested.
Even as we read these words, we have 'in secret' been making love – and
hopefully our response has been better than Gelvin's.

If poetry is the language which Babs is trying to realize herself in, she
admits that she rarely finds lovers appreciative enough to create her
properly. When Gelvin leaves, she says: 'he did not, in his address, at any
time, construct me. He made nothing, I swear. Empty I began, and empty I
remained' (White Section, 4). Indeed, she even observes some
inadequacies in our own response when she asks: 'Is that any way to make
love to a lady, a lonely one at that, used formerly to having put the
choicest portions of her privates flowered out in pots and vases' (Red
Section, 3). The main problem, as Babs observes, is simply that we have
forgotten how to make love appreciatively:

> You can't make love like that anymore – make love or manuscript. yet
> I have put my hand upon this body, here as no man ever has, and I
> have even felt my pencil stir, grow great with blood. But never has it
> swollen up in love. It moves in anger, always, against its paper.
>
> (Red Section, 3)

Today readers and writers alike approach lady language in the wrong
spirit. The pencil, the writer's phallic instrument of creation, grows great
nowadays only with blood, never with love. After intercourse, Babs is left
alone; she sits and ponders her fate: 'They've done, the holy office over,
and they turn their backs on me, I'm what they left, their turds in the

toilet. Anyway, I mustn't wonder why they don't return. Maybe I should put a turnstile in' (Red Section, 3).

Lonely and often ignored, Babs spends a good deal of time considering her own nature. Like many twentieth-century philosophers, she is very interested in the relationship between words and the world. In the Olive Section (2) she quotes (or quasi-quotes) John Locke's discussion of the way in which language develops from sense to impression to perception to concept. Locke shows the way our understanding sorts out our perceptions, and then concludes that we give proper names to things 'being such as much have an occasion to mark particularly'.[18] Babs has obviously taken Locke to heart, for she is constantly musing over the appropriateness of names in just this fashion. She wonders, for instance, why men do not assign proper names to various parts of their anatomy:

> They ought to name their noses like they named their pricks. Why not their ears too? – they frequently stick out. This is my morose Slav nose, Czar Nicholas. And these twins in my mirror, Rueben and Antony, they have large soft lobes ... If you had nice pleasant names for yourself all over, you might feel more at home, more among friends.
>
> (Blue Section, 1)

The passage shows that Babs confers upon language the same magical potency which Stephen Dedalus gave it in *A Portrait of the Artist as a Young Man*: she exalts the habit of verbal association into a principle for the arrangement of experience. Of course, she is right – words help arrange our experience and often exhibit the power to make us 'feel more at home, more among friends'. Naming something gives us a sort of power over it, just as we become the master of a situation by putting it into words. On the other hand, Babs confronts 'the terror of terminology' (Blue Section, 1) when she considers specific occasions when words fail to suggest what they are supposed to. As might be expected, Babs' example of an inappropriate word is drawn from a sexual context: 'Screws – they say *screw* – what an idea! did any of them ever? It's the lady who wooves and woggles. Nail – bag – sure – *nail* is nearer theirs' (Blue Section, 1).

Because of her envy of poetic language, Babs is especially interested in circumstances – as with the language of Shakespeare or any great poet – where words become something more than simply Lockean devices for calling to mind concepts. Babs thinks a good deal about the 'poetic ideal': the word which lies midway between the 'words of nature' (which constitute reality) and the words of ordinary language (which are nothing in themselves but arbitrary symbols which direct our minds elsewhere). Babs explains her view of what qualities ordinary words have:

What's in a name but letters, eh? and everyone owns *them* ... the
sound SUN or the figures S, U, N, are purely arbitrary modes of
recalling their objects, and they have the further advantage of being
nothing *per se*, for while the sun, itself, is large and orange and
boiling, the sight and the sound, SUN, is but a hiss drawn up through
the nose.

(Olive Section, 2)

At times Babs tries to exploit the sound of words at the expense of their
sense (or referential quality) in a way which may remind us of the
symbolist poets. For example, she takes one of her favorite words
('catafalque') and repeats it for several lines; she follows up by creating a
lovely-sounding but totally non-sensical poem: 'catafalque catafalque
neighborly mew/Ozenfant Valery leonine nu' (Olive Section, 2). What
Babs is obviously looking for, especially in creating herself, is the kind of
fusion of sound and sense found in the best poets. She says admiringly of
Shakespeare at one point that 'Now the language of Shakespeare ... not
merely recalls the cold notion of the thing, it expresses and becomes a part
of its reality, so that the sight and sound, SUN, in Shakespeare is warm
and orange and greater than the page it lies on' (Olive Section, 2). Nearly
all the strategies of *Willie Masters'* are closely related to the idea that in
literature words should not merely point somewhere else but should be
admired for themselves.

Willie Masters', then, is a remarkably pure example of metafiction. As we
watch 'imagination imagining itself imagine' (Blue Section, 1), we are
witnessing a work self-consciously create itself out of the materials at hand
– words. After Babs has endured still another unsatisfactory encounter
(with Gelvin – but possibly with us as well), she sums up some of the
problems she faces by quoting Dryden:

The rest I have forgot; for cares and time
Change all things, and untune my soul to rhyme.
I could have once sung down a summer's sun;
But now the chime of poetry is done;
My voice grows hoarse; I feel the notes decay,
As if the wolves had seen me first today

(White Section, 4)

Babs finishes the poem by adding a final, optimistic line of her own – she
will 'make a start against the darkness anyway'. In the concluding pages
Babs makes an eloquent plea for a new kind of language capable of
provoking the kind of loving response she so desires. Her plea concludes
her narrative and provides a brilliant example of the sort of language she
is calling for:

Then let us have a language worthy of our world, a democratic style where rich and well-born nouns can roister with some sluttish verb yet find themselves content and uncomplained of. We want a diction which contains the quaint, the rare, the technical, the obsolete, the old, the lent, the nonce, the local slang of the street, in neighborly confinement. Our tone should suit our time: uncommon quiet dashed with common thunder. It should be as young and quick and sweet and dangerous as we are. Experimental and expansive ... it will give new glasses to new eyes, and put those plots and patterns down we find our modern lot in. Metaphor must be its god now gods are metaphors ... It's not the languid pissing prose we got, we need; but poetry, the human muse, full up, erect and on the charge, impetuous and hot and loud and wild like. Messalina going to the stews or those damn rockets streaming headstrong into stars.

(White Section, 4)

As the best metafiction does, *Willie Masters' Lonesome Wife* forces us to examine the nature of fiction-making from new perspectives. If Babs (and Gass) have succeeded, our attention has been focused on the act of reading words in a way we probably have not experienced before. The steady concern with the *stuff* of fiction, words, makes Gass's work unique among metafictions which have appeared thus far. At the end of the book, we encounter a reminder from Gass stamped onto the page: 'YOU HAVE FALLEN INTO ART – RETURN TO LIFE.' When we do return to life, we have, hopefully, a new appreciation – perhaps even love – of that lonesome lady in Gass's title.

Notes

1. JEAN ROUSSET, '*Madame Bovary*: Flaubert's Anti-Novel,' in *Madame Bovary*, ed., PAUL DE MAN (New York: W.W. Norton, 1965), p. 439.

2. WILLIAM GASS, 'Philosophy and the Form of Fiction,' *Fiction and the Figures of Life* (New York: Random House, 1972), p. 25. Two critics who have recently used the term are ROBERT SCHOLES, 'Metafiction,' '*Iowa Review*, 1 (Fall 1970), 100–15, and NEIL SCHMITZ, ROBERT COOVER and the Hazards of Metafiction,' *Novel*, 29 (Spring 1974), 210–19.

3. Among significant additions to the list would be STEVE KATZ's *The Exaggerations of Peter Prince* (1968), EARL M. RAUCH's *Dirty Pictures from the Prom* (1969), RON SUKENICK's *The Death of the Novel and Other Stories* (1969), RAYMOND FEDERMAN's *Double or Nothing* (1971), ALAN FRIEDMAN's *Hermaphrodeity* (1972), STEPHEN MILLHAUSER's *Edwin Mullhouse* (1972), GILBERT SORRENTINO's *Imaginative Qualities of Actual Things* (1972), RON SUKENICK's *Out* (1973), and JERRY ANDREWS' *The Story of Harold* (1974).

4. Gass, p. 24.

5. Roger Shattuck, 'The Art of Stillness,' *The Banquet Years* (New York: Random House, 1968), p. 328.

6. William Gass, *Willie Masters' Lonesome Wife* (designed by Lawrence Levy and photographed by Burton L. Rudman) was first published in *Tri-Quarterly Supplement*, 2 (1968); it was re-issued by Alfred A. Knopf in 1971. All the special effects of the original edition (differences in page texture and color) are not present in the Knopf edition. Although neither edition has pagination, the book is divided into four clearly distinct sections or chapters. In the *Tri-Quarterly* edition these sections are easily distinguished by differed page colors; in the Knopf edition the first three sections cannot be distinguished by color or texture (the fourth section has the same white glossy finish as the first edition), but the divisions are still fairly evident: the first section (the 'Blue Section') ends with the picture of the nude woman with the caption, 'OO-OOO-OO my Mister Handsome how could you?; the second section ('Olive Section') consists largely of the closet drama and concludes on the page before the appearance of the picture of the woman's leg and representation of the coffee stain – which opens the third section ('Red'), concluded in both editions when the white, glossy fourth section begins. References here indicate both the section color and number (the Blue Section is 1, the Olive 2, the Red 3, and the White 4).

7. William Gass, 'The Clairvoyant,' *Location*, 1, 2 (1964), 59–66; and 'The Sugar Crock,' *Art and Literature*, 9 (1966), 158–71.

8. Gass, 'The Clairvoyant,' p. 62.

9. William Gass, 'The Medium of Fiction,' *Fiction and the Figures of Life*, p. 27.

10. William Gass, 'In the Heart of the Heart of the Country,' *In the Heart of the Heart of the Country and Other Stories* (New York: Harper and Row, 1968), p. 202.

11. Among contemporary works of fiction which have used typographic experimentation, the most interesting are Michael Butor's *Mobile* (1963), Steve Katz's *The Exaggeration of Peter Prince* (1968), Raymond Federman's *Double or Nothing* (1971), and Kobo Abe's *The Box Man* (1974).

12. Hugh Kenner, *Flaubert, Joyce, and Beckett: the Stoic Comedians* (London: W.H. Allen, 1964), p. 47.

13. Michael Butor, 'The Book as Object,' *Inventor* (New York: Simon and Schuster, 1968), p. 44.

14. Kenner, p. 47; Butor refers to basically the same thing with his term 'the book as object'.

15. Kenner, p. 40.

16. Paul Valery, 'Discourse on the Declamation of Verse,' *Selected Writings* (New York: New Directions, 1964), p. 157.

17. Donald Barthelme, *Snow White* (New York: Atheneum, 1967), p. 6.

18. John Locke, 'An Essay Concerning Human Understanding,' (Book II, Chapter XI, Section 9), *Selections* (Chicago: Univ. of Chicago Press, 1956), p. 144.

11 'Metafiction, the Historical Novel and Coover's *THE PUBLIC BURNING*'*

RAYMOND A. MAZUREK

Raymond Mazurek's analysis of *The Public Burning* clearly influenced Linda Hutcheon's account of Postmodernism in *A Poetics of Postmodernism* (see section 2 of this volume). According to Mazurek, Coover's novel is one in a wave of new historical novels, most of which appeared in the 1970s, which aimed to challenge the empirical concepts of history, and to conceive of history instead as a kind of discourse. In this respect, Mazurek's analysis can be compared to Onega's 'British Historiographic Metafiction' (Chapter 5) which identifies the same tendency in the British novel of the 1980s. Mazurek's interest is in the juxtaposition of metafictional techniques with historical content as a way of staging a paradox in what he calls the 'structuralist model of history': that history is at the same time 'real' and 'discursive'. This model of history, brought to light by commentators such as Hayden White during the 1970s in North America (see Part Two), is the non-fictional correlative of historiographic metafiction. Taken together, these attitudes to history represent an assault on the boundary between history and fiction. In this context, Mazurek claims that *The Public Burning* brings into focus the textual form of history. Thus the years of Nixon's presidency are used by Coover as a way of blurring the distinction between the empirical events of history and their representation in discourses such as novels and newspapers, thereby foregrounding certain problems of historical interpretation.

Robert Coover's *The Public Burning* (1977), a fictionalized account of the Rosenberg case told largely from the point of view of Richard Nixon, combines metafictional techniques with a critique of American history and ideology. Among the many recent examples of serious historical fiction, Coover's novel seems unusual in the extent of its satire and the bitterness of its vision. As the often perplexed and sometimes hostile response of readers and critics indicates, *The Public Burning* is an 'explosive object'.[1] Whatever our difficulties in responding to Coover's text, it is well worth

---

*Reprinted from Mazurek, Raymond A., 'Metafiction, the Historical Novel and Coover's *The Public Burning*', *Critique:Studies in Modern Fiction* 23, 3 (1982), 29–42.

examining, for it reveals the problems confronted by a new kind of historical novel that has emerged in recent years.

The 'major novels of the last decade or so,' a critic has noted, 'have tended strongly toward the apparently worn-out form of the historical novel'; yet the novels by such writers as Pynchon, Barth, Garcia-Marquez, and Fowles, as well as Coover, 'are not novels based upon the empirical concepts of history that dominated Western thought in the nineteenth century'.[2] What is 'new' in the new historical novel is its treatment of history as a form of discourse. Extending the metafictional critique of the realistic novel, novels like *The Public Burning* imply not only that the realistic novel is a series of conventional signs masking as reality, but that history itself depends on conventions of narrative, language, and ideology in order to present an account of 'what really happened'. The new historical novel, then, differs from the traditional historical novel defined by Lukács, which aims to present a 'total' model of a society undergoing historical change, and which avoids reminding the reader of its limitations as a textual version of history.[3]

The example of *The Public Burning*, however, suggests that the metafictional historical novel cannot completely efface the problems of other historical narratives. Insofar as it is an historical novel, *The Public Burning* makes use of actual historical materials, and its irony is often predicated on the reader's awareness of those documents. Moreover, its treatment of history is not merely parodic, for *The Public Burning* is built upon a basic paradox; while presenting history as discursive, it also presents a model of the history within which Nixon and the Rosenbergs act and are trapped. The bridge between the metafictional techniques and historical content of Coover's novel is provided by its criticism of American ideology: by emphasizing the limits of historical discourse in the America of the 1950s, it points to the limits of American ideology and the use of language as power.

The model of history that *The Public Burning* embodies is a structuralist model: history becomes the story of cultural signs and ideological constrictions which appear autonomous and self-generating. Indeed, *The Public Burning* and other metafictional historical novels bear a considerable similarity to the 'metahistorical' analysis of history by recent theorists.[4] While such parallels suggest that Coover's novel deserves more serious treatment than it has received, and while structuralist approaches to history are certainly productive in an age saturated by information, *The Public Burning* is beset by the dilemma which has troubled structuralism: to the degree that history is analyzed only in terms of discourse, historical change – the processes of history itself – cannot be accounted for. History, we are reminded, 'is *not* a text, for it is fundamentally non-narrative and nonrepresentational,' notwithstanding 'the proviso that history is inaccessible to us except in textual form'.[5] Perhaps the irreducible otherness of history, the resistance of the complex events and practices of human existence to being completely reduced to narrative form, makes the analysis of history as discourse so powerful an insight, capable of pointing to the gaps in any given historical account.

The Public Burning repeatedly reminds us of the textual form through which history is mediated, but when it needs to evoke the social situation within which historical narratives operate, it instead offers further, increasingly outlandish, 'rewritings' of historical events. Obviously, a novel cannot be expected to provide a coherent historical argument; however, the aesthetic problems of *The Public Burning* are closely related to its historical incoherence. The failure of its political critique of recent American history to coincide with its almost obsessive exploitation of the possibility of treating history as discourse is what makes *The Public Burning* so exasperating a novel for many readers.

The Public Burning has achieved notoriety primarily by its extensive – and rather free – use of actual people, documents, and events, which has seemed particularly disturbing to critics who would prefer a clear distinction between 'fact' and 'fiction'.[6] In particular, the use of Richard Nixon has provoked controversy, and although the most striking feature of the novel, Coover's Nixon presents only about half the text. Structurally, the novel consists of about thirty chapters divided into a prologue, four main sections ('Wednesday-Thursday,' 'Friday Morning,' 'Friday Afternoon,' and 'Friday Evening'), and an Epilogue. Three interruptions or 'Intermezzos,' written either in verse or as dramatic scenes, separate the four main sections. Every second chapter is presented from 'Nixon's' point of view. The other sections use a variety of styles to depict the global and national events leading to and including the execution of the Rosenbergs. A mass of journalistic detail with obvious sources in the media of the fifties is presented, though with a parodic exaggeration most clearly embodied in the fantastic activities of Uncle Sam. Sam, a garrulous, mean, arrogant creature with supernatural powers, is Coover's strangest creation, combining the crudest American humor with the attributes of Superman and other comic-book heroes. A shape-changer who 'incarnates' himself into those he chooses to become President, and whose speech is a motley of American clichés, Sam is, to a degree, Protean; however, the possibilities which Sam represents prove to be narrowly circumscribed. Beneath his apparent plurality, Sam represents a one-dimensional American ideology, a body of ideas and practices which (at least in the world of Coover's text) have established hegemony within American society.

As Coover presents it, that ideology includes a combination of paranoiac anti-communism and an almost child-like belief in American superiority. The Rosenbergs are to be burned in the electric chair in Times Square for being infected with the spirit of the 'Phantom,' the dark power that opposes Uncle Sam throughout the world. Sentenced under a law that reads that 'any man who is dominated by demonic spirits to the extent that he gives voice to apostasy is to be subject to the judgment upon sorcerers and wizards,' the Rosenbergs are to be publicly executed for reasons that are 'theatrical, political, whimsical.'[7] The Rosenbergs, entrapped within the categories of Uncle Sam's world, are the victims of an ideological closure of political discourse. When Justice William O. Douglas creates a temporary crisis by issuing a stay of execution, Uncle Sam appears to Douglas to accuse him of treason, only to disappear when the janitor enters the room, leaving Douglas, symbolically, talking to himself. Similarly, in the most interesting of the 'Intermezzos,' Eisenhower and Ethel Rosenberg appear on stage together in a confrontation reminiscent of absurdist drama and the cartoons of Jules Feiffer: Eisenhower's refusal of clemency is interspersed with Ethel's plea for life, but both characters speak monologues. Neither succeeds in addressing the other: Ethel is not given the opportunity; the President, Coover's stage directions indicate, does not 'even acknowledge her presence on the same stage' (247).

Coover's Nixon is in a better situation than Ethel Rosenberg, but the difference is one of degree, not of kind. He, too, is hardly 'acknowledged on the stage' by Eisenhower and the President's symbolic surrogate, Uncle Sam. Nixon's narrative presents his repeated attempt to overcome his position as outsider and to arrive at the center, even to become the author, of history. Despite the constant irony produced by our awareness of the identity of the speaker, the 'Nixon' sections of the novel closely resemble traditional first-person narrative. But Nixon's grandiose hopes, fears, and plots – as well as his surprisingly sentimental moments – serve only to emphasize the failure of the egocentric world view often implied in the traditional novel. Nixon's hope to change history only reminds us of his insignificance. Coover's choice of Nixon as metaphor seems related to Nixon's inflated significance in the popular press; however, Coover alters Nixon's conventional image by attempting to conjoin Nixon and the Rosenbergs as victims.

Coover's Nixon is a victim of Uncle Sam's ideology as well as one of its executioners. Like the reader, he approaches the Rosenbergs with a post-Watergate consciousness; he identifies with the Rosenbergs (especially Julius) as 'the Generation of the Great Depression' (143) and as fellow victims of American history: 'Our purposes, after all, were much the same: to convince a stubbornly suspicious American public – our judges – of our innocence. And we *were* innocent' (309). Nixon is purportedly speaking about the accusations which led to the Checkers speech, but the words Coover gives him have a larger resonance. Coover's re-environing of history juxtaposes Watergate, the Rosenberg case, and the sense of American history as conflict so characteristic of the Vietnam era. Though

the noisy demonstrators outside Coover's White House and in his Times
Square are numerous, much of the conflict occurs within Nixon himself
while he attempts to tell his story. Oddly enough, the technique becomes
part of a significant refusal to join in the 'scapegoat' interpretation of
American history (i.e., 'throw the bum out, so we can get on with the
bicentennial') that seemed so common at the time Coover's novel
appeared.[8] Instead of attacking or excusing Nixon as an individual,
Coover focuses on the ideology that formed Nixon, in a context which
foregrounds the problematic (and rhetorical) nature of historical
interpretation.

Many of the discussions of the limitations of historical interpretation in
The Public Burning focus on the presentation of current history by the
media. In Chapter 10, 'Pilgrimage to *The New York Times*,' the disjunction
between the concepts and descriptions which become 'news' and the
reality they evoke is repeatedly stressed. *The Times* is described as a group
of sacred tablets, an institution to which millions make their morning
pilgrimage, including Julius Rosenberg:

> Often enough ... he has discovered himself here on these slabs, or
> something they said was himself ('the accused,' they call him, but the
> words keep melting and blurring on him, and what he sees there is
> 'the accursed'), but he has not recognized his own image, grown
> gigantesque, eviscerated, unseeing: it's like looking into some weird
> funhouse mirror that stretches one's shape so thin you can see right
> through it. He used to think that if he could just find his way onto
> these tablets everything would be all right, but now he knows this is
> impossible: nothing living ever appears here at all, only presumptions
> ... within which a reasonable and orderly picture of life can unfold.
> No matter how crazy it is.
>
> (192)

Julius' nightmarish experience of seeing 'himself' in print illustrates that
Coover's attack is not merely on the limits of historical narrative but on
the ideological function of the ' orderly and reasonable picture of life' *The
Times* presents. The presentation of history ('the times') as news, then, is
the occasion of Coover's most sustained discussion of historical narrative.

The Times, as an institution which defines the 'facts' in a spirit of
'objectivity,' is satirized, and its readers are compared to 'mystics' for
whom

> the Spirit, annunciating reality, displaces it, and the tangible world
> dissolves even as it is being proclaimed ... People press themselves
> against the Father's Day advertisements and crisis tabulations, fail to
> notice the people leaping out of buildings, girls being raped on

subway platforms ... cannot see the crowds gathering outside the
Supreme Court building, the writing on the subway walls:
OBJECTIFICATION IS THE PRACTICE OF ALIENATION'

(194)

Using the language of Hegel ('Spirit,' 'objectification,' 'alienation'), *The
Public Burning* suggests that uncritical acceptance of the reality
'annunciated' as a picture of 'the times' in the fifties becomes a way of not
knowing those parts of reality that are excluded from the news. Thus, the
apparent 'objectivity' of *The Times* conceals an idealism which mistakes its
own language for reality and is unable to recognize the alienation which
results.

The process of 'objectification' creates a monolithic version of history
which has a hegemonic function, regardless of the intentions of those who
write the news. Listing questions like 'Is Alger Hiss a Communist? Is Joe
McCarthy a Fascist? Is Justice Douglas a Traitor?' Coover notes that what
'matters is: where are such questions being asked?' (195). While the
twentieth century has come 'to accept the objective reality of time and thus
of process – history does not repeat ... and out in that flow all such
assertions may be true, false, inconsequential, or all at the same time,' *The
Times* reifies this 'time-process into something hard and – momentarily
anyway – durable' (195). The repeated presentation of predications which
make 'Hiss' equivalent to 'Communist' transforms them into
unquestioned truths. The act of selection – the ritual of inclusion and
exclusion which constitutes the news – belies objectivity: ' "Objectivity" is
in spite of itself a willful program for the stacking of perceptions ...
Conscious or not, *The New York Times* statutory functions as a charter of
moral and social order ... defining meaningful actions merely by showing
them' (191). The 'objectivity' of *The Times* creates a silent reinforcement of
the hegemony of American ideology in a world where true mimesis is
impossible.

Most of the historiographical comments in *The Public Burning* are made
by Coover's Nixon; much of the plot consists of his belated attempt to
'save' the Rosenbergs after he discovers the ambiguity of historical
interpretation in the fantastic nature of their trial. Absorbed by the
numerous parallels between his life and those of the Rosenbergs, Coover's
Nixon sees through the efforts of the prosecutor 'to make what might later
seem like nothing more than a series of overlapping fictions cohere into a
convincing semblance of historical continuity and logical truth' (122).
Endowed by Coover with a considerable capacity for reflection and
fantasy, Nixon repeatedly described history as writing and as theater.
Everyone in the trial was, he notes, 'behaving like actors ... in a play'
(117). After a detailed discussion of the trial, Nixon asks: 'What was fact,
what intent, what was framework, what was essence? Strange, the impact

of History, the grip it had on us, yet it was nothing but words. Accidental accretions for the most part, leaving most of the story out' (136).

Nixon replaces Sam's and Eisenhower's Manichean interpretation of American history as a 'War Between the Sons of Light and the Sons of Darkness' (149) with the familiar idea of unbounded American open-endedness and freedom: any 'rewriting' of the 'script' of history seems possible to him:

> And then I realized what it was that had been bothering me: that sense that everything was somehow inevitable, as though it had been scripted out in advance. But bullshit! There were no scripts ... no final scenes, there was just *action*, and then more *action*! Maybe in Russia History had a plot because one was being laid on, but not here – *that was what freedom was all about.*
>
> (362)

Nixon, who once aspired to be a playwright, sees himself as the potential writer of an otherwise patternless history – although in the world of *The Public Burning*, a plot is clearly 'being laid on', a structure of cultural relationships in which Nixon is contained. Staring at the mass of paper strewn around his office, Coover's Nixon characterizes the Rosenbergs as trapped by 'the zeal for pattern. For story. And they'd been seduced by this. If they could say to hell with History, they'd be home free' (305). To some extent, Nixon functions to place the Rosenbergs, too, in an ironic perspective. However, Coover's irony falls much more heavily on Nixon, who is unable to transcend the idea that history is unbounded discourse and free, self-determined action. Although he is bounded by the cultural ideology *The Public Burning* describes, his version of history is a private one, in which he is the central character.

Armed with his ironic conception of history, Coover's Nixon goes to Sing Sing to try to persuade the Rosenbergs to confess to something, in return for having their persecutors partly exposed and their lives saved. Having discovered that historical truth is relative and that identity involves role-playing, Nixon attempts to play all roles simultaneously, to stand on both sides of the conflict. The result, if read too literally, is perhaps the most tasteless scene in American literature, as Nixon attempts to seduce Ethel Rosenberg. In the process, Nixon discovers that he shares the other American history, which he envisions as the dream of the common man who was 'America itself' but who 'awoke – we both awoke – to the nightmare of poverty, neglect, and despair' (438). Yet he achieves these insights while his 'tongue roamed behind Ethel's incisors' (438) in a sophomoric rediscovery of sex.

In this passage, Coover's style oscillates between black humor and an attempt to reconcile the novel's oppositions. On one level, Nixon's insight into the 'other America' is what might be called a 'structuralist epiphany'.[10] Coover's Nixon attains insight into the common humanity of his opponent by seeing the opposition's view as a script, a possible and plausible version of reality which he is capable of sharing. On another level, Nixon is satirized: he is unaware of the lust which has motivated his trip, of the necessity of choice, and of the choices, within the social structure, he has already made.

Nixon's failure is dramatized through the somewhat over-explicit satire of the novel's final chapters, where Ethel becomes a symbol of resistance. Nixon is spirited away to Times Square (where only one version of time is permitted) with his pants down to speak before the assembled mob and is eventually raped by Uncle Sam, who literally 'incarnates' himself in Richard to symbolize his selection for eventual Presidency, Ethel, we learn, has managed to write 'I am a scamp' on Richard's posterior, and like the Rosenberg trial, she refuses to die easily. When she was not killed by the first charge of electricity, her body flaps defiantly in the breeze at the end of the execution, as it is subjected to jolt after jolt.

If one cannot quite reconcile this Ethel with the Ethel of the seduction scene or the cynical Nixon who mouths cliches to save himself in Times Square with the thoughtful Nixon who dissects the trial, the problem is rooted in Coover's technique. At one point, Coover's Nixon reflects on the way associations from the previous night's dream 'opened up the gates and flooded the syntax routes. ... it could be fun, if you didn't do it too often' (181). 'Flooding the syntax routes' is an appropriate metaphor for the structure of *The Public Burning*, which simultaneously presents the same action from various points of view and in multiple literary styles. The use of multiple, even contradictory, narrative units appears to be characteristic of Coover's metafiction; in Coover's story, 'The Baby Sitter,' he 'presents not only what "does happen" ... but all the things which *could* happen'.[11] The result is a spatialization that denies the validity of a single sequence which constitutes 'what happened' and makes any single linear track or implication of the narrative difficult to follow to its logical end.

In *The Public Burning*, such technique acquires a specific thematic function in the attack on the 'single vision' which sentenced the Rosenbergs. Coover's Eisenhower, an architect of that vision, claims in the poem that comprises the second 'Intermezzo' that 'the one capital offense against freedom' is 'a lack of staunch faith' (156). Eisenhower's faith denies the multiplicity of language; in Nixon's narrative, Ike is characterized as an ignorant cowboy who is unable to see that words, especially words like 'freedom,' 'sincerity,' and 'decency' are not simple and unambiguous (230). Similarly, the 'Phantom,' Uncle Sam's and Ike's enemy, is described as the 'Creator of Ambiguities' (336) and seems a reflection of America's lack of critical self-awareness, its insistence on an unambiguous, linear story. Coover's Nixon, on the other hand, is self-conscious in several senses: he is the 'bumbling' Nixon, an inept outsider; reflective and ironic, he seems almost aware of himself as a character in a fiction. He is a Nixon aware of himself as Nixon, a post-Watergate scapegoat, a series of media clichés, and a source of much of the novel's humor.

Often, as in the Times Square scenes, the reflective irony of *The Public Burning* is displaced by slapstick. Even here, the dreary repetitiveness which drives readers away from the novel's 'public' chapters is thematic, related to the monolithic tendencies that characterize Uncle Sam's America. The overwhelming bitterness of Coover's vision finds little that is affirmative in post-war America. The mob assembled in Times Square is there, for the most part, to witness the burning of the Rosenbergs as the ultimate media event. Entertained by the execution jokes of the Marx Brothers and the singing of the Mormon Tabernacle Choir, they wait for the sacrificial killing through which, they privately hope, their individual resentments can be purged. Like the Supreme Court Justices who slide in the dung of the Republican elephant on stage, the reader is not excused but forced to confront the dreck of American culture.

At times, *The Public Burning* 'tests one's capacity for embarrassment rather too cruelly'.[12] The characters 'are shaped almost exclusively by the domination-subjugation pairing',[13] brought to consciousness in the text itself. Inserted between parodies of Jack Benny and Charlie McCarthy, Coover notes:

> ... America laughs. At much the same things everybody laughs at
> everywhere: sex, death, danger, the enemy, the inevitable, all the
> things that hurt about growing up, something that Americans
> especially, suddenly caught with the world in their hands, are loath to
> do. What makes them laugh hardest, though, are jokes about sexual
> inadequacy – a failure of power – and the cruder the better, for
> crudity recalls their childhood for them: the Golden Age.
>
> (450)

In passages like this, *The Public Burning* recalls the 'epic theater' of Brecht, simultaneously presenting a caricatured reduction of reality and a comment on the significance of that reduction.[14]

Even some of the novel's most outlandish scenes are complex, involving the ironic juxtaposition of discordant texts. Nixon's appearance with his pants down before the assembled mob in Times Square brings together the 'public' and ' private' narratives at a moment when, for Nixon, both worlds threaten to disintegrate. We are given a bewildered Nixon's private thoughts as he fights 'to drag myself back to myself, my old safe self, which was – who knows? – maybe not even a self at all, my frazzled mind reaching out for the old catchwords, the functional code words of the profession' (471). Simultaneously, we are given in italics the 'code words,' the empty rhetoric which he desperately employs.

The scene is an obvious reference to Watergate, to the actual Nixon's public entrapment in verbal duplicity with his 'pants down,' but the speech he gives is also a parody of the 'Checkers' speech. Many of the 'code words' that Coover's Nixon utters echo directly from the famous televised address in which Nixon defended himself against accusations that he used a campaign fund for personal purposes. In 'Checkers' Nixon speaks repeatedly of the 'smears' against his reputation and of how difficult it is 'to come before a Nation-wide audience and bare your life, as I have done.'[15] Coover's Nixon, ass to the crowd, feels Ethel's lipstick inscription on his posterior and declaims (verbatim from 'Checkers'): '*I know that this is not the last of the smears!*' (476), and eventually suggests '*that under the circumstances, everybody here tonight should come before the American people and bare himself as I have done!*' (482). Similarly in 'checkers,' Nixon asks that Stevenson and Sparkman come before the people with their personal financial histories and claims that 'if they don't it will be an admission that they have something to hide.' At the end, Coover's Nixon asks the crowd for '*support*' in a number of high-minded patriotic endeavors, finally exhorting '*everyone tonight to step forward ... and drop his pants for America!*' (482). 'Checkers' also ends with an appeal for support, for telegrams saying whether or not Senator Nixon should stay on the Republican ticket.

The parallels between the two texts can be extended, suggesting that 'Checkers' is a source for *The Public Burning* as a whole. In the actual speech, Nixon accused Stevenson of reducing the Communist threat to a matter of 'phantoms among ourselves,' thus providing Coover with a name for the novel's principle of opposition. Moreover, 'Checkers' is famous for Nixon's sentimental personal narrative, in which he relates his 'Horatio Alger' past – and simultaneously draws attention to himself in doing so, parenthetically noting 'this is unprecedented in American politics' (a claim Coover's Nixon echoes – 474). Nixon's actual text thus invokes itself as unique at precisely the point at which it is most clearly circumscribed within the limits of a traditional American ideology (reinforcing Coover's theme). In 'Checkers' Nixon speaks of his work in exposing Hiss, who (like the Rosenbergs) allegedly sold atomic 'secrets' to the Russians. In a classic example of implying guilt by association, Nixon claims that his primary work has been 'exposing the Administration, the communism in it, the corruption in it.' The abrupt insertion of grammatically parallel elements in a speech which repeatedly notes the necessity of getting down to the simple 'facts' – of telling the whole, literal
truth – recalls Coover's analysis of history as a rhetorical 'force-field maker' in Chapter 10. The actual Nixon provides a more telling example of the reification of history in political language than any Coover could invent.

Coover's use of the 'Checkers' speech points to the central idea of *The Public Burning*: the attempt to move the 'exposed' Nixon of Watergate (the Nixon who has become our cliché) from the contest of a 'tragic' personal mistake and make him representative of an American ideology gone wrong. As his use of 'Checkers' illustrates, Coover tries to get inside the rhetoric of that ideology, using the metaphors it takes so literally and expanding them to the point of the absurd. *The Public Burning*, then, tries to make the hegemonic use of that rhetoric, dramatized in the victimization of the Rosenbergs *and* Nixon, into an appropriate metaphor for contemporary America.

Unfortunately, the process becomes clear only when we can stop and look at it in slow motion; too often, *The Public Burning* simply bombards us with the metaphors it seeks to distance us from. Coover's portrayal assumes the reader's familiarity with the rhetoric of the fifties. Moreover, the attempt to get inside that rhetoric is not matched by an attempt to evoke the society within which it functions. The search for an opposing principle to Sam is quite unresolved, even with William O. Douglas (to whom the novel is dedicated), the horde of demonstrators who recurrently appear (but who seem almost incidental), and Ethel's symbolic death. To some extent, the Rosenbergs themselves present an alternative to repression – yet, like all Coover's characters except Nixon, they appear as caricatures. Nixon, his attempt to 'rewrite' history, and the narrator's comments on historical representation become the focus of the novel and, oddly, the source of a critical perspective in Coover's America, as the analysis of history as text displaces an analysis of history.

The novel, then, leaves the reader with a confusion of response. The Ethel–Nixon scene, its most unforgettable, points in every direction at once. The comic employment of the Rosenbergs' situation momentarily included seems inappropriate to the novel's generally left-liberal politics. Difficult to assimilate on the level of content, it is best understood as part of Coover's treatment of history as text, which serves as an ironic comment on the Manichean tendencies within Coover's own myth (or anti-myth) of America. The difficulty with *The Public Burning* remains the collision between its metafictional technique and its political content. One cannot, finally, make Richard Nixon and Ethel Rosenberg embrace. The more specific the political impulse of the text, the more difficult the dramatization of that purpose through metafiction – otherwise, politics becomes reduced to the celebration of liberation in the 'openness' of the text, in the act of writing itself. *The Public Burning* is a novel in which Coover has taken great risks, one which helps to define the tension between the presentation of history as writing and the writing of history.

Notes

1. THOMAS R. EDWARDS, 'Real People, Mythic History,' *New York Times Book Review*, 14 August 1977, p. 9.

2. ROBERT SCHOLES, *Fabulation and Metafiction* (Urbana: Univ. of Illinois Press, 1979), p. 205.

3. GEORGE LUKÁCS, *The Historical Novel*, trans. HANNAH and STANLEY MITCHELL (Boston: Beacon Press, 1963), pp. 90–92.

4. See HAYDEN WHITE, *Tropics of Discourse* (Baltimore: Johns Hopkins Univ. Press, 1978), especially pp. 1–23; also, the bibliographical essay in *The Writing of History; Literary Form and Historical Understanding*, eds. ROBERT H. CANARY and HENRY KOZICKI (Madison: Univ. of Wisconsin Press, 1978), pp. 151–58.

5. FREDRIC JAMESON, *The Political Unconscious: Narrative as a Socially Symbolic Act* (Ithaca: Cornell Univ. Press, 1981), p. 82.

6. See NORMAN PODHORETZ, 'Uncle Sam and the Phantom,' *Saturday Review*, 4 (17 September 1977), 34. While Coover's earlier novel, *The Universal Baseball Association, Inc. J. Henry Waugh Prop* (New York: New American Library, 1971), also presents history as a 'game' similar to fiction and myth, it is less clearly an historical novel than *The Public Burning*.

7. ROBERT COOVER, *The Public Burning* (New York: Viking Press, 1977), p. 3. Subsequent references are to this edition.

8. See ROBERT SCHEER, *American After Nixon* (New York: McGraw-Hill, 1974), pp. xi–xxii.

9. Coover's analysis of the trial appears to draw heavily on MIRIAM and WALTER SCHNEIR, *Invitation to an Inquest* (Garden City: Doubleday, 1965), the standard study of the trial.

10. See ROBERT SCHOLES, *Structuralism in Literature* (New Haven: Yale Univ. Press, 1974), p. 192.

11. JEROME KLINKOWITZ, *Literary Disruptions: The Making of a Post-Contemporary Fiction* (Urbana: Univ. of Illinois Press, 1975), p. 17; also Coover, 'The Baby Sitter,' in *Pricksongs and Descants* (New York: New American Library, 1969), pp. 206–39.

12. ROBERT TOWERS, 'Nixon's Seventh Crisis', *New York Review of Books*, 24 (29 September 1977), 9.

13. Towers, p. 9.

14. See WALTER BENJAMIN, *Understanding Brecht*, trans. ANNA BOSTOCK (London: NLB, 1977), pp. 1–11.

15. 'Text of Senator Nixon's Speech,' *Washington Post*, 24 September 1952, Sect. 1, p. 4. Subsequent quotation is from this text.

12 The novel, illusion, and reality: the paradox of omniscience in *The French Lieutenant's Woman**

FREDERICK M. HOLMES

John Fowles's *The French Lieutenant's Woman* is often seen as the first British historiographic metafiction (see Onega in Part Two of this volume), though it could be argued that certain Modernist novels – Joyce's *Ulysses* or Woolf's *Orlando* – were exploring the paradoxes of fictional history long before. This study of Fowles's 'modern novel about a Victorian novel' analyses the way that fictionality can be exposed without being destroyed, the interweaving of historical and literary sources, and the paradoxes generated by a godlike author who attempts to bestow freedom on his own characters. The analysis illustrates many of the characteristics considered definitive of metafiction by the essays in this volume, notably the ability of a novel to become what Barth calls 'a metaphor for itself' (Part Three) and the persistent contradiction of history as real and discursive, as advanced by Hutcheon, Onega and White (Part Two).

Some readers have found *The Magus* more compelling than *The French Lieutenant's Woman*,[1] even though the latter is clearly the more controlled and shapely novel. *The French Lieutenant's Woman* is also a more successful blending of a traditional narrative, presented with documentary realism, and self-conscious devices which disrupt the illusion of reality in order to permit an investigation of its status as fiction. It is a superior novel in this regard because it surmounts a difficulty Fowles encountered in *The Magus*, where Conchis's dual role as realistic character and novelist-surrogate necessitated that he perform in action what the novelist does with language. In other words, because he exists within the illusion of real life created by Fowles, Conchis carries out a facsimile of the novelist's task by creating for Urfe 'real' as opposed to literary experiences. Because the reader recognizes that *The Magus* employs many of the conventions of the thriller, the exotic setting and implausible action do not inhibit his willingness to suspend disbelief. A problem does arise, however, from the fact that, in order to demonstrate to Urfe that his enterprise is, like a novelist's, fictional, Conchis must destroy the reality of each stage of the godgame before moving on to create a new illusion involving his company

*Reprinted from *Journal of Narrative Technique*, 11, 3, 184–98.

of actors. It becomes increasingly difficult for the reader to submit imaginatively to successive illusions inasmuch as he becomes increasingly aware that they will soon be punctured.

In *The French Lieutenant's Woman*, on the other hand, the illusionist element does not strain our credulity because its fictionality is exposed in a way that does not require its destruction. The self-conscious narrator–novelist is not a character in the same sense that Conchis is. Rather, the narrator identifies himself as the author,[2] and, accordingly, it is apparent from the start that he does not exist within the confines of his narrative (although at two points he does enter it briefly as a character). Consequently, he can periodically point up the artificial nature of his story without destroying it.[3] Having momentarily dispelled the illusion that his characters have a reality apart from the book, he can then continue to delineate the plot without needing to create an entirely new set of fictional circumstances. The reader, therefore, soon forgets the narrator's warning, once again becoming immersed in the verisimilitudinous account of a Victorian love triangle and its effects on the lives of the characters.

The adjective 'Victorian', of course, suggests an important respect in which *The French Lieutenant's Woman* is paradoxical, for as Patrick Brantlinger explains, its modernity is achieved from its pastiche of old-fashioned novelistic practices: 'As an experimental work, it paradoxically assumes the form of a Victorian novel. Fowles, goes crab-backwards to join the avant-garde, imitating George Eliot as a way to emulate "Alain Robbe-Gillet and Roland Barthes."'[4] This statement requires qualification in that Fowles' novel is as much a critique of the assumptions of the French new novelists as it is an application of them.[5] Fowles is able to have it both ways; in the very act of resurrecting an outmoded sort of novel, he indicates that it is an anachronism, and so manifests the kind of uneasiness about the activity of fiction writing that we have come to recognize as characteristic of contemporary writers. By exposing the artificiality of the form in the very act of using it, by showing that he does not view it as transparently representational, he avoids writing in bad faith. And yet simultaneously he is able to exploit the very facets of the novel that he is questioning by imitating the Victorians – morally sensitive omniscience, plot, character, and the illusion of an objective reality, a set of historical circumstances open to empirical investigation. He is interested, as Bradbury claims, in preserving 'as much humanism for the novel as can be got,'[6] while at the same time confronting the forces which have threatened both humanistic beliefs and the elements of fiction allied with them.

Fowles's strategy is like John Barth's. A similarity is apparent between the double-edged use Fowles makes of an antiquated fictional form and Barth's experiments with the conventions of the picaresque novel. *The Sot-Weed Factor* in particular bears comparison with *The French Lieutenant's*

Woman: not only do both employ narrative conventions derived from earlier historical periods, but both are set in the past as well. There are significant differences, of course. The most obvious is that Barth's is the more comical and blatantly parodic novel. Another is that Fowles's narrator, far more intrusive than Barth's, brings an explicitly modern understanding to bear on his nineteenth-century subject matter, whereas Barth's authorial voice pretends to be of the historical period during which the action takes place. Of course, *The Sot-Weed Factor*'s ignorance of modern history is disingenuous since the book uses its turn-of-the-eighteenth century content as a metaphor for twentieth-century concerns. Fowles's narrator, on the other hand, juxtaposes nineteenth- and twentieth-century modes of thought, feeling, and behaviour, enabling each to comment upon and qualify the other. His intention in doing so is to make them converge for the reader in an intensely alive fictional present.

These differences aside, the two novels treat history in a somewhat similarly ironical fashion. Neither aspires simply to weave a narrative into a historically accurate representation of a bygone age. For both the evocation of history is a means, not an end it itself.[7] Each ostensibly aligns itself with the documentary tradition of the novel in recreating a densely particularized social milieu and alluding to (and even incorporating into the story) real historical events and personages. Yet, having done so, each paradoxically dissolves the illusion of solid actuality that the conventions of formal realism were designed to create. Both novels thereby try to persuade us, not simply that the versions of history they present are fictional, but that all conceptions of objective reality are in some sense human fabrications with no underlying solidity. For Barth, whose sense of life's ephemerality is more developed than Fowles's, this is a terrifying state of affairs. But for Fowles it is potentially redemptive because it means that all of life can be invested with the significance of good art, for which he makes exalted claims.[8]

By imitating the Victorian novel Fowles is able to create the paradoxical effect of a narrative at once credible on a realistic plane and self-consciously artificial. He exploits the anomaly that, although the nineteenth century is usually regarded as the great age of realistic fiction, many of the conventions of the Victorian novel have fallen into disfavour, even amongst writers committed to social realism. Fowles's use of out-of-date conventions enables us to perceive their conventionality; they remind us that we are reading an unusual sort of novel, not witnessing the unfolding of actual events. That novelistic practices have shifted from the nineteenth to the twentieth centuries in understandable, since history has so altered the political, social, and cultural structures of England that the mental and social landscapes depicted by modern writers are quite different from those of their Victorian predecessors. As L.P. Hartley writes in the opening sentence of *The Go-Between*, 'The past is a foreign country:

they do things differently there.'[9] In short, both the forms of life and the literary conventions fashioned to represent them have altered radically since the 1860s, and Fowles exploits this shift for his own purposes. He even exaggerates the strangeness of the Victorian world, as his comments on the novel's dialogue attest:

> the genuine dialogue of 1867 (in so far as it can be had in books of the time) is far too close to our own to sound convincingly old. It very often fails to agree with our psychological picture of the Victorians – it is not stiff enough, not euphemistic enough, and so on; and here at once I have to start cheating and pick out the more formal and archaic elements of spoken speech.[10]

The word 'cheating' is instructive here, for Fowles is intentionally duplicitous in elaborating a fictional world which on the one hand is realized with documentary realism but which on the other hand bears slight resemblance to contemporary social realities. By doing so he invites the reader to feel that he is entering a solid, factually-based environment and therefore to delude himself that he is responding in a morally engaged way to serious human concerns. But, as Dwight Eddins claims, the book actually raises within the reader the desire to experience history 'as romanticized and archaic ideation,' implicitly lulling him into believing 'that he is embarked on nothing more threatening than a field trip into the safely-frozen past'.[11] He is in actuality comfortably removed in time and circumstances from the Victorian subject matter and might even feel immune from the moral plight of the more sexually repressed central characters. Accordingly, Fowles dispels the reader's complacent security by dissolving the solidity of the narrative, exposing the fictionality of the work by discoursing on the processes of its creation and by providing multiple endings.[12]

By making the reader sensitive to the work as a fabrication composed of words rather than as a transparent window to a real-seeming human drama, the novel's literary self-consciousness enables him to see that the apparently solid, historically accurate evocation of the Victorian age is as much a product of our collective imagination as it is of fact. Fred Kaplan shows that the novel's mood, themes, and character types are derived, not directly from life, but from nineteenth-century literature, and he also remarks that Fowles's portrait of the era is constructed more from the use of excerpts from imaginative literature than from historical documents. Kaplan's conclusions are incisive:

> The history, then, is more in the fiction than in the fact, more in the literary products of the age than in the factual documents of the historians. Fowles has succeeded in writing a fiction, a historical novel

of sorts, that is true to our knowledge of the period revealed through the period's imaginative literature ... The premise seems to be that we know an age not through its so-called facts but through the impact its imaginative literature has on us. It is as if Fowles wants to redefine 'facts' in the light of his attempt to relate the past to the present. The past that exists, in this case the Victorian past, is the product of our present immersion in the only aspect of the past that still has life, its art.[13]

But the ultimate effect of the novel's alienating devices is not merely to expose the story's fictitiousness, its basis in letters rather than in life. Rather, it is to intensify the significance of the fiction for the reader. Fowles punctures one illusion, then, only to create another: that the reader is collaborating in the fashioning of a story involving, not quaint Victorian men and women whose problems are safely distant from the reader's experience, but two proto-existentialists inhabiting his moral universe, sharing a living present made anxious by the burden of choice, and facing an equally uncertain future.[14] Although Linda Hutcheon seems not to notice that the reader is meant periodically to feel removed from the quandaries of Charles, Sarah, and Ernestina in order to give his eventual moral engagement more force, her description of the ultimate thrust of the book seems apt: 'The real and the imaginary, the present and the past merge for the reader.'[15] And if the novel suggests that the real and the imaginary are in the last analysis indistinguishable, it also implies that the imaginary may constitute the highest form of truth.

The importance of the authorial voice in creating the paradoxes described above cannot be overemphasized. The intrusive narrator is, of course, standard in may Victorian novels, and Fowles's imitation of this convention is no less paradoxical than the previously discussed aspects of the book. In the work of writers such as George Eliot or Trollope, the narrator is the medium through whom novelistic authority is established. The source of this authority is the narrator's omniscience – his access to the inner lives of the characters – and the confidence, reasonableness, subtlety, and withering irony with which moral, cultural, and psychological generalizations are advanced. Fowles provides the reader with this sort of guidance, broaching a wide range of topics from the follies of clothing styles to the scientific and moral importance of the discoveries of Darwin and Lyell. Kaplan comments aptly on the way the narrator's seemingly digressive remarks expand the book's significance without detracting from the main plot: 'entire chapters imitate the Victorian proclivity for incorporating historical and sociological generalization into the fabric of their fictions, amplifying the dimensions of the novelist's interests, creating a fiction that is almost encyclopedic in its absorption of all aspects of culture'.[16]

While availing himself of the benefits of the intrusive narrator, however, Fowles simultaneously undermines his authority in the very act of making him speak at times as a Victorian figure who veritably proclaims himself an anachronism with his formal, courtly locution. Listening to his voice, the reader is keenly aware, not only that he is reading an imitation Victorian novel, but also that he is doing so in an era when, for certain reasons, Victorian-style novels are no longer written. In this respect, Eddins's description of *The French Lieutenant's Woman* as 'a "Victorian" novel that is a contemporary novel "about" the Victorian novel' is just.[17] It is not only the narrator's antiquated practices and idiom which make one suspicious. Because he also speaks from a modern perspective, the narrator can tell the reader explicitly what is no longer viable about the Victorian novel: the convention 'that the novelist stands next to God' (p. 80). Since Fowles believes that the metaphysical assumptions about the universe upon which the analogy is based have broken down, leaving man in a position of uncertainty, he believes that the analogy has lost its usefulness and that it should be altered:

> The novelist is still a god, since he creates (and not even the most aleatory avant-garde modern novel has managed to extirpate its author completely); what has changed is that we are no longer the gods of the Victorian image, omniscient and decreeing; but in the new theological image, with freedom our first principle, not authority.
>
> (p. 82)

Fowles' treatment of the narrator, then, is reminiscent of his penchant in *The Magus* for building up Conchis as a figure of wisdom and power only to make the reader doubt him in this respect. About both there is a suggestion of the charlatan, the flashy impresario orchestrating baseless illusions. Indeed, late in *The French Lieutenant's Woman* the narrator appears overtly in this role in order to expose the illusory nature of the penultimate ending by introducing a final one (p. 362). If both Conchis and the narrator are gods, they are so only 'in the new theological image': 'There is only one good definition of God: the freedom that allows other freedoms to exist' (p. 82). Accordingly, the function of the author – surrogates is paradoxical in that both seek authority only to eschew it. Both manipulate others in order to bestow the freedom which must of necessity terminate their control.

Of course, as Fowles says, the novelist can never actually cease to manipulate characters; he can only create the illusion of having done so. Since inspiration cannot be commanded at will, however, there is a sense in which the development of a novel's characters may actually be beyond a writer's conscious control. Novelists, states Fowles, 'cannot plan. We know a world is an organism, not a machine. We also know that a genuinely created world must be independent of its creator; a planned world (a world that fully reveals its planning) is a dead world. It is only when our characters and events begin to disobey us that they begin to live' (p. 81). But this sort of independence of the created from the conscious intentions of the creator is not the same as the absolute freedom espoused by the narrator. His argument here seems deliberately specious. After all, the fictional worlds of the great Victorian novels surely are organic in Fowles's terms, but their narrators do not for this reason reject the convention of omniscience and proclaim the autonomy of their characters.

Fowles, however, desires to create a sense, not only that the springs of his characters' motivations and actions lie too deep within himself for rational understanding, but also that they are free of his control. Although whenever it suits his purposes his narrator provides a god's-eye view of his characters' innermost thoughts and feelings and draws our attention to his primacy as creator of the novel's world, he nonetheless adopts a posture opposite to that of Thackeray's puppet-master-novelist in *Vanity Fair*. While Fowles' strategy is not as extreme as Flann O'Brien's in *At-Swim-Two-Birds* (where the characters plot to end the despotism of the novelist-persona at night as he sleeps), Fowles' narrator does at times trumpet the recalcitrance of his characters. Moreover, by providing three separate endings he tries to convey the suggestion of indeterminacy, impart the notion that the characters have been freed from the tyranny of his plot. But Christopher Ricks argues rightly that this liberation is more apparent than real:

> Once the novelist says 'I'm in no position to insist that such-and-such happened,' he is in no position to insist that either such-and-such or such-and-such happened. For there would not be, in life, two possibilities, but virtually an infinity of them. To reduce this infinity to two alternatives is no less manipulatory or coercive ... than was the Victorian novelist's reduction of the infinity to one eventuality.[18]

Furthermore, as Elizabeth Rankin observes, even the illusion of indeterminacy is undermined inasmuch as the final ending is both a logical resolution of the novel's themes and the only one not vitiated by the narrator's irony.[19] Fowles only seems, then, to grant his characters and readers an equal partnership in the creative process. Bradbury perceives what he actually does, which is to demonstrate the importance of freedom, not literally to bestow it: 'Authorial authority is relativized, not in order to lighten responsibility for the characters, thrusting it on the reader, but rather to take full responsibility for showing their freedom, their faculty of choice.'[20]

Fowles is, naturally enough, fully aware of these contradictions, the artful management of which contributes to the book's success. They are meant to be perceived by the attentive reader. The narrator-novelist informs us explicitly that he has the look of 'an omnipotent god' (p. 317), and his absconding in a landau shortly before the last ending is acted does not blind us to the fact that in the act of setting his watch back fifteen minutes he has ordained Sarah's rejection of Charles. He is no less the god-like novelist in pretending not to watch the scene he has written played out.

The world 'paradox' also comes to mind if we think of Fowles's sleight-of-hand, not in terms of the extent of his control over the characters, but in relation to the way he invites the reader to surrender to or disengage himself from the illusion of an actual human drama unfolding. One quality of the Victorian novelist which Fowles lacks is an unselfconscious faith in the truth and significance of his own fictional representations of life. This confidence is manifested in, not belied by, the way the nineteenth-century novelists characteristically use the convention of the omniscient author. One might think that authorial intrusiveness necessarily interferes with a verisimilitudinous narrative by reminding the reader of the story's fictionality.[21] But with Victorian writers the practice actually strengthened the illusion of reality because intrusive commentary was used typically to make connections between life as the reader knew it and the fictional world, broadening its base and suggesting its factual solidity and moral relevance. In places Fowles employs authorial commentary in this fashion too, but his narrator also intrudes to distinguish between modern reality and his Victorian story, thus underscoring its character as a fabrication. Or perhaps one should say that he pretends to discriminate between fiction and reality in the process of actually doing the opposite: confusing the two. This is certainly the intent of one of his apostrophes, bearing echoes of Baudelaire and T.S. Eliot, to the reader, here imaged as a no-nonsense devotee of facts:

> A character is either 'real' or 'imaginary'? If you think that, *hypocrite lecteur*, I can only smile. You do not even think of your own past as quite real; you dress it up, you gild it or blacken it, censor it, tinker with it … fictionalize it, in a word, and put it away on a shelf – your book, your romanced autobiography. We are in flight from the real reality. That is a basic definition of *Homo sapiens*.
>
> (p. 82)

Like the Victorian writers, Fowles here links his book with the world outside of it, but he achieves an opposite result. Whereas the Victorians appealed to their readers' sense of reality in order to validate the reality of their fictions, Fowles sensitizes the reader to the fictionality of his work in order to emphasize his view that all life is a web of fiction.

The point of the disruptive commentary is finally illusionist, 'part of the

prestidigitation,'[22] as Barth would say, not anti-illusionist. 'You are not the
"I" who breaks into the illusion,' Fowles reminds himself, 'but the "I"
who is a part of it'.[23] It originally seems that the purpose of the intrusive
narrator in pointing up the fictionality of the work is simple if paradoxical.
The paradox is that he seems to be violating what was originally designed
as a realist mode of fiction because it does not do justice to reality: 'The
story I am telling is all imagination. These characters I create never existed
outside my own mind' (p. 80). This seems at first simply to be a philistine
objection issuing from a preference for hard, factual realities over art,
which is fanciful and untrue in a literal sense. But Fowles goes on to
overturn this implication: 'I have disgracefully broken the illusion? No.
My characters still exist, and in a reality no less, or no more, real than the
one I have just broken. Fiction is woven into all' (p. 82). By seeming to
belittle the significance of his fiction as ephemeral illusion, Fowles actually
begins to establish its relevance to the reader's life, which he also portrays
as a tissue of fictions. He thwarts the reader's urge to take 'flight from the
real reality,' the ever-present need to claim one's freedom and confront the
attendant dangers and responsibilities. This he does by frustrating the
reader's escapist desire to submit whole-heartedly to the reality of a safely
distant narrative presided over by a comforting omniscient god who
provides certain knowledge and sees to it that things work out. He
establishes a context within which the reader becomes aware of the
potency of the fiction as a fiction in a world of fictions and, conversely, of
the destructiveness of fictions created in bad faith, those which have come
to be, to use one of the novel's dominant metaphors, fossilized, accepted
as unambiguous realities. The ultimate effect is to heighten, not diminish,
the immediacy and power of the Victorian subject matter and to foster the
illusion that the reader is participating in its creation.

By concentrating mainly on only a few pages of authorial commentary,
my analysis to this point might seem to distort the essential nature of *The
French Lieutenant's Woman*, the bulk of which is a traditional narrative.
Walter Allen, for example, who believes that Fowles' real achievement in
the novel is the evocation of history, states: 'The significance of *The French
Lieutenant's Woman* doesn't lie in its "experimental" features. These are
much more apparent than real, and in my view, are a boring red
herring.'[24] In its vividness, rightness of detail, and assurance of tone,
Fowles' recreation of the Victorian past is, as Allen avows, a triumph in its
own right. But it is worth reiterating that Fowles' purpose in reviving the
Victorian fictional traditions is, in part, anti-traditional. Moreover, the
matter of the fiction mirrors the manner of its telling. Bradbury is simply
wrong in asserting of the novel's resolution that 'the substantial action
seems to end in one world and the substantiating *machinery*, the technical
modes and means, in another'. Neither is he persuasive in arguing that the
novel 'has something of the air of forcing itself towards a formal self-

consciousness of surface, rather than inherently needing it'.[25] William Palmer more astutely observes that the meta-fictional concerns raised by the narrator are woven into the very fabric of the story itself: 'the plot and the characters ... comprise a metaphor for Fowles' aesthetic theme. It is a novel about the past and future of the novel genre.'[26] In Barth's terminology, then, Fowles' novel is 'a paradigm of or metaphor for itself'.[27]

As in *The Magus*, in *The French Lieutenant's Woman* Fowles turns to his own advantage a potentially debilitating circumstance by building into the novel apocalytpic forces antagonistic to a human-centered world view which fosters the creation of art. In his essay on writing the novel he identifies this threat, its implications for Victorian society, and what he takes to be its modern equivalent:

> The great nightmare of the respectable Victorian mind was the only too real one created by the geologist Lyell and the biologist Darwin. Until then man had lived like a child in a small room. They gave him – and never was a present less welcome – infinite space and time, and a hideously mechanistic explanation of human reality into the bargain. Just as we 'live with the bomb' the Victorians lived with the theory of evolution. They were hurled into space. They felt themselves infinitely isolated. By the 1860's the great iron structures of their philosophies, religions and social stratifications were already beginning to look dangerously corroded to the more perspicacious.[28]

It is through Smithson, the amateur scientist and champion of Darwin, that Fowles makes these concerns explicit in the novel. Charles uses his insider's knowledge of the then very recent theory of natural selection as a refuge from his vague fears of a misspent life and entrapment in a sterile social order. As the quoted passage would suggest, there is considerable irony in finding solace in Darwinism, for its implications reduce the importance and dignity of man in the overall scheme of things. Moreover, there is dramatic irony in an awareness shared by the narrator and reader but lacking in Charles: that the Darwinian principle of general extinction can be used to explain the near demise of Smithson's own social class in our own century. Rankin sees that it is the process of evolution which forces upon Charles the painful ordeal of choosing to become a social outsider, an existentialist before his time.[29] At first Charles mistakenly believes that he has been naturally selected as the fittest to survive, that his way of life and social status are sanctioned by immutable natural laws (p. 45). He misinterprets the full import of evolution, conceiving of life along discredited Linnean lines as a fixed order in which his own place is exalted rather than as a ceaseless, mysterious flux (p. 45). This propensity the novel depicts as characteristic of the era, and, despite the comfort derived from its 'iron certainties,' the narrator presents this aspect of the Victorian age as life-denying (p. 285). It finally is doubly paradoxical that, as in *The Collector* and *The Magus*, confronting the hazardous uncertainty of existence proves to be the means of attaining authenticity. As long as Charles deludes himself that he has a clear and reassuring insight into the truth about life, he exhibits, in existentialist jargon, *mauvais foi*.

The process whereby Charles learns to question and reject some of the rigid Victorian conventions and structures of thought corresponds to the narrator's determination to overturn the canons of the Victorian novel, to reveal the fiction *as* fiction and to deny the reader at times the certain knowledge of an omniscient guide. Both cases involve the refusal to treat products of the imagination as if they had a prior objective existence, a rock-bottom reality. Charles has an insight into the illusory character of all interpretive structures in conjunction with his discovery that evolution is horizontal, not vertical: 'Time was the great fallacy; existence was without history, was always now ... All those painted screens erected by man to shut out reality – history, religion, duty, social position, all were illusions, mere opium fantasies' (p. 165).

What Charles must learn in the novel, however, is not to do without the 'painted screens' of fiction, but to reinvigorate them, to employ them to enhance life, to bring out its vibrancy and mysteriousness and infinite significance. Again, this is analogous to what Fowles hopes to achieve by altering, rather than abandoning, the conventions of the Victorian novel. He may assert the unreality of history, but, because he knows that we cannot dispense with it, his response is not to repudiate it but to evoke the Victorian past in a way that lets us see its relevance to the present. Despite his championing of hazard, he has no intention of entrusting his novel – which is in fact highly structured and planned – to contingency. Fostering the illusion that his novel has been freed from the tyranny of artistic structuring is a way, not of doing away with, but of bringing new life to the forms of art, making them flexible and open to the surprises hazard brings. Fowles does not believe one can or should discover a reality more substantial than the fabrications which he imposes on experience. This is not an available option. Kerry McSweeney describes the choice that is, according to Fowles, open to man – to live by inert, dead metaphors or to create of one's life a rich and vital fiction: 'one's perception of reality, one's phenomenological world, is the work of the imagination. The failure to replace culturally and socially conditioned metaphors of reality by one's own, or to move beyond stale metaphors, is an imaginative failure.'[30]

The novel makes clear that it is also an imaginative failure to endeavour to use metaphors to evade the flux and contingency of life, to impose a fixed order and certainty where in reality there is mystery and unending change. This destructive urge, appropriately called 'collector-consciousness' by Palmer,'[31] is the desire for a proprietary relationship to the truth. It is the wish to possess, to control, to understand totally; this is the sort of mentality Keats denigrated as lacking negative capability.[32] The central symbol for this flight from reality, Smithson's collection of fossilized tests, conveys what Fowles believes to be its deadening, life-denying character. By seeking absolute knowledge and control, one kills whatever life made the object under scrutiny desirable in the first place. 'We murder to dissect,'[33] said Wordsworth, and Fowles would certainly agree. Indeed, in *The Collector* the demented Clegg literally kills Miranda in an attempt to possess her.

A woman is also the focus for Smithson's less extreme form of 'collector-consciousness', his inclination to fictionalize in bad faith. As Palmer explains, because Charles fears his broadly sexual attraction to Sarah, he at first tries to conceptualize her in a framework which will make her entirely comprehensible in a negative way and so defuse her mysterious power over him: 'Charles wants to dehumanize his relationship with Sarah and turn it, as Dr Grogan would, into a neatly labeled psychological "case."'[34] The profile constructed by Grogan, in which Sarah's behavior is unambiguously pathological, is in actuality a hypothesis or theory, a species of fiction which is at best a partial and metaphoric explanation of the workings of her psyche, but both men would like to accept it as factual. In a like manner, the townspeople who categorize her as the French Lieutenant's whore mistake a faulty hypothesis for a fact, and Mrs Poulteney confuses her lubricious fantasies about Sarah's misbehavior in the Undercliff with reality. But Sarah slips through the conceptual nets Charles and others would trap her in, forcing him to perceive them as destructive fictions.

Sarah's thematic function in the novel has been identified by several critics;[35] it is to embody a mysterious vitality which defies rigid intellectual formulation. 'I am not to be understood' (p. 354), she tells Charles, and certainly the narrator and reader fare no better in this respect than he does. Even after Charles succumbs to her blandishments, he continues to try to dispel Sarah's mystery, to possess her by creating around her an explanatory fiction which he hopes to realize in action. This is how he fantasizes about the joys of a honeymoon abroad with Sarah: 'The Alhambra! Moonlight, the distant sound below of singing gypsies, such grateful, tender eyes ... and in some jasmine-scented room they would lie awake, in each other's arms, infinitely alone, exiled, yet fused in that loneliness, inseparable in that exile' (p. 313). Hutcheon notes that Charles' use here of romantic clichés tonally undercuts his dream of the future, which, in any case, is soon to be shattered by Sarah's disappearance.[36] Charles' fantasy of a beautiful marriage which could mitigate the essential loneliness of life corresponds exactly to the happy ending, which is first parodied by means of excessively romantic rhetoric

(p. 360) and then revoked by the narrator (pp. 362–366). Once again the novel's content and its meta-fictional form reflect each other.

Finally, because his attempts to control and possess Sarah fail, Charles does come to recognize that his ideas about her are not literal truths: 'he became increasingly unsure of the frontier between the real Sarah and the Sarah he had created in so many ... dreams' (p. 336). Granting her the freedom to be autonomous does not diminish the positive effect she has on his life. Indeed, painful though it may be, Smithson's growth depends upon his willingness not to treat Sarah as a goddess who can be commanded to solve all of his problems and make him happy. Like the speaker of Tennyson's *Maud*, with whom Charles identifies (p. 334), he must leave the garden (symbolized in the novel by the Undercliff) and make his way alone in the world. He must face the anxiety of freedom by himself, without the intervention of a protective, quasi-divine presence. Analogously, by means of the techniques of literary self-consciousness, Fowles tries to foster within the reader the illusion that he must undertake the creative chores without the novelist's god-like aid.

The positions of Charles and the reader on the one hand and Sarah and the narrator on the other are, as Rankin states,[37] clearly parallel. Hutcheon describes Sarah's relationship to the narrator succinctly: 'Sarah is the narrating novelist's surrogate within the fictional world.'[38] Unlike the other characters, she is aware that the fiction she creates (that she has been seduced by Vargueness) is a fiction, and her motivation differs as well. Whereas the other characters often fictionalize in order to produce comforting delusions which will relieve them of the burden of their own freedom, Sarah designs a fiction to move herself beyond the pale of conventional Victorian morality. Her purpose in deliberately courting the pains of social ostracism is to claim her uniqueness, to grow as a free individual. In the process, as Eddins remarks,[39] she spurs Charles on to pursue his own human potential. Her effect on him is similar to Conchis' influence on Urfe, and it is equally paradoxical. Both magus-figures knowingly use, manipulate, and lie to their disciples in order to liberate and enlighten them. Sarah is perhaps less disinterested and aware of the possible consequences of her actions, but her effect in the end is the same as Conchis'. The intent of the narrator is, of course, identical; his self-conscious trickery, duplicity, and manipulation of the reader is aimed at leading him to the truth and making him choose to be free. The illusion is fostered that both Charles and the reader, in assuming responsibility for their destinies, become authors of their own lives. Paradoxically, life is more real, then, when art is perfected, not when it is transcended. The view that a reality more real than art can be attained is in this context a delusion created in bad faith.

The French Lieutenant's Woman resolves itself so as to insist upon the ambiguities and paradoxes surrounding the relation of art and life, not to repudiate them. Paradoxically, the novelist undermines his own authority as a sage who has a special insight into reality in the ultimate interest of establishing that authority. Because Fowles broaches the meta-fictional concerns from the outset, explores them interestingly, and makes them a part of the living tissue of the narrative in a way that increases its dramatic intensity and significance for the reader, the success of his novel is inseparable from its reflexive character.

Notes

1. MALCOLM BRADBURY, for instance, states that *The Magus* is the more mysterious and commanding of the two novels. 'The Novelist as Impresario: John Fowles and His Magus,' *Possibilities: Essays on the State of the Novel* (London: Oxford University Press, 1973), p. 263.

2. It would be a mistake, however, to equate the narrator narrowly with Fowles, as he himself states in his essay on writing *The French Lieutenant's Woman*: 'the "I" who will make first-person commentaries here and there in my story, and who will finally even enter it, will not be my real "I" in 1967; but much more just another character, though in a different category from the purely fictional ones.' 'Notes on an Unfinished Novel,' reprinted in *The Novel Today: Contemporary Writers on Modern Fiction*, ed. MALCOLM BRADBURY (Great Britain: Fontana, 1973), p. 142.

3. For example, at one point the narrator justifies his refusal to enter Sarah's consciousness by explaining that he does not at this moment have access to her thoughts, which in any case have no existence apart from his own: 'These characters I create never existed outside my own mind.' *The French Lieutenant's Woman* (New York: Signet, 1969), p. 80. All future references to *The French Lieutenant's Woman* will be to this edition.

4. PATRICK BRANTLINGER, IAN ADAM, and SHELDON ROTHBLATT, 'The French Lieutenant's Woman: A Discussion,' *Victorian Studies*, 15 (1972), p. 339.

5. In this respect, see Fowles' criticisms of Robbe-Grillet's argument in *Pour un Nouveau Roman*. 'Notes on an Unfinished Novel,' p. 139.

6. Bradbury, 'Novelist as Impresario,' p. 263.

7. The following comment by Fowles on *The French Lieutenant's Woman* is instructive in this regard: 'I don't think of it as a historical novel, a genre in which I have very little interest.' 'Notes on an Unfinished Novel,' p. 136.

8. See *The Aristos*, rev. ed. (New York: New American Library, 1970), p. 184.

9. L. P. HARTLEY, *The Go-Between* (Harmondsworth: Penguin Books, 1958), p. 7.

10. Fowles, 'Notes on an Unfinished Novel,' p. 139.

11. DWIGHT EDDINS, 'John Fowles: Existence as Authorship,' *Contemporary Literature*, 17 (1976), p. 219.

12. He also explicitly debunks the notion that our own supposedly enlightened sexual attitudes and practices are superior to those of the Victorians (pp. 212–213).

13. FRED KAPLAN, 'Victorian Modernists: Fowles and Nabokov,' *Journal of Narrative Techniques*, 3 (1973), p. 111.

14. See Fowles' comment on Charles and Sarah as existentialists before their time. 'Notes on an Unfinished Novel,' p. 141.

15. LINDA HUTCHEON, 'The "Real World(s)" of Fiction: *The French Lieutenant's Woman*,' *English Studies in Canada*, 4 (1978), p. 84.

16. Kaplan, 'Victorian Modernists,' p. 113.

17. Eddins, 'John Fowles,' p. 217.

18. CHRISTOPHER RICKS, 'The Unignorable Real,' *New York Review of Books*, 12 Feb. 1970, p. 24.

19. ELIZABETH RANKIN, 'Cryptic Coloration in *The French Lieutenant's Woman*,' *Journal of Narrative Technique*, 3 (1973), p. 205.

20. Bradbury, 'Novelist as Impresario,' p. 257.

21. Such was the view of Ford Madox Ford, for example, who held that the novelist's job was 'to render and not to tell'. *The English Novel: From the Earliest Days to the Death of Joseph Conrad* (London: Constable and Co., 1930), p. 122.

22. JOE DAVID BELLAMY, 'Having It Both Ways: A Conversation Between John Barth and Joe David Bellamy,' *New American Review*, 15, p. 143.

23. Fowles, 'Notes on an Unfinished Novel,' p. 142.

24. WALTER ALLEN, 'The Achievement of John Fowles,' *Encounter*, 35 (1970), p. 67.

25. Bradbury, 'Novelist as Impresario,' p. 257 and p. 263.

26. WILLIAM PALMER, *The Fiction of John Fowles: Tradition, Art, and the Loneliness of Selfhood* (Columbia: University of Missouri Press, 1974), p. 30.

27. JOHN BARTH, 'The Literature of Exhaustion,' reprinted in *The Novel Today: Contemporary Writers on Modern Fiction*, ed. Malcolm Bradbury (Great Britain: Fontana, 1977), p. 78.

28. Fowles, 'Notes on an Unfinished Novel,' pp. 140–1.

29. Rankin, 'Cryptic Coloration,' p. 199.

30. KERRY MCSWEENEY, 'John Fowles's Variations in *The Ebony Tower*,' *Journal of Modern Literature*, 8 (1981), p. 311.

31. Palmer, *The Fiction of John Fowles*, p. 51.

32. JOHN KEATS to George and Thomas Keats, 21, 27(?) Dec. 1817, *Selected Poems and Letters by John Keats*, ed. Douglas Bush (Boston: Houghton Mifflin, 1959), p. 261.

33. WILLIAM WORDSWORTH, 'The Tables Turned,' *Selected Poems and Prefaces by William Wordsworth*, ed. Jack Stillinger (Boston: Houghton Mifflin, 1965), p. 107.

34. Palmer, *The Fiction of John Fowles*, p. 51.

35. See IAN ADAM, 'The French Lieutenant's Woman: A Discussion,' p. 347, and Eddins, 'John Fowles,' p. 220.

36. Hutcheon, '"Real World(s)" of Fiction,' p. 88.

37. Rankin, 'Cryptic Coloration,' p. 197.

38. Hutcheon, '"Real World(s)" of Fiction,' p. 90.

39. Eddins, 'John Fowles,' p. 222.

13 'A Novel which is a Machine for Generating Interpretations'*

Elizabeth Dipple

Dipple's *The Unresolvable Plot*, of which this is a chapter, is an excellent resource for any student of metafiction, including studies of the 'masters of metafiction': Borges, Calvino and Beckett. This chapter focuses on Eco's *The Name of the Rose*, taking its title from his *Reflections on the Name of the Rose* (see Part Three), and elaborates from Eco's reticence about authorial interpretation in that work. Like Lodge's 'The Novel Now' (see Part Three), Dipple focuses her discussion on the problems of a theorist writing a novel, beginning from the view that a novel is capable of achieving more than a work of theory, narrating that which cannot be theorized. For this reason, Dipple reads Eco's novel as a didactic work which aims to teach semiotic and interpretative theory to its readership at the same time as narrate a medieval tale. The didactic aim is not fulfilled by the successful transmission of ideas between author and reader as much as by a kind of interpretative openness: the novel generates interpretations which are almost infinite in number to demonstrate the 'infinite semiosis' that Eco argues for, but cannot show, in his critical writings such as *Opera Aperta* and *The Role of the Reader*. The argument here makes some use of Eco's own disbelief in authorial interpretation and its ability to provide authoritative commentary, and might therefore be considered alongside Eco's own discourse about his novel and the argument made by Lodge in relation to the work of Mikhail Bakhtin against interpretative closure, both in Part Three of this volume.

When a theorist writes a novel, problematic issues are raised in the never stable relationship between text and reader, as the theories of the author are in a sense unavoidably imposed on the reader. We may actively rebel against the overlordship of the author at any time as, for example, so many receptors have to the strident narrative voices of John Fowles or Saul Bellow. But, in our acquiescence to the author's narrativity – that is, in the fact that we read the novel ardently enough to carry on with it – we succumb to being dominated at least temporarily by the impact of the

*Reprinted from Dipple, E. *The Unresolvable Plot: Reading Contemporary Fiction* (London: Ron Hedge, 1988), pp. 117–39.

theory in question. By 1980, at the age of 47, Umberto Eco had established an international scholarly reputation for his work in semiotics – the theory of signs and signifiers – with such books as *Opera Aperta* and *The Role of the Reader*. In that year the Italian edition of Eco's now famous novel, *The Name of the Rose (Il Nome della Rosa)* appeared under the imprint of Bompiani, the publishers of his scholarly work. The novel was quickly translated into many languages to wide and almost universal acclaim, with the English edition coming along rather belatedly in 1983, elegantly translated by the American expatriot, William Weaver. Its reception in the English-speaking world is a publishing phenomenon. Popular in Britain, the novel exploded on the American market, with something like 1,700,000 copies sold in the first two years of its life.

Given the problem of private coterie self-indulgence in much self-consciously Postmodernist contemporary fiction and the resulting dwindling of readership, the success story of this very good and intellectually ambitious novel presents an almost unanalyzable situation. It is not simply that the popularity and extravagant sales of *The Name of the Rose* throughout the western world – and the figures are astounding – indicate to many that the novel at hand should not be very good, or must at least be suspect for all serious novel readers. But ironically *The Name of the Rose* is a particularly demanding novel that not only asks its reader for impassioned attention to the intellectual milieu of the fourteenth century, it also taps Eco's Peircean theories of infinite semiosis and illustrates his idea of the 'model reader' in a polysemous act of intertextuality. Such a dose of specialized vocabulary is dismaying when applied to a bestseller, but fortunately for the majority of non-academic readers, such technical terms never emerge from the smooth narrative drive of the text. For those who persist through the daunting first hundred pages (Eco says in *Postscript to* (or *Reflections on*) *The Name of the Rose* that 'those first hundred pages are like penance or an initiation, and if someone does not like them, so much the worse for him. He can stay at the foot of the hill'), the book is superb entertainment and splendidly evocative at many levels. Even the inevitable negative backlash that follows such an unpredictable success is inadequate as a counter-force to the power of a work that persists in satisfying and exciting a wide range of readers.

One way of estimating the book's success is to stress its *jouissance*, to misuse Roland Barthes's term somewhat – its ideological celebration of human laughter against an Antichrist who would destroy it, as well as its demonstration of the joyous energy of its author. At various points in his works and interviews, Eco has said that what cannot be theorized about must be narrated, and certainly this text erupts with a clean energy that achieves much more for more sorts of thinkers than his theoretical work has been able to manage. Unfortunately this statement would be wounding to Eco, who has been irritated by the dominance granted this novel which he sees as a game, a minor exercise composed in the interstices of his serious – and to him much more important – semiotic-philosophical work. Unlike a writer like Iris Murdoch, who dislikes having her philosophical thought brought up in the context of her novels, Eco appears to assume that his reputation will rest on the semiotic work, and that the novel should be put into a minor context within that realm.

Nevertheless, Eco has been a constant popularizer, and if fiction is seen as an act of popularizing, it can be categorically stated that he has reached a wider audience and in many ways – when one includes the positive response of medievalists and historians – a more responsive one through *The Name of the Rose* than his structuralist semiotics could do. As in the case of Italo Calvino, the peculiar circumstances of Italian culture and its media dispensation have had much to do in molding a writer like Eco. Like the other handful of Italian cultural heroes, Eco has a longstanding journalistic career aside from his professorship at the University of Bologna and frequent lecture trips to Germany, France, and particularly America. As writer of a popular column in the magazine *L'Espresso*, he has had another means of reaching a large audience than his technical books and essays; as a journalist his theme has been consistent with the thought promulgated in the more inaccessible texts. Basically he wishes for an open cosmos of understanding in which all of culture will be seen not as something frozen, closed, disciplined into a rigid myth, but reverberative, used as an infinite, polysemous, interlocking system of signs to lead the mind fluidly forward. The conventional enshrining and codification of cultural fact or artifact for him are systems generated by simple allegory and leading to tyranny, frozen logic, and the sort of rigid theocentric dogma that *The Name of the Rose* is dedicated to breaking.

The strength of Eco's ideological commitment can be frankly and directly expressed in journalism and especially in theoretical criticism. His theory of the tasks of narrative and of the occlusion of the author within the realms of fiction raises other problems, however, that challenge his consistency in talking about readers' reception of *The Name of the Rose*. As a literary critic he has always argued that no text can move into being by itself: the interpretative role of the reader is central, and indeed the polysemy of a work can only be achieved by the reader, whose productive reading of the text is what really counts. In semiotic theory in general, no text is in itself a condition for its own signification. It depends on the interaction of reader and text, or even text and other texts for its emergence. This reciprocal process produces the idea of intertextuality, which, through Eco's constant evocative, unfootnoted quotations from 'anterior' texts, is the dominant stylistic mode of *The Name of the Rose*. This novel gives effective reinforcement to the idea of texts infinitely talking to and illuminating each other. Dominantly, however, there is the reader, whose mind is in constant activity as (s)he reads the authorially implanted signs through the lexicon of his/her own knowledge and necessity.

For Eco, the reader must be 'free'. Although the author implants the signs and imagines the possibilities that the 'model reader' might pursue, the authorial task is essentially finished when the book is written. Eco, who in the wake of his novel's mammoth popularity was excessively present to his readers through media interference, has repeatedly said that the author must not interpret. Indeed his efforts not to do so have been both stalwart and ironically disingenuous. When asked for the ultimate code that would transform the philosophical metaphysic of the novel into a statement, Eco claims that he doesn't know what it is, or indeed what the novel is about, and he constantly throws the task of interpreting to the reader. Unfortunately, Eco quickly and it seems unconsciously broke his consistency with the rapid publication of a little explanatory book entitled *Postscript to* (in Britain, *Reflections on*) *The Name of the Rose* (it appeared in English, translated by William Weaver, in 1984, one year after the novel). The resulting contamination of the reader's freedom despite Eco's claims to the contrary cannot be underestimated, for almost every fact he gives us directs the reader in a predetermined way.

To begin with, in *Postscript to The Name of the Rose*, Eco describes and, in keeping with his critical bias, limits all novels as 'machine[s] for generating interpretations'. Surely only a literary critic could ever conceive of a novel in such a way. Even more surely, only a writer also paid an annual university salary would allow his view of the reader's response to art – what Nabokov tellingly described as 'aesthetic bliss' – to be darkened by the professional aspects of interpretation that characterize so much of what Eco himself has subsequently said written about his justly famous, tantalizingly entitled first novel. All his demurrals about authorial interference tend to disappear when the novel becomes a machine and its product nothing but interpretation. But Eco cares passionately about interpretation, about the sort of sign-reading advocated by the American philosopher C.S. Peirce that led to the field of semiotics, Eco's chosen academic speciality and passion, into which he has here poured his passion for the Middle Ages.

Perhaps the production of an adjunct text like *Postscript* seemed necessary for reasons having to do with Eco's urgent sense of the need for more elaborate interpretations from his readers. He himself describes it as a permissible text in which some of the primary ideas and genesis of the novel could be made visible without authorial interference. Indeed, the surprisingly low analytical level of most of the Anglophone reviews, even by major reviewers like Richard Ellmann, indicated that in fact many vague commentaries occurred, but few complex, interesting, or original interpretations were generated. Continental reviewers on the other hand were much more eager to interpret and particularly to impose contemporary political meanings on *The Name of the Rose*. Eco claims that *Postscript* had its origin during a period when he was doing a lecture tour in Germany after the novel's first success there; he was boringly asked the same questions over and over again until he and his translator began referring to the reiterated questions as # 1, # 5, etc. According to his account, *Postscript* was a published attempt to stave off the same questions.

Under any circumstances, anyone teaching the novel (and it seems made for the academy, so eagerly does it welcome a wide range of pedantic quirks in various academic minds) quickly discovers that for readers the reaction of marvel is much greater than that of interpretation. Partly because of problems with decoding, serious contemporary fiction has spoken to an increasingly narrow audience, with worrisome consequences such as the proliferation of coteries and a sad diminution of receptivity on the part of the well-educated average reader. Here, however, was a complex book that great numbers of people wanted to read for pleasure, and although one can perhaps argue that *The Name of the Rose* is the most unread bestseller in history, it aroused a variety of responses throughout Europe and America that unexpectedly cut across many boundaries of interest.

This is far from the first time an academic has turned his theories into fiction, but not since Sartre has the resulting ideological narrative so deeply seized the imagination of the reading public. It generated intellectual excitement in almost all quarters, and for once united the idea of a 'university' or élitist novel with the ideal of a fiction for all readers. European reviewers saw it as political and topical; murder mystery fans were delighted; lovers of the historical novel were given their heart's desire; medievalists were generous in their admiration; learned readers celebrated its intertextuality – its apparently endless evocation, through direct quotation, of text after text from the past, from the Bible to Augustine to Wittgenstein, from Aristotle to St Hildegard of Bingens to Borges. The busiest commentators of all were the academics, particularly in Europe but in America as well, and an Eco industry was begun, tracing down every allusion to Eco's extensive critical publications and to his semiotic theories, and identifying all of the often obscure literary, theological, and philosophical texts incorporated as *disiecta membra* into the deceptively 'unified' surface of *The Name of the Rose*.

Indeed, interpretations show themselves to be uncommonly tightly controlled in advance by Eco's framework; paradoxically, this novel has turned out decidedly *not* to be in any straightforward way a free 'machine for generating interpretations' as its author claimed in his *Postscript to the Name of the Rose*. Interesting interpretations on the whole have only recently begun to be generated, and perhaps a 'free' interpretation is impossible. The first responses were off-center and useful only in small local terms – in the way, for example, that individual phrases, pages, and sections of the novel could be reacted to by the individual reader, or in the way that a critic and disciple like Teresa de Lauretis, for example, could slavishly connect to a theoretical context planned and planted by Eco. The problem lies partly in Eco's lexicon of critical theory, in the fact that the term 'interpretation' means different things for the ordinary reader or critic than it does for the theoretical semiotician. Eco does not want his novel ruined by excessive concentration on the theoretical concerns, but he is a fictionist whose double expertise, in a way imposed upon the reader, divides and obscures his intention, whatever it may be.

Most theorists believe that Eco's intention is the proving and illustration of his semiotic theories, and probably, teacher that he is, Eco began with this in mind. But he also obviously had a thoroughly good time in writing the novel, and it is to this and to its narrativity that most readers respond. John Freccero, in 'the fig tree and the laurel,' points out that St Augustine, as Eco well knows, talked about *uti* versus *frui* in respect to aesthetics, *tui* = use (the proper ethical or typological response) versus *frui* = enjoyment (an almost impious self-indulgence), and Eco merges the two in new and contemporary terms. What emerges from the well-earned success of this novel is a double argument or bifurcated response, in which theoreticians will choose the route of use and in doing so will be tightly controlled by Umberto Eco, the theorist. Readers of fiction, also but more subtly manipulated by the authorial voice, will go off in the other direction and receive the book with the pleasure the text generously delivers. But what does one do with this duplicity? Where and when ought the reader to feel that his/her job is to try to follow the hidden argument decodably primarily by the scholar or theorist, and when by contrast do more purely literary pleasures present us with a better or more authentic means of talking or writing about the text?

This nervous ambiguity about response was, but did not dramatically seem to be, a great problem when we had only *The Name of the Rose* itself – before, that is, Eco chose to interfere openly *in propria persona*. Like most successful authors unappeased by the enormous international critical and financial success of their novels, Umberto Eco also shows a negative side. He has seized every chance to rush through academic and popular high-priced international lecture circuits, and shows poor judgment in using the popularity of his novel to push into translation and print such early and meretricious books as his dated essays on James Joyce's aesthetics (*Aesthetics of Chaosmos*, originally published in Italian in 1966), as well as his 1952 dissertation on St Thomas Aquinas (recently issued by Harvard University Press) and glossy collections of his journalistic semiotic essays. At the same time he also continues to produce good scholarly work, including a rapid flow of books on semiotics – most recently, *Semiotics and the Philosophy of Language*. It remains clear at most levels that Eco sees his fiction as a tool for his theory, and that his desire is to be mammothly known in both realms simultaneously – as useful semiotician and theorist, and as famous novelist. This may be megalomania, but on the whole the case is more interesting than that, inasmuch as Eco, unlike most successful novelists, seems to consider the general public educable within his theoretical standards, and understands those standards as socially, politically, and culturally ameliorative.

It is troubling, however, to turn attentively to the tiny, expensively produced volume mentioned above, *Postscript to The Name of the Rose* (1984), an essay of considerable charm that denies one of its own central tenets – namely that the author should leave his original text alone. The form of publication itself presents a curious aspect, in that *Postscript* is published separately – and therefore not seen as integral – only in languages other than Italian. It Italy, Bompiani now binds it in one book with the novel as an adjunct to all editions, rather like Mann's afterword, *Die Entstehung* is now bound in most German editions of *Doktor Faustus*.

As it turns out, *Postscript* may be moderately useful to the relatively few non-Italian general readers who read it, but the condition of being pre-empted by the author, *hors de texte* so to speak, is interestingly reflective of a central problem in the reader's fate *vis-à-vis* contemporary fiction in general, where the author can be, and often is, competitively and noisily present. It is also a telling symptom of the nervous indeterminacy of the place of the novel in a reader's universe, or to reverse this into a more subtle issue, the reader's place in the writer's or novel's world. In spite of his theoretical statements to the contrary, Eco cannot limit his lexicon, let his reader go, or completely allow the text its own route.

Postscript raises problems on many levels, from the simplest to the most complex, and certainly is a unique moment in interpretative as well as in recent publishing history, a moment that goes beyond the standard interviews that most fictionists are willing to give to literary critics, journalists, and TV talk show anchormen. Much more pointed then Mann's description of *Doktor Faustus* or Nabokov's short, ironic, question-begging essay ('On a book entitled *Lolita*') published regularly in all editions of *Lolita* since 1958, Eco's supposedly serendipitous *libellus* has some of the same intentions Mann's and Nabokov's essays had – such as clarifying the publishing history, accounting for backgrounds, providing information about genesis and process, and, most significantly, directing the reader whose perusal of the original text is not considered trustworthy. At the same time it is evident that the project of writing an afterword was for Eco an ineluctable part of either the ambiguous original intention or the popular post publication result of *The Name of the Rose*. And whereas neither Mann nor Nabokov had demurrals about straightening out the reader. Eco has noisily proclaimed many, and continues to claim himself innocent of interference.

It seems to me programmatic that the novel needed something like the *Postscript*, in that the fiction itself imposes the following negative situations on the majority of the book's receptors: (1) this complex and scholarly book was not aimed at the general reader who only doubtfully knows why (s)he has been so absorbed by it; (2) the bookish non-scholar, or the reader not interested in current theoretical literary criticism such as Eco's own studies in semiotics, will automatically be bewildered and perhaps even feel resentment at the possibly excessive literary-textual aspects inherent in the putative murder-mystery's dénouement; (3) the extensive use of incompletely translated Latin throughout feels like a deliberate attempt to exclude all but certain kinds of readers – those whose knowledge of Latin is in good order, literary medievalists, and historians of the philosophical problem of the long Nominalist–Realist debate in the Middle Ages and how it might, through Peircean inversions, relate to current ideas of epistemology.

Since the scholarly-specialist group constitutes a fit audience though few, it apparently became obvious to Eco that more explanation could or should justifiably be forthcoming. The fact that he originally chose not to translate the last lines of the novel – the most telling Latin quotation in the book – makes it clear that from the beginning he intended secretiveness or refined decoding. The words '*Stat rosa pristina nomine, nomina nuda tenemus*' conclude the novel, and the intrinsic signs contained in these words are, in the book's original unpostscripted form, clear only to a mandarin few.

With scholarly problems lurking behind, but not in any way affecting, the popularity of *The Name of the Rose*, the question of authorial responsibility as opposed to the task of the reader/critic must be raised. Eco is fond of referring to Joyce's puzzles in *Finnegans Wake*, and reiterating that the ideal reader of Joyce – and he hopes of this novel too – is afflicted with an 'ideal insomnia'. But surely that insomnia is productive of decoding, of a thoroughly intelligent, participatory reading of Joyce's linguistic signs, of the reader's being, in short, the best of all possible semioticians. Although altogether too many critics have published 'keys' to Joyce's work, the process of enjoyment so strongly celebrated by Eco's commentary on his own novel and in his references to Joyce comes not from such crutches, but from the ideal reader's doing his/her job well. To put it another way, Joyce certainly helped out his critics in the 1930s, but did we ever want or need Joyce as author to publish an oblique commentary, even on a book as endlessly allusive as *Finnegans Wake*? Inevitably we must also ask if we want Eco to have written his *Postscript*, and into what category he has put his readers as the result of it.

In *Postscript*, Eco says (I wish him health and long life), 'The author should die once he has finished writing. So as not to trouble the path of the text.' In our deconstructionist time, it is easy to see this simply as a straightforward death-of-the-author statement. The useful conversation produced by a novel is not a dialogue between author and reader, but between text and reader (the author being at least metaphorically dead), and the restless urgency many contemporary writers feel to explain their work to their public is, at least theoretically, deplored by Eco. But he also subtly modifies his position, calling on Edgar Allen Poe in his own defence: 'The author must not interpret. But he may tell why and how he wrote the book.' The area of the licit should be fairly clear throughout this constraint, but in effect the amount and kind of information Eco gives both contaminate interpretation and impose significant limits on it. Just as one can be irritated when Thomas Pynchon deliberately and ironically misreads his recently issued early short stories in his 1984 preface to *Slow Learner*, so the reader of *Postscript* cannot avoid observing the tyranny imposed by Eco in his graceful giving and withholding of crucial information in this quasi-explanatory, only putatively non-interpretive essay. An easy example of this tricky area of friendly tyranny lies in the fact that the Latin of the final quotation of *The Name of the Rose* is identified by Eco as coming from Bernard of Morlay and is then set in a vaguely broad rather than precise context. '*Stat rosa pristina nomine, nomina nuda tenemus*' literally means 'the former rose remains through its name; we keep only pure names.' But Eco tells us in *Postscript* that

> the verse is from *De contemptu mundi* by Bernard of Morlay, a twelfth-century Benedictine, whose poem is a variation on the *ubi sunt* theme (most familiar in Villon's later *Mais où sont les neiges d'autun*). But to the usual topos ... Bernard adds that all these departed things leave (only, or at least) pure names behind them. I remember that Abelard used the example of the sentence *Nulla rosa est* to demonstrate how language can speak of both the nonexistent and the destroyed. And having said this, I leave the reader to arrive at his own conclusions.

No educated medievalist can think about the name of the rose without knowing that the evocation is Nominalist; Eco mentions Abelard, but in fact queers the direction of enquiry toward the more casual aspects of a *carpe diem* theme, which can indeed lead to a simple and comfortable reading for those who do not wish to enquire too far into the possible stretch and play of the text. But the mention of Abelard most indicate to the next level of reader that Abelard too should be checked out within an unweaving of the referential frame, and of course the educated medievalist will known that all roses in the Middle Ages were shadowed by Abelard's use of that example in laying the Nominalist groundwork. Just as the novel's hero, William of Baskerville, contrasts the religious and political comprehension available to the 'simple' of his time to that practiced by the learned, Eco here firmly guides the two poles of his audience.

I would argue strongly that Eco does not leave the reader 'to arrive at his own conclusions, 'but that in deciding how much information to give in the *Postscript* he engineers a simple reading for the simple and complex but precise work for the *cognoscenti*. He follows his controlled dispensing of limited information with the following statement:

> A narrator should not supply interpretations of his work; otherwise he would not have written a novel, which is a machine for generating interpretations. But one of the chief obstacles to his maintaining this virtuous principle is the fact that a novel must have a title.

If a novel is indeed a 'machine for generating interpretations,' then an authorially controlled range of possibilities should in honesty not be externally presented beyond the highly connotative title, simply because such an apparatus closes the possibilities of still further readings, and holds the reader in the author's interpretative grasps.

From his first book on semiotics and criticism, *Opera Aperta* (1962), Eco has been obsessed with the contrast between 'open' and 'closed' texts, and all his subsequent theoretical works have tried to explain the difference between the two. If a novel is 'a machine for generating interpretations,' some definition of an open text, requiring polysemous or infinite interpretation, is in order. In lectures, Eco delights in tracing the closed idea of allegory and contrasting it with the open system of symbol, proving the progression by working from Augustine to the pseudo-Dionysus and Giordano Bruno. His emphasis is theological, separating *allegoria in verbis* (rhetorical/grammatical criticism) from *allegoria in factis*, which deals with the increasing need in the Middle Ages and Renaissance to interpret Christ polysemously.

What precisely Eco means by terms like an open text or infinite semiosis remains rather obscure, however, and finally the exact nature of the contrast between open and closed texts is sharply modified by the fact that Eco tends to think like a hybrid cross between Thomas Aquinas and C.S. Peirce. In other words, his idea of infinite semiosis or interpretation cannot at all be generalized by the reader into an interpretational Abbaye de Thélème, where, to quote Eco's beloved Rabelais, *Faicts ce que Voudras* (interpretational chaos) is the order of the day. Eco argues that in any given text the symbol (the vehicle whereby we formulate an interpretation) is anchored to the terms of that text, and therefore infinite semiosis is possible only insofar as the text controls the terms of the interpretation the reader might make. To put it directly and rather negatively, there can be infinity only within prior constraints: any number of readings is possible except those that deny the text's basic mandate.

Let me modify this negative statement by putting it more exactly into the context of Eco's idea of infinite 'interpretation': arguing from a predominantly historicist bias in his theoretical works, Eco claims that interpretation has always depended on the 'encyclopedia' of knowledge within which the text was composed or is received. This encyclopedia of knowledge can be assumed to a degree within the text's milieu and immediate historical period, but in a changeable world, something automatically happens every day that over a period of time challenges our models and makes our interpretations shifting and ultimately unstable. The encyclopedia of assumed knowledge for reading a text is generally taken for granted by the author, but (s)he cannot assume its universality or persistence. Nevertheless, in positing the idea of a 'model reader,' the author can assume at least temporarily that (s)he and the reader exist within the same encyclopedic frame, and indeed that the author is godlike in positing a world/cosmos and educating the reader in its terminology. Thus Eco creates a model reader who will respond positively to the Middle Ages and the Nominalist-scientistic-progressive world he posits. Readings that belong in other free-floating categories are basically excluded.

In conjunction with this sort of thinking about the creation of the 'model reader,' Eco closes other doors without apparently noticing them. In all of his work including *Postscript*, and especially in *The Role of the Reader*, he presents the author's task in creating the *model reader* as a project that at first glance looks quite benign. The model reader is apparently one whose interpretative fluidity is such that the author can write for him/her, foreseeing and building into the text every possible reaction or reading conceivable. Under such subtly and fluidly predetermined circumstances, the Eco-esque reader is at the opposite extreme to the now fashionable Nietzschean idea that interpretation is not found within the autonomy of the text, but made by the creative reader. Eco cantankerously or paradoxically argues that the reader is free to make his/her own interpretation, but not creatively: (s)he is bound by the manipulation of the providential author. His is most decidedly not the line of the current catch phrase of 'creative reading,' where the reader challenges the author as an equal maker of the text, although Eco does allow the reader small private originalities (what, for example, is the nature of William of Baskerville's pity, if he has any?). Observe the author as maker/creator of the model reader in *Postscript*:

> What model reader did I want as I was writing? An accomplice, to be sure, one who would play my game. I wanted to become completely medieval and live in the Middle Ages as if that were my own period (and vice versa). But at the same time, with all my might, I wanted to create a type of reader who, once the initiation was past, would

become my prey – or, rather, the prey of the text – and would think he wanted nothing but what the text was offering him. A text is meant to be an experience of transformation for its reader. You believe you want sex and a criminal plot where the guilty party is discovered at the end, and all with plenty of action, but at the same time you would be ashamed to accept old-fashioned rubbish made up of the living dead, nightmare abbeys, and black penitents. All right, then, I will give you Latin, practically no women, lots of theology, gallons of blood in Grand Guignol style, to make you say, 'But all this is false; I refuse to accept it!' And at this point you will have to be mine, and feel the thrill of God's infinite omnipotence, which makes the world's order vain. And then, if you are good, you will realize how I lured you into this trap, because I was really telling you about it at every step, I was carefully warning you that I was dragging you to your damnation.

'God's infinite omnipotence, I was dragging you to your damnation': surely this is the rhetoric of a medieval, theologized version of the very attractive nineteenth-century idea of the passive reader whose intelligence and sensibility are controlled by the writer-god into whose hands we submit ourselves with no deconstructionist intention. All is foreseen, all providential in a world where infinity and freedom in their usual definitions are disallowed. Only the plurality of worlds (historical periods, special interests, ideological preconceptions, etc.), productive of a plurality of encyclopedias, can open the text beyond the author's evocations as he designs the model reader.

The Name of the Rose, then, is a controlled book in spite of Eco's ambiguous protestations, didactic or perhaps even propagandistic in its design. The medieval idea of *sentential* or meaning contained in and even obscured by the husk of entertainment for the simple is paramount. Its agent is William of Baskerville, the Franciscan monk hero of *The Name of the Rose*, who talks and talks, consistently teaching the young Benedictine novice Adso who, in old age, becomes our narrator. Through a brilliant sequence of narrative ordering, these progressive verbal lessons become the novel's ideological vehicle, and as such subvert the text's ostensible task of solving the mystery of the increasing number of dead monks. William's conversations and explanations give us both historical and philosophical information, and once the original or primary pleasure of the novel, finding our whodunnit, has been served, it is with increasing care that the reader returns to the magisterial words of this unambiguous and utterly trustworthy secondary narrator. The book's real narrator – Adso of Melk in old age remembering and modifying the Adso he was in youth – is of course transparently untrustworthy, like Nellie Dean in *Wuthering Heights* or Serenus Zeitblom in Thomas Mann's *Doktor Faustus* (a source Eco mentions). But like other narrators in the venerable reportorial tradition, Adso renders the words of his subject faithfully, even while he undercuts him judgmentally.

An ambiguous thread in the labyrinth of William's pedagogy is the contrast between the simple and the learned. The beliefs of the simple spring from their unprescient desires to link the social miseries of their lives to the shifting theological fashions rising with unequal authority from the philosophical disputes of the learned. The contrast William's cogitations set up between the simple and the learned can ironically be applied to the two audiences Eco has succeeded in addressing, and indeed dualities and bifurcations are central to all the thinking that this rich novel gives rise to. Although the substance of this book firmly and aggressively addresses the learned, its saving strength and marvelous possession are its educational kindness to the simple, its sense of function within a novelistic rather than a purely semiotic-theoretical-philosophical frame.

In spite of Eco's theoretical leanings, the popularity of *The Name of the Rose* surely comes from its 'husk' qualities rather than its *sententiae*, and the inevitable backlash against it has begun with naive practical (as opposed to theoretical) critics re-evaluating it and claiming crankily that it is contrived. All books within the detective-novel genre are, or else they would not be capable of being thus described by Eco: 'And since I wanted you to feel as pleasurable the one thing that frightens us – namely, the metaphysical shudder – I had only to choose (from among the model plots) the most metaphysical and philosophical: the detective novel.' When the American critic Edward Mendelson seriously but bizarrely states that *The Name of the Rose* is inferior because of its contrivance and shallowness to a small, contained novel like John Fuller's medieval-monastery metaphysical fantasy, *Flying to Nowhere*, he is obviously arguing from premises that are more innocently novelistic and less ambitiously ironic than Eco's. Given the aspirations and achievements of the two novels, he is comparing apples and oranges on the basis of the mere and barren facts that both texts are set in the Middle Ages and have a monk detective hero. This desire to read the novel merely novelistically cannot, of course, be considered a fault, since the book is indeed a novel and the only, far from debased, means by which Eco's name and ideas could ever have come so dramatically to the forefront of international contemporary attention. It is nevertheless essential to a just reading of *The Name of the Rose*, to uncover some of its message to the *cognoscenti* before turning to the pleasures it also grants to the simple, to the ranks of eager and even naive readers of novels, among whom I count myself an enthusiastic member.

It would be monomania indeed if Umberto Eco's primary didactic attention in this novel were directed toward an exposition of an arid strip of semiotic theorizing. But his voracious appetite for the objects and ideas of culture – Aristotle, the Middle Ages, comic strips, current film, etc. – indicates that his theory is largely a means of making the history of human insight coherent and subject to analysis. In an important incident in *The Name of the Rose* the narrator Adso, caught by the hallucinatory drugs that protect the forbidden library of the Aedificium, is given a sudden, bookish illumination in the midst of the labyrinth, quite different from the illuminations of the gorgeous medieval texts on which he has been fixing his eyes:

> My eye became lost, on the page, along gleaming paths, as my feet were becoming lost in the troublous succession of the rooms of the library, and seeing my own wandering depicted on those parchments filled me with uneasiness and convinced me that each of those books was telling, through mysterious cachinnations, my present story. 'De te fabula narratur,' I said to myself, and I wondered if those pages did not already contain the story of future events in store for me.

The idea that one is oneself the subject of all tales told – *de te fabula narratur* (the tale is told about *you*) – takes Baudelaire's *hypocrite lecteur – mon semblable, mon frère* back in history to the Middle Ages and stresses the book's – any book's – primary ability to cancel the boundaries of time. This medieval tale laced with the history of a period apparently so separated from ours enforces our identity with its world rather than our historical alienation. Italian reviewers were not wrong when they claimed that Eco's novel was politically apt to the late twentieth century; it is equally true that its intellectual directions are those that Eco sees as pertinent to and urges upon contemporary thinkers.

It is significant that whereas William thinks, Adso, his pupil-grown-old, writes, making a book that will be the only agent of communication. William's thought processes, ideas, conclusions, skills, and drive toward truth would be terminal without the existence of a book that talks of him and, even more crucially, of the other books through which he learned to make his mind function at its high level of achievement. The fiction that Adso innocently and ignorantly presents about his master is, like so much medieval fiction, an employment of larger, general truths that Eco wishes to communicate. The major point of the novel is that no book is an independent entity, and private existential self-referentiality is an impossibility. The degree to which the mind is formulated by written data and our perusal of them is immeasurable. As William explains it to Adso:

> 'Often books speak of other books. Often a harmless book is like a seed that will blossom into a dangerous book, or it is the other way

around: it is the sweet fruit of a bitter stem. In reading Albert, couldn't I learn what Thomas might have said? Or in reading Thomas, know what Averroës said?'

'True,' I said, amazed. Until then I had thought each book spoke of the things, human or divine, that lie outside books. Now I realized that not infrequently books speak of books: it is as if they spoke among themselves. In the light of this reflection, the library seemed all the more disturbing to me. It was then the place of a long, centuries-old murmuring, an imperceptible dialogue between one parchment and another, a living thing, a receptacle of powers not to be ruled by a human mind, a treasure of secrets emanated by many minds, surviving the death of those who had produced them or had been their conveyors.

This is certainly non-novelistic thinking, even in a period like our own where all sense of definition or genre imposed by the nineteenth century was lost long ago in the rising mists of Modernism. The novel has always assumed that 'each book spoke of the things, human or divine, that lie outside books.' Realism depended on mimetic correspondence, and even after Joyce's parataxis or fragmentation, some kind of correspondence theory has been essential. The post-structuralist argument that language is always the subject of language has created a plethora of fictive ironies, but the idea that books are always about books and not about knowledge of either human or divine things is even for the modern mind as unbalancing as Adso's perception of it. Even more significantly, the idea that all books narrate us (*de te fabula narratur*) pushes us into a non-existential area where we live only within the mythos of books and die in and by texts. *The Name of the Rose* is almost endlessly about books, that 'treasure of secrets emanated by many minds, surviving the death of those who had produced them or had been their conveyors,' in that it consists of an extended collection of quotations, and whispers at every point of the books our culture knows and which this text endows with extended resonance.

Near the end of *The Name of the Rose*, Adso tells us that he returned to the ruins of the monastery many years after its destruction by fire, wandering about picking up torn bits of surviving parchment that he carried back to Melk. These disordered, tragically partial shreds of the great library reflect the theme of *disiecta membra*, ill-assorted, cast-aside fragments of a once unified whole, that is so important to the ironies inherent in this novel. Adso's pitiable collection of verbal fragments cannot be pieced together into coherence, just as the monk Salvatore's language cannot become other than a nearly incomprehensible *maccedonia* of the various languages and dialects – French, Provençal, Italian, and Latin – that he has picked up in a scrambling, politically wretched struggle from poverty into his present comfort as a permitted hanger-on in the abbey.

When the idea of the scattered fragments or *disiecta membra* is combined with the trope of the world-turned-upside-down (semiotic adynaton), it becomes clear why the particular form of *The Name of the Rose* is so useful as an ideological vehicle. Within the framework of Eco's thought, one might say that the text is an ingenious strategy to produce a model reader who will see that avenues through the labyrinth opened by the collection of quotations, which constitute the *disiecta membra* of the novel. Moreover, it is then the quest of the model reader to transform the metaphysical mysteries, as well as the real ones, into a tentative statement, and in this case the statement must irreducibly be one that asserts a disordered world of fragments in which system and thought are only intermittently successful. If there is any firm message in this novel, it is about the calamitous impossibility of statement or order in a chaotic, constantly shifting universe.

Of the many sub-genres of the novel genre from Victorian times to the present, none has been as pervasive among authors purporting to write beyond the merely popular than the idea of the detective novel. One thinks automatically of Dickens, Poe, Collins, and Conan Doyle in the nineteenth century and Nabokov, Spark, Murdoch, Calvino, and Greene in the twentieth. And of course it was the power of detective fiction that first began the deterioration of the rigid European-art separation between high and low culture. Part of the attraction came from the sheer perspicacity of Edgar Allen Poe's detective, C. Auguste Dupin, who was almost a fictional alter ego for the American philosopher C.S. Peirce, with his passion for empirical observation and the conclusions such sign-reading automatically lead to. Even more popular and attractive was the creation of Sir Arthur Conan Doyle's foolproof sleuth, Sherlock Holmes (a worthy successor to the English medieval cognitive empiricists, Roger Bacon and William of Occam, celebrated in *The Name of the Rose*), whose genius spawned whole collections of twentieth-century detective heroes and heroines. Eco of course invokes the shade of Conan Doyle's tale, 'The Hound of the Baskervilles,' when he names his sleuth William of Baskerville. Indeed the first episode of *The Name of the Rose*, in which William guesses that the abbot's horse is lost and locates it, is comically parodic of any Sherlock Holmes story. Eco, who is not above dallying with his readers' intelligence, thus falsely formulates in many readers from the beginning the expectation that this will be a tidy account of a solved murder mystery.

And things are duly unraveled, but almost by mistake, for this book turns the detective novel (and everything else) upside down by showing how fragile and chancy William's deductions are, and how skewed and almost defeated he is in following his bookish theories. Early in the novel,

Adso gives us a clue to the strangeness of this novel's world when he stops the narrative to express in his own words and many borrowed from medieval sources his extended aesthetic delight at the sculpted stone doorway of the abbey church. The long, eloquent passage illustrates one of Eco's many successes in this fiction – his splendid ability to free medieval visual representation from mannered rigidity into vividly felt beauty of form – but it also shows how apt a vehicle for thematics such contemplation can be.

An apocalyptic vision of the Last Judgment, the stone sculpture (Eco's model is the entrance to the abbey church at Moissac in Gascony) reveals to the ecstatic Adso an anonymous image of ordered justice and cosmos. The judging figure is of course the Christ of the Apocalypse, but is identified neutrally as the 'Seated One' and the figures of mankind, evangelists, prophets, etc., are torqued and twisted as they writhe inward toward the throne, the object of attention. The ornamentation surrounding the sculpture is of the grotesque world-turned-upside-down sort reminiscent of the Boschian bestiary that Adelmo, the monk-illustrator whose corpse begins the series, had typically painted in his manuscript illuminations. As Adso suddenly loses his capacity to name Christ and neutralizes him by calling him simply the Seated One, he inverts his elsewhere obvious, obedient, conventionally held faith, and the torque of the bodies of men and animals in the sculpture indicates an almost baroque twisting of order, a *discordia concors* or reversal of unified harmonic order.

Within the framework of this aesthetically enrapturing medieval sculpture, then, Adso perceives or constructs a partial semiotic adynaton or world reversal that illustrates the structure and intention of this novel. The naive reader, expert in the art and craft of reading murder-mysteries, will search in van for the orderly world of well-contained cause and effect in *The Name of the Rose*, where the vagaries of fragmentation are triumphant, and where every object has to be looked at with an insight and vividness not typical of conventional perception. This need to look carefully is, of course, endemic to an alert reading of the detective novel in general and is characterized by this book's detective-hero, William. But William is in crucial ways a failed hero: he stumbles on his dénouement while his reasoning has demonstrated its limitations, and much of his intelligence is vainly deployed. Eco makes it clear in *Postscript* that he assumes a process of reader transformation, that it is his will to alter the perceptions and expectations of those who are following the text, and obviously he wishes to alter and in certain ways enrich cant notions of hero and solutions:

> The reader was to be diverted, but not di-verted, distracted from problems. *Robinson Crusoe* is meant to divert its own model reader,

telling him about the calculations and the daily actions of a sensible *homo oeconomicus* much like himself. But Robinson's *semblable*, after he has enjoyed reading about himself in the novel, should somehow have understood something more, become another person. In amusing himself, somehow, he has learned. The reader should learn something either about the world or about language: this difference distinguishes various narrative poetics, but the point remains the same.

Among the many things necessarily learned by a reader following Eco's signposts is that the closed, terminal logic of preconceived designs or theories impedes the ability of the observer to see what is actually in front of him. So William, like Borges's detective Eric Lönnrot in 'Death and the Compass,' is led astray for altogether too long by his bookish ingenuity – in this case his knowledge of the Book of Revelation and the fact that the monastery is famous for its quantity and quality of illuminated moralized Apocalypse manuscripts. A rigid pattern of killings reflecting the images of the seven trumpets of Revelation appears fascinating but is wrong. While he concentrates on such a preconceived set piece, William temporarily fails in other much more crucial tasks like solving the riddle to the opening of the *finis Africae* and locating the proper identification of the mysterious and lethal book. Eco's point here is transparently pedagogical and in keeping with his essential idea of open as opposed to closed texts. William, in assuming even temporarily that the solution to the murders might lie in the closed text of the Apocalypse, becomes a bad reader reliant on a limited anterior text rather than working under the aegis of infinite possibility. The interesting point is that William has been trained in openness and scientism, and his lapse into pattern or closedness gives a stern example of how treacherous the inaccurate use of signs is for even the best mind.

When Eco talks about openness, he implies that any response accurately reflective of the referential encyclopedia of both author and reader should be allowed equal freedom or primacy. For this reason, apparently, he claims that he as author does not and should not interpret. Hence those who wish to read the novel as detective fiction may do so without violating the boundaries or *a priori* function of the text; but in interview Eco claims that the naive readers have carried this aspect too far, seeing *The Name of the Rose* only or primarily as a detective novel. The implication is that the integrity of the book has somehow become darkened in the process. At the same time, he acknowledges this novel as both detective and historical fiction, and much authorial energy is devoted to making it both. Nevertheless, the percipient reader of *The Name of the Rose* should find his/her way fairly quickly to another mode of reading that indicates the marginality of the novel's detective story cast. Put briefly, this latter aspect is primarily tonal and functional, associated with the semiotics of Peirce and Poe, as well as medieval empirical scientism in the English tradition of William of Occam and Roger Bacon. Once a sense of sign-reading is gained through William's complex example of success and failure, the reader can then work on the more pointed directions of the fiction.

Here there can be little doubt that, despite all of Eco's deflections of this subject, his real purpose is didactic to a quite extraordinary extent. He claims that in the written word there is only one authorial intention (*intentio auctoris*) which is the book itself, its textual existence being its only interpretational boundary. At the same time he argues that as author of *The Name of the Rose* he has permitted or guided the recipient toward a vast plurality of interests and interpretations pursuable by the reader who is free to choose any one possibility from the multitude presented. But in fact the various dominant subjects meet not in infinity but within the logical extensions of the text itself, and one can give fairly objective descriptions of the almost propagandistic thrust of the thematics of the novel.

If there is a thoroughly wrought and stable theme in our time it is that of indeterminacy as opposed to the tyranny of the absolute. In textual terms, this means that freedom of interpretation fights against the idea of an anterior, established truth, and Eco in this novel is one of its most adamant and interesting exponents. His passion for the Middle Ages allows him the presentation almost *sub rosa* (allow me the pun) of an intellectual situation very much analogous to our own, whether we think of ourselves as mere citizens or active critics of the present. Eco gives his motivating signal through the title of the novel with its Nominalist connotations, and there can be no doubt that the medieval Nominalists were the ancestors of our relativist world of whirling symbols and constantly realigned models. Nominalist thought automatically led to scientism in that Nominalism denies that abstract thought can be based on other than names (or models). These must be altered, decoded, rethought because empirical evidence and relentless Aristotelian logic, applied to both abstract names and concrete experience, progressively render such rethinking necessary.

The enemies to the Nominalists, the Realists, bear no real resemblance to the novelistic or Auerbachian tradition of realism, but are in fact Platonist-Augustinian in impulse. The Realists are so named because their constant reference is to an anterior reality such as the world of forms or God – in Christian terminology, a Logos whose stability is eternal, unquestionable, and separated from the empirical experience of our world. Their automatic referent is the divine; their psychological frame that of *contemptus mundi*.

Eco's espousal of the Nominalist background is obvious from his title, but he allows his naive narrator, Adso, to open the novel with the evocation of the Logos from the Gospel according to St John: 'In the beginning was the Word and the Word was with God, and the Word was God,' thus beginning *The Name of the Rose* with a strong text for the Realists and closing the book with a strong text for the Nominalists. Adso sees himself as 'the transparent witness of the happenings that took place in the abbey,' but he does not perceive as an old man and only dimly as a youth the lessons his master tries to teach him through the events and conversations of the book. The detective-Nominalist Williams sets himself progressively against the set pieces of medieval doctrine, the idea of the comprehensibility of the Logos that makes God exist, and reliance on an anterior text like the Apocalypse. The idea of an absolute anterior text can give explanation and comforting coherence to a world-turned-upside-down, composed of *disiecta membra* or fragments that William's contemporaries too easily identify as signs of the devil in the world.

Adso as narrator assumes that eventually coherence in a world apparently ruled by evil will be revealed by or resolved in God, and that he, now an old moribund monk, will in death enter the world of mystic bliss so luminously expressed by fourteenth-century saints. His flight into the divine nothingness is an anti-interpretational escape from a largely meaningless, disjointed world imaged by his senseless parchment fragments collected from the ruins of the monastery. This disjointed world is, on the other hand, one that the hard empiricist mind – like William of Baskerville's – sees as necessary and something to be worked with. Adso's report of his fragmentary, meaningless parchment sheets is throughout the novel ironically paralleled by the intertextual congeries of quotation that comprises the fiction, and the idea of chaotic indeterminacy is textually reinforced. As Adso describes it and as readers accept it, the hopeless compulsion to work on the fragments and partial signs of the universe is illustrated by the, for Adso, incomprehensible text of the novel itself:

> The more I reread this list the more I am convinced it is the result of chance and contains no message. But these incomplete pages have accompanied me through all the life that has been left me to live since then; I have often consulted them like an oracle, and I have almost had the impression that what I have written on these pages, which you will now read, unknown reader, is only a cento, a figured hymn, an immense acrostic that says and repeats nothing but what those fragments have suggested to me, nor do I know whether thus far I have been speaking of them or they have spoken through my mouth.

Had Adso followed William's teaching closely and precisely, he could have perceived the irony intrinsic to the human situation which William is at such pains to illustrate. As the monastery burns to the ground, the master and the novice, in the novel's most important conversation, discuss the errors of William's initial techniques:

'I have never doubted the truth of signs, Adso; they are the only things man has with which to orient himself in the world. What I did not understand was the relation among signs. I arrived at Jorge through an apocalyptic pattern that seemed to underlie all the crimes, and yet it was accidental. I arrived at Jorge seeking one criminal for all the crimes and we discovered that each crime was committed by a different person, or by no one. I arrived at Jorge pursuing the plan of a perverse and rational mind, and there was no plan, or, rather, Jorge himself was overcome by his own initial design and there began a sequence of causes, and concauses, and of causes contradicting one another, which proceeded on their own, creating relations that did not stem from any plan. Where is all my wisdom, then? *I behave stubbornly, pursuing a semblance of order, when I should have known well that there is no order on the universe* ... The only truths that are useful are instruments to be thrown away ... It's hard to accept the idea that there cannot be an order in the universe because it would offend the free will of God and His omnipotence. So the freedom of God is our condemnation, or at least the condemnation of our pride.'

(italics added)

This statement of semiotic necessity leads Adso to a desperately brief moment of insight that summarizes the torque of human existence in a medieval world in which the concept of God is demonstrated as impossible:

I dared, for the first and last time in my life, to express a theological conclusion: 'But how can a necessary being exist totally polluted with the possible? What difference is there, then, between God and primogenial chaos? Isn't affirming God's absolute omnipotence and His absolute freedom with regard to His own choices *tantamount to demonstrating that God does not exist?*

(italics added)

All of *The Name of the Rose* leads to this skeptical conclusion, a conclusion that Adso can speak momentarily, but then forgets forever. William answers the question by positing another sort of ironic necessity and Adso's final questions go unanswered except by inference:

William looked at me without betraying any feeling in his features, and he said, 'How could a learned man go on communicating his learning if he answered yes to your question?' I did not understand the meaning of his words. 'Do you mean,' I asked, 'that there would be no possible and communicable learning any more if the very criterion of truth were lacking, or do you mean you could no longer communicate what you know because others would not allow you to?'

This conversation implies Eco's situation as didactic writer and ironic apologist for a skewed, indeterminate, necessary world. The human mind has materials to work with, but through logical inference no God (i.e. absolute anterior text) and no perfect unraveling of reality. If reality is temporarily found in a small way – as, for example, Jorge is found at the base of most of the monastery murders – it happens partly by chance and partly by semiotic decoding. Human intelligence makes us sign-readers but does not guarantee our courage to be accurate or our consistency; this novel offers us a parody (and Eco is quite aware of the parasitic nature of parody) of the tightly contained structure of the murder mystery, and in doing so proves definitively that the very existence of the genre is a mental fiction, and an illustration in its own unrealistic way of an anterior idea whose dominant quality is easy certainty rather than the ambiguous, indeterminate world in which life is incomprehensibly led. This ultimate labyrinth of the monastery's library, and as Eco subtly shows, an orderly view of life is to reality what the tidy murder mystery is to this novel's detailed and extensive exploration of the indeterminacy of the world and the limited possibilities of the human mind.

There are other areas of ideology within *The Name of the Rose* that must not be overlooked in estimating its intellectually didactic nature. As an historical novel it involves the reader in some of the major disputes of the fourteenth century, notably the controversy about apostolic poverty and the quarrels about the laughter of Christ. At the same time, William's presence as imperial legate challenges the injustice of inquisitorial methods in the Church as practised by men like Bernard Gui, and his position ultimately indicates the need to break the secular power of the papacy so misused by John XXII in Avignon.

The wealth of material about the 'heretical' Fraticelli and Dolcinians, and parallel controversies within the Franciscan order, give a rich and firm texture to the irreducible political ramifications of the novel which are socialist and ameliorative in nature. In *Postscript*, Eco says that early in his thinking about the fiction he wanted to make his investigating hero a contemporary priest who read the left-wing Italian newspaper *Il Manifesto*, but there can be little doubt that this is another red herring thrown at the reader to divert him/her from the larger issues. Certainly a socialist inclination toward change in society is an automatic outgrowth of the novel's emphasis on seeing human beings as part of a mobile system in which empiricism must discover whatever routes there might be toward justice. And the dominant idea that dogmas represent closed, repressive texts automatically argues against both right-wing establishmentarianism and doctrinaire Marxism.

But *The Name of the Rose*, despite its historical strengths, never wanders very far from its bookish inclinations. Behind its structure is not only the necessary fourteenth-century opposition between medieval Realism and Nominalism, but also between Platonism as a fixed mode and Aristotelianism as a steady movement toward change and amelioration. Most of the deaths in the monastery occur because of the ideological duel being fought by William and his arch intellectual adversary Jorge of Burgos; the two adverse characters were obviously essentially created as allegorical representations of the two schools of thought that are thrown into absolute conflict in so many ways in this novel. Whereas William represents a manifold idea of openness, Jorge fights to the death against Aristotle's opening out of the Platonic system, and in a stroke of ingenious bookishness Eco builds his whole dénouement on the lost second part of Aristotle's *Poetics*, the book on comedy whose argument fits so well into the quarrel about the laughter of Christ.

Early in the novel, William makes it clear that the monkish love of books in this library world can lead to death, and petty quarrels arise about the nature of bookishness and its power. Indeed, the monks in the abbey are more likely to have a point of view about the knowledge obtained from the specific kinds of books that interest each of them than they are to have a character in any traditional novelistic sense. But in spite of its intertextuality and vast allusive frame, *The Name of the Rose* does not immediately impress on many of its readers the degree to which its task is the presentation of the primacy of books. Books and their denotation in the life of the mind, of the spirit, of society, and of the individual can actively lead to death which, in this novel, easily comes from ideological controversies and from pursuing the wrong text of forbidden knowledge. As a result, some readers have proclaimed their disappointment that the real culprit could be a blind, atavistic old man whose hatred of Aristotelian progressive thought could lead to moral destructiveness on a hugely impenitent scale. Some put it more bluntly, disliking the idea that all of the murders in the abbey could connect to nothing more 'serious' than the lost book on comedy in Aristotle's *Poetics*.

But for Jorge the destruction of that book is major to the maintenance of Christian faith; for William its survival is equally important for its ironic potentiality and the connexion of that potentiality to ameliorative steps forward for the questing mind. As the two adversaries confront each other in the *finis Africae* of the library for their final 'shoot out,' Jorge desperately explains why Aristotle's treatment of laughter – laughter that would overturn the world in a senseless anti-Logos or Anti-Christ – must destroy the eternal certainty of Christianity:

> 'Because it [the treatise on comedy] was by the Philosopher. Every book by that man has destroyed a part of the learning that Christianity had accumulated over the centuries. The fathers had said everything that needed to be known about the powers of the World, but then Boethius had only to gloss the Philosopher and the divine mystery of the Word was transformed into a human parody of categories and syllogism ... We knew everything about the divine names, and the Dominican buried by Abo [Thomas Aquinas] – renamed them, following the proud paths of natural reason ... Before, we used to look to heaven, deigning only a frowning glance at the mire of matter; now we look at the earth, and we believe in the heavens because of earthly testimony. Every word of the Philosopher, by whom now even saints and prophets swear, has overturned the image of the world. But he had not succeeded in overturning the image of God. If this book were to become ... had become an object for open interpretation, we would have crossed the last boundary ... from this book many corrupt minds like yours would draw the extreme syllogism, whereby laughter is man's end! Laughter, for a few moments, distracts the villein from fear. *But law is imposed by fear, whose true name is fear of God*. This book could strike the Luciferine spark that would set a new fire to the whole world ... and from this book there could be born the new destructive aim to destroy death through redemption from fear ... this book – considering comedy a wondrous medicine, with its satire and mime, which would produce the purification of the passions through the enactment of defect, fault, weakness – would induce false scholars to try to redeem the lofty with a diabolical reversal: through the acceptance of the base. This book could prompt the idea that man can wish to have on earth (as your Bacon suggested with regard to natural magic) the abundance of the land of Cockaigne. *But this is what we cannot and must not have'*.
>
> (italics added)

Jorge's frantic belief that the loss of the central, authoritative Logos must mean the loss of all knowledge and certainty is countered by William's optimistically progressive notion that 'I would match my wit with the wit of others. It would be a better world than the one where the fire and red-hot iron of Bernard Gui humiliate the fire and red-hot iron of Dolcino.'

But Jorge is adamant, and in his wonderfully mad bibliophagy as he tears the poisoned pages of the linen book and stuffs them into his mouth, Aristotle's text is lost – and so is the splendid library, in a holocaust of ecpyrosis that reflects a new sort of apocalypse, the end of a cosmos of books that in the fourteenth century still cannot be used as a vital source to forge an enlightened world.

It remains palpably true at the end of *The Name of the Rose*, however, that the stylized character of William of Baskerville has achieved success of a major sort. Eco is scrupulously accurate in creating this twentieth-century fourteenth-century man, giving him thoughts that could be historically possible in a world that had created cognitive scientists like Roger Bacon and philosophers like William of Occam. Yet William is of necessity defeated by history and by an overriding ideology whose adversaries were not yet ready to take the progressive steps necessary to create the empirical world already implied in Nominalism. At the same time, his triumph lies in self-analysis and in the fact that he has seen clearly and justly the whole episode. William of Baskerville passes the tests set by Peirce in talking about 'the ideal inquirer'. He is not yet – nor are we – in an adequately advanced position to imagine what the philosopher Hilary Putnam might 'idealize' as life at the end of enquiry, but he accomplishes the ameliorative aim of Eco's novel.

The reader of this carefully designed novel should, if (s)he follows the author's thorough instructions, be transformed into a being ready for the next steps necessary in a neo-enlightenment of contemporary man that is Umberto Eco's most aggressive and kindly task. Only a churlish reader would be unwilling to allow him his success at this point in his mission.

Bibliography

For reasons made clear in the Introduction, this list does not attempt to name metafictions as primary or fictional sources. Instead it aims to indicate texts not included in this volume which are relevant to its themes of self-consciousness, historiographical self-consciousness and the figure of the writer/critic, as well as case studies of metafictional writings. The first section includes work explicitly dealing with the concept of metafiction. The second lists works of related interest. Relevant materials also appear regularly in journals such as the *Journal of Narrative Techniques, Novel, Critique, Modern Fiction Studies, Triquarterly, Boundary 1*, and the *Partisan Review*.

Works on metafiction

ALTER, ROBERT, *Partial Magic: the Novel as a Self-Conscious Genre* (London and Berkeley: University of California Press, 1975.

CHRISTENSEN, INGER, *The Meaning of Metafiction: a Critical Study of Selected Novels by Sterne, Nabokov, Barth and Beckett* (Bergen: Universitetsforlaget, 1982).

HASSAN, IHAB, *The Dismemberment of Orpheus: Toward a Post-Modern Literature* (New York and Oxford: Oxford University Press, 1979).

HUTCHEON, LINDA, *Narcissistic Narrative: the Metafictional Paradox* (London: Methuen, 1980).

HUTCHEON, LINDA, *A Poetics of Postmodernism: History, Theory, Fiction* (New York and London: Routledge, 1988).

IMHOF, RUDIGER, *Contemporary Metafiction: a Poetological Study of Metafiction in English since 1939* (Heidelberg: Carl Winter Universitatsverlag, 1986).

MCCAFFERY, LARRY, *The Metafictional Muse* (Pittsburgh: University of Pittsburgh Press, 1982).

ROSE, MARGARET, *Parody/Meta-fiction: an Analysis of Parody as Critical Mirror to the Writing and Reception of Fiction* (London: Croom Helm, 1979).

SCHOLES, ROBERT, *Fabulation and Metafiction* (Chicago: University of Illinois Press, 1979).

WAUGH, PATRICIA, *Metafiction: the Theory and Practice of Self-Conscious Fiction* (London and New York: Methuen, 1984).

ZAVARZADEH, MAS'UD, *The Mythopoeic Reality* (Urbana, Ill. and London: University of Illinois Press, 1976).

Further reading

BAR, EUGEN, 'Things are Stories: a Manifesto for a Reflexive Semiotics', *Semiotica*, 25, 3–4 (1979), 193–205.

BARTH, JOHN, 'The Literature of Replenishment: Postmodernist Fiction', *Atlantic Monthly*, June (1980), 65–71.

BARTHES, ROLAND, *Image, Music, Text* in Stephen Heath (trans. and ed.) (London: Fontana, 1977).

BRADBURY, MALCOLM, (ed.), *The Novel Today: Contemporary Writers on Modern Fiction* (London: Fontana, 1977).

BROOKE-ROSE, C. *A Rhetoric of the Unreal: Studies in Narrative Structure especially of the Fantastic* (Cambridge: Cambridge University Press, 1981).

BROOKER, PETER (ed.), *Modernism/Postmodernism* (London and New York: Longman, 1992).

CAMPBELL, JAMES, 'An Interview with John Fowles', *Contemporary Literature*, 17, 4, Autumn (1976), 455–69.

COHN, D., 'Fictional vs. Historical Lives: Borderlines and Borderline Cases', *Journal of Narrative Technique*, 19, 1 (1989), 3–24.

DALESKI, H.M., 'Imagining Revolution: The Eye of History and of Fiction', *Journal of Narrative Technique*, 18, 1 (1988), 61–72.

CONNOR, STEVEN, *Postmodernist Culture: an Introduction to Theories of the Contemporary* (Oxford: Basil Blackwell, 1989).

DE LAURETIS, T., 'Gaudy Rose: Eco and Narcissism', *SubStance*, 47, (1985), 13–29.

DIPPLE, ELIZABETH, *The Unresolvable Plot: Reading Contemporary Fiction* (London and New York: Routledge, 1988).

DOCHERTY, THOMAS, (ed.), *Postmodernism: a Reader* (New York and London: Harvester Wheatsheaf, 1993).

ECO, UMBERTO, *The Role of the Reader: Explorations in the Semiotics of Texts* (London: Hutchinson, 1981).

EIERMACHER, KARL, 'The Problem of Metalanguage in Literary Studies', *Philosophy and the Theory of Literature*, 4, 1 January (1979), 145–78.

FEDERMAN, RAYMOND, *Surfiction: Fiction Now ... and Tomorrow* (Chicago: University of Illinois Press, 1975).

FOKKEMA, DOUWE and BERTNES, HANS, (eds), *Approaching Postmodernism: Papers presented at a workshop on Postmodernism 21–23rd September 1984* (Amsterdam and Philadelphia: Benjamins, 1986).

FOWLES, JOHN, 'Notes on an Unfinished Novel', in T. McCormack (ed.) *Afterwords* (New York and London: Harper & Row, 1969).

GRAFF, GERALD, *Literature Against Itself: Literary Ideas in Modern Society* (Chicago: University of Chicago Press, 1979).

GRIFFITH, J., 'Narrative Technique and the Meaning of History', *Journal of Narrative Technique*, 3, 1, January (1973), 3–19.

HASSAN, IHAB, *Paracriticisms: Seven Speculations of the Time* (Urbana: University of Illinois Press, 1975).

HECKARD, MARGARET, 'Robert Coover, Metafiction and Freedom', *Twentieth Century Literature*, 22, May (1976), 210–27.

HICKS, W., *The Metafictional City* (Durham, NC: University of North Carolina Press, 1981).

HOLQUIST, MICHAEL, 'Whodunnit and Other Questions: Metaphysical Detection Stories in Post-War Fiction', *New Literary History*, 3, 1 Autumn (1971), 135–56.

HUTCHINSON, P., *Games Authors Play* (London: Methuen, 1983).

JAMESON, FREDRIC, *Postmodernism, or The Cultural Logic of Late Capitalism* (London: Verso, 1991).

JAMESON, FREDRIC, 'Metacommentary', *PMLA*, 86 (1971), 9–18.

KAPLAN, F., 'Victorian Modernists: Fowles and Nabokov', *Journal of Narrative Technique*, 3, 2 (1973), 108–20.

KELLMAN, S., 'The Fiction of Self-Begetting', *MLN*, 91, December (1976), 1243–56.

KRIEGER, MURRAY, 'Fiction, History and Empirical Reality', *Critical Inquiry*, 1, 2 (1974), 335–60.

LAWSON, HILARY, *Reflexivity: the Post-modern Predicament* (London: Hutchinson, 1985).

LACAPRA, DOMINIC, *History and Criticism* (Ithaca and London: Cornell University Press, 1985).

LIPSKI, J.M., 'On the Metastructure of Literary Discourse', *Journal of Literary Semantics*, 5, 1 (1976), 53–61.

MCHALE, BRIAN, *Postmodernist Fiction* (New York and London: Methuen, 1987).

MERRELL, FLOYD, *Pararealities: the Nature of Our Fictions and How we Know them* (1983).

PARAMESWARAN, UMA, 'Handcuffed to History: Salman Rushdie's Art', *Ariel*, 14, 4, 34–45.

PAVEL, THOMAS, *Fictional Worlds* (Cambridge, Massachusetts and London: Harvard University Press, 1986).

RIFFATERRE, MICHAEL, *Fictional Truth* (Baltimore and London: Johns Hopkins University Press, 1990).

RABKIN, ERIC, 'Metalinguistics and Science Fiction', *Critical Inquiry* 6, 1, Autumn (1979), 79–97.

ROVIT, EARL, 'The Novel as Parody: John Barth', *Critique* 4, 2, Fall (1963), 77–85.

RUSSELL, CHARLES, 'The Vault of Language: Self-Reflective Artifice in Contemporary American Fiction', *Modern Fiction Studies*, 20, 3, 349–59.

SARUP, MADAN, *An Introductory Guide to Post-Structuralism and Postmodernism* (London: Harvester Wheatsheaf, 1988).

SCHMITZ, NEIL, 'The Hazards of Metafiction', *Novel: a Forum on Fiction*, 7, 3, (1974), 210—19.

SCHOLES, ROBERT, *The Fabulators* (New York and Oxford: Oxford University Press, 1967).

SCHOLES, ROBERT, *Structural Fabulation: an essay on the Fiction of the Future* (Notre Dame and London: University of Notre Dame Press, 1975).

SCHOLES, ROBERT, *The Nature of Narrative* (Oxford: Oxford University Press, 1966).

SEARLE, JOHN, 'The Logical Status of Fictional Discourse', *New Literary History*, 6, 2, Winter (1975), 319–32.

SMYTH, EDMUND, *Postmodernism and Contemporary Fiction* (London: Batsford, 1991).

SPANOS, WILLIAM, 'The Detective and the Boundary: Some Notes on the Postmodern Literary Imagination', *Boundary 1*, 1, Fall (1972), 147–68.

SARK, JOHN, *The Literature of Exhaustion: Borges, Nabokov and Barthes* (Durham, NC: University of North Carolina Press, 1974).

TANNER, TONY, *City of Words: American Fiction 1950–1970* (London: Cape, 1971).

THIHER, ALLEN, *Words in Reflection: Modern Language Theory and Postmodern Fiction* (Chicago and London: University of Chicago Press, 1984).

WAUGH, PATRICIA, *Feminine Fictions: Revisiting the Postmodern* (London and New York: Routledge, 1989).

WESTERVELT, L., 'Teller, Tale, Told: Relationships in John Barth's Latest Fiction', *Journal of Narrative Technique*, 8, 1 (1978), 42–55.

WHITE, HAYDEN, *Metahistory: The Historical Imagination in Nineteenth Century Europe* (Baltimore and London: Johns Hopkins University Press, 1973).

WILDE, ALLEN, *Horizons of Assent: Modernism, Postmodernism and the Ironic Imagination* (Baltimore and London: Johns Hopkins University Press, 1981).

WILLIAMS, JOHN, 'Fact and Fiction: Problems for the Historical Novelist', *Denver Quarterly*, VII, 4, Winter (1973), 1–12.

INDEX